INTERIOR DETAILING

INTERIOR DETAILING

CONCEPT TO CONSTRUCTION

David Kent Ballast, FAIA, CSI

WILEY

John Wiley & Sons, Inc.

This book is printed on acid-free paper. ♾

Copyright © 2010 by John Wiley & Sons, Inc. All rights reserved.

Published by John Wiley & Sons, Inc., Hoboken, New Jersey.
Published simultaneously in Canada.

For general information on our other products and services, or technical support, please contact our Customer Care Department within the United States at 800-762-2974, outside the United States at 317-572-3993 or fax 317-572-4002.

Wiley also publishes its books in a variety of electronic formats. Some content that appears in print may not be available in electronic books.

For more information about Wiley products, visit our Web site at http://www.wiley.com.

Library of Congress Cataloging-in-Publication Data:

Ballast, David Kent.
    Interior detailing : concept to construction / David Kent Ballast.
        p. cm.
    Includes index.
    ISBN 978-0-470-50497-0 (cloth : alk. paper); ISBN 978-0-470-91642-7 (ebk);
    ISBN 978-0-470-91643-5 (ebk); ISBN 978-0-470-91644-3 (ebk)
    1. Building–Details. 2. Interior architecture. I. Title.
TH2025.B36 2010
729—dc22   2010003427

Printed in the United States of America.

10 9 8 7 6 5 4 3 2 1

CONTENTS

PART 1 ROADMAP TO SOLVING DETAILING PROBLEMS

3 FUNCTION 41

PART 2 ELEMENTS

5 DIVIDING AND CREATING SPACE WITH PERMANENT BARRIERS _____ 105

LIST OF TABLES

LIST OF ILLUSTRATIONS

PREFACE

Throughout my professional career, I have noticed that the best interior design and architecture is a combination of innovative, creative thinking coupled with solid technical proficiency. A good design alone is not sufficient; it must be combined with the best construction technology and detailing techniques. Without good detailing and the best selection of materials, the most imaginative design will suffer by not adequately meeting the function for which it was intended, being unsafe, costing more money than it should, making construction difficult, wearing out over time, and being a maintenance problem.

Conversely, a perfectly executed technical solution is not enough if the designer has failed to fully explore options and creative ways to solve the problem before starting the construction drawings. Solutions to problems approached this way may serve their basic function but will miss their potential to fully express design possibilities and targeted, client-oriented solutions.

During my many years of teaching interior construction, I realized that the reason for the dichotomy often seen between conceptual design and construction design is the way the human brain works. This is based on the left brain/right brain theory, which in simple terms, suggests that the left brain hemisphere handles analytical, logical thinking, and the right hemisphere is the creative, intuitive side. The work and questions of my students suggested that if someone is predominately right or left brained he or she cannot be as good a designer as someone who has the ability to use both sides of the brain almost simultaneously. This ability is typically learned in school and during the early stages of a designer's practice, but many times a person stays with one more than the other to the detriment of good design problem solving.

This book is an attempt to bridge the gap between broad, conceptual design thinking and the specific requirements of designing all the necessary aspects of an interior space. Both are necessary for a successful design and one cannot really exist without the other. I hope that both students and practicing interior designers can benefit from viewing both sides of the issue, especially if they tend to focus on one more than the other. This simultaneous thought process is really one of the most valuable skills that interior designers and architects can offer their clients when they undertake to solve the wicked problems of design discussed in Chapter 1. Not many people can juggle the creative and the technical to solve environmental problems while creating interiors that are a joy in which to work, play, and live.

The first part of the book provides a general approach to designing a detail that is applicable for any design problem and includes the many factors that must be considered. The second part of the book discusses some of the primary elements of interior design and gives both conceptual and technical ways to fulfill the design intent of the project. The last part of the book provides some conceptual ideas for making the connections between individual interior elements and offers some starting points to make these connections.

Because so much of interior design is proprietary—that is, specific manufacturer's products are used to solve specific problems—I have included some of these with the manufacturers' web sites as a starting point so the reader can get more ideas and information. These listings are by no means complete, so I encourage readers to explore some of the general building product web sites given in the back of the book to do further research for specific design problems. By applying the guidelines I provide in the first part of this book with other details in the book and specific manufacturer's information, you can approach any design problem wisely and competently.

David Kent Ballast, FAIA, CSI

ACKNOWLEDGMENTS

I would like to thank the many people who contributed to the making of this book. For the publisher, Amanda Miller, vice president and publisher, and John Czarnecki, Assoc. AIA, senior editor, were instrumental in helping me through an idea I had many years ago. Thanks also to the other fine people at John Wiley & Sons: Nancy Cintron, senior production editor; Sadie Abuhoff, editorial assistant; Foxxe Editorial Services, for copy editing, and Aptara for design and page layout. My thanks also to the many students I have instructed over the years for helping me see how designers learn and how to logically think through the process of design.

INTRODUCTION

Interior Design and Detailing—Concept to Construction provides interior designers, architects, and others involved in the making of the interior environment a unique resource for creating interior details that work. Design alone is not sufficient for a successful interior, nor is a strictly technical solution. Solving interior design problems and crafting successful interiors requires imaginative thinking *and* the efficient application of technical knowledge to design ideas.

Good details can make or break an interior project. Properly designed details can contribute to the overall design intent of the project and provide functional use and long-lasting serviceability while being beautiful in their own right. Poorly designed details can break, chip, leak, and collapse. They can create fire and safety hazards, violate codes, transmit noise, wear poorly, and exceed the budget. Bad details can also be hard to build, difficult to clean, toxic, and impossible to repair. The list of potential problems is long. At the very least, poor detailing can make a client unhappy. In the worst case, bad detailing can result in lawsuits, financial loss, and a bad reputation for the designer.

This book connects design with detailing and shows how to move from one realm to the other. It offers suggested ways to look at broad conceptual approaches to developing details for the major interior design elements common to all projects. It also provides specific ways to work through the detailing process and apply universal principles to any detailing problem.

An overemphasis on design without sufficient thought about detailing is just as bad as too much technical detailing without enough thought given to design. Many design offices and designers place too much emphasis on design or detailing, but not enough on both. Without competent detailing the best design ideas will be, at best, weakly implemented and, at worst, may fail.

Interior Design and Detailing—Concept to Construction is, in ways, similar to the detailing process itself. In some areas, it is broadly conceptual and presents alternatives to approaching detailing problems, and in other areas, it is more technical. This book offers those who may be more technically oriented some suggested ways to look at larger design issues. Conversely, for those who are mainly design oriented, this book gives some resources for making their design ideas into better technical solutions.

Students as well as practicing professionals can use this book to broaden their perspective and improve their design and detailing skills. Rather than being just a compilation of material information and standard details, this book connects the disciplines of design and technical detailing that are typically treated separately. It shows how to logically think through the design and development of an assembly so that it conforms to the designer's intent and meets all the other practical requirements of good construction. It describes and illustrates how a relatively small number of design responses can be used to solve nearly any problem. In addition, this book can be used to review and check the work of others and to diagnose problems with existing details.

Interior Design and Detailing—Concept to Construction provides a one-of-a-kind approach to interior detailing. Part 1, *Roadmap to Solving Detailing Problems*, describes how to solve *any* detailing design problem in a rational way, giving consideration to all the pertinent aspects of the detail. Chapters are included that describe the efficient process of designing details, how creative intent factors into the work, typical constraints of detailing, functional requirements, and the many constructability issues that are involved.

Part 2, *Elements*, contains conceptual and practical approaches to designing and detailing the major construction components that define interior space. These include permanent and temporary vertical barriers, the overhead plane, the ground plane, and how a spatial connection is made with openings, doors, and glazing. Each chapter describes element concepts, functional requirements, common constraints, the coordination required, and specifics for beginning the detailing of the elements.

Part 3, *Transitions*, shows design and detailing approaches to making the transitions and connections between interior elements. These include the transition of partitions to the ceiling and floor planes; the transition of floors, partitions, and ceilings to other elements in the same plane; and structural transitions of columns and beams.

The book can be read in any order. For a good review of basic requirements for any detail or for how to logically think through a new design problem refer to Part 1. For some creative ideas for jumpstarting early design work refer to Parts 2 and 3. Use the index to find information about specific topics that may be spread throughout the book. Any way you use this book you will find it a useful addition to your library and a good resource for better design, construction, and project delivery.

HOW SI UNITS ARE USED
IN THIS BOOK

This edition of the *Interior Design and Detailing—Concept to Construction* includes equivalent measurements, using the Système Internationale (SI), in the text and illustrations. However, the use of SI units for construction and book publishing in the United States is problematic. This is because the building construction industry in the United States (with the exception of federal construction) has generally not adopted the metric system, as it is commonly called. Equivalent measurements of customary U.S. units (also called English or inch-pound units) are usually given as soft conversions, using standard conversion factors. This always results in a number with excessive significant digits. When construction is done using SI units, the building is designed and drawn according to hard conversions, where planning dimensions and building products are based on a metric module from the beginning. For example, studs are spaced 400 mm on center to accommodate panel products that are manufactured in standard 1,200-mm widths.

During the transition to Système Internationale units in the United States, code-writing bodies, federal laws (such as the ADA), product manufacturers, trade associations, and other construction-related industries typically still use the customary U.S. system and make soft conversions to develop SI equivalents. Some manufacturers produce the same product using both measuring systems. Although there are industry standards for developing SI equivalents, there is no consistency for rounding off when conversions are made. For example, the International Building Code shows a 152-mm equivalent when a 6-in. dimension is required. The *ADA Accessibility Guidelines* shows a 150-mm equivalent for the same dimension.

For the purposes of this book, the following conventions have been adopted.

Throughout this book, the customary U.S. measurements are given first and the SI equivalents follow in parentheses. In the text, the unit suffixes for both systems, such as ft or mm, are shown. In the illustrations, the number values and U.S. unit suffixes are given first (in., ft., etc.) and the SI value after that in parentheses, *without* units if the number is in millimeters but *with* the unit if it is meters or some other unit except millimeters. This follows standard construction practice for SI units on architectural drawings; a number is understood to be in millimeters unless some other unit is given. The exception to this convention occurs when a number is based on an international standard or product. In this case, the primary measurement is given first in SI units with the U.S. equivalent in parentheses. The unit suffix is shown for *both* in the text, as well as in the illustrations, to avoid confusion.

When there is a ratio or some combination of units where it might be confusing, unit suffixes are used for all numbers; for example, 6 mm/3 m.

When a standards-writing organization or a trade association gives dual units for a particular measurement, those numbers are used exactly as they come from the source. For example, one group might use 6.4 mm as the equivalent for 1/4 in., while another organization might use 6 mm.

When an SI conversion is used by a code agency, such as the International Building Code (IBC) or published in another regulation, such as the *ADA Accessibility Guidelines* (ADAAG), the SI equivalents used by the issuing agency are printed in this book. For example, the IBC uses a 152-mm equivalent when a 6-in. dimension is required, while the ADAAG gives a 150-mm equivalent for the same dimension.

If a specific conversion is not otherwise given by a trade association or standards-writing organization, when converted values are rounded, the SI equivalent is rounded to the nearest millimeter for numbers under a few inches unless the dimension is very small (as for small tolerances like 1/16 in.), in which case a more precise decimal equivalent is given.

For dimensions over a few inches, the SI equivalent is rounded to the nearest 5 mm and to the nearest 10 mm for numbers over a few feet. When the dimension exceeds several feet, the number is rounded to the nearest 100 mm.

PART 1

ROADMAP TO SOLVING DETAILING PROBLEMS

CHAPTER 1

THE DESIGN/DETAILING PROCESS

1-1 INTRODUCTION

Detailing is that part of the project delivery process that lies roughly between initial conceptualization and final construction documentation. It is the point where the grand ideas of the designer meet the hard realities of construction fact. Although detailing is not spelled out as a separate design activity on proposals and invoices, happening mainly during design development but also during schematic design and construction drawing production, it is one of the most important aspects of a designer's skill set. Detailing is really "designing a detail."

Good detailing has many advantages. In addition to improving and enhancing design, it can reduce construction costs, minimize the designer's liability, and speed the production of construction drawings. Detailing can also be a valuable link for outsourced work, either onshore or offshore, because it provides the vital aspect of good communication required for successful collaboration with outside production assistance. A design office can also use detailing as a training vehicle for young designers and as a way to create a signature style.

In many ways detailing has a schizophrenic nature. It is pure design as well as technics, intuitive as well as analytical, holistic as well as compartmentalized, left brain as well as right, fun as well as hard work, and quickly inspirational as well as time-consuming. The best detailers are those who can simultaneously occupy the worlds of creative designer and knowledgeable technician, switching from left brain to right brain as they work.

1-2 WHAT IS DETAILING?

Detailing can be thought of as a subset of interior design in general. It is a *creative process* of problem solving with constraints and choices aimed at translating broad design concepts into construction reality. Sometimes there are more constraints than choices and sometimes more choices than constraints. It is the designer's task to know how to make the best choices and attempt to make constraints into assets. It is not just a technical activity but also a creative process.

Although detailing means different things to each designer, there are three basic things detailing does. First, it is a way fitting the pieces together. There must be a way of physically

3

and visually connecting the various components of an interior space or architectural feature. For example, a doorframe must attach to a wall opening in some fashion regardless of how simple or complex the detail may be. Second, detailing solves functional problems, responding to the specific needs the interior space is trying to fulfill. For example, providing a moisture-resistant, durable surface is something a bar countertop must do, but there are innumerable ways that such a surface can be created. Thirdly, detailing is one of the most important ways to enhance the overall design intent of the project. The basic elements and principles of design, as well as broad design concepts, can be reinforced with the design of the smaller-scale details that make up a space.

Detailing as a Wicked Problem

Like interior or architectural design in general, detailing is a type of wicked problem. The term *wicked problem* was coined in 1973 by Horst Rittel and Melvin Webber. Rittel was a theorist of design and planning at the University of California, Berkeley. Webber was an urban planner and professor of urban and regional planning, also at UC, Berkeley. Although the term often refers to very large-scale economic or political problems, like ending world hunger or improving the healthcare system, a design problem is also a perfect example of a wicked problem. An interior designer must understand the nature of wicked problems to be a good detailer while maintaining a practical business orientation toward completing a project on time and on budget.

There are several aspects to wicked problems that Rittel and Webber identified that are characteristic of interior design and architectural problems. Some of these are the following, in no particular order:

- There is no right or wrong solution. Given the same basic design or detailing problem with the same client, program, and constraints, 10 different designers will come up with 10 different solutions, all of which may be acceptable and generally solve the problem. Even with a very narrowly defined detailing problem, such as a wood doorframe placed in a wood stud partition, there may be one very *common* solution used by all designers in most situations, but never *just* one.
- There is no definite stopping point. Every designer has experienced the situation of wanting more time to improve the solution. Because there are so many variables to design problems, there are always more alternatives to explore or research to be done. However, the realities of interior design, including the designer's budget, dictate that the best solution be selected at a particular time to complete the project. Often, this is the area where designers lose their business sense and spend more design time than they have budgeted.
- Constraints and resources to solve the problem change over time. In spite of the most detailed program and understanding of a problem, many things can change during a project. The client may change the budget or project requirements, new materials may come on the market or become scarce, construction costs may rise, or building codes may change. The designer is almost always shooting at a moving target.
- Often, a solution is required to fully understand the problem. Although various types of modeling, such as three-dimensional drawings, physical models, or full-size mockups may be used, the true test is to build the facility and see how it works. Modeling or even existing, similar facilities only provide a partial view of how the proposed solution will work.

- Every problem is unique. Interior design and architectural projects are, by their vary nature, unique. Even the same building type with the same client and the same program will vary depending on geographical location, budget, or time of construction. When looking at smaller detailing problems, such as how to design and install a kitchen cabinet, there may be identical ways of building the cabinet and mounting it on the wall, but it will still have variations in materials, finish, and hardware.

Although wicked design problems present many challenges to the interior designer, they are also what make the process and the profession valuable, interesting, and enjoyable.

1-3 THE DRAWING-THINKING-DRAWING CYCLE

Like other aspects of interior design, detailing is, for the most part, graphic problem solving. Designers use various types of graphics methods to study and resolve the issues they face. This is a cyclical process in which the designer begins with a thought, no matter how minor or undeveloped, sketches a representation of it on paper, looks at the image, and thinks about it and its implications. See Fig. 1-1. The cycle repeats, with each cycle refining the image until a complete resolution of the issue being studied is resolved. With each cycle three things, or some combination of the three, happen. The designer explores ideas, learns something, or makes a decision.

There are many ways that someone may represent their thoughts, but it usually takes the form of marks on paper, typically tracing paper. When the problem being investigated is a design or construction detail, multiple layers of tracing paper should be used to help refine the design. The first sketch may be a very rough idea of the solution, while successive tracings refine the image, retaining (tracing) those elements that seem to work and drawing new lines to reflect new or modified ideas.

One of the most important aspects of this type of graphic problem solving is that it must be done with the hand and on paper. The problem-solving process works in a unique way when eye, hand, paper, and brain are intimately connected through this technique. Contrary to what some designers may believe, a computer is not a good instrument for this type of work. Like using a sharp pencil, the computer, regardless of the drawing or sketching program being used, slows the process of recording ideas and is too precise early in the problem-solving process. Manipulating a computer generally gets in the way of the rapid, multilevel thought

Figure 1-1 The drawing-thinking-drawing cycle

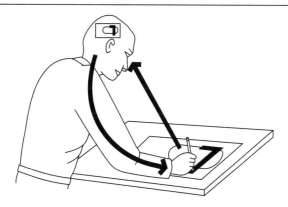

that the brain is capable of. Although there are several good sketching programs available, both two-dimensional and three-dimensional, the best method is still marker on tracing paper. No other method can respond to the variety of graphic methods of representing problems that designers use. A computer is most useful when a designer alternates between paper sketching for rough ideas and computer-aided design for exploring three-dimensional models that can be quickly developed and manipulated to view the image from multiple points of view.

1-4 PROCESS TOOLS AND TECHNIQUES

Process Tools

Partly because design and detailing are types of wicked problems with no single answer or algorithm for solving them designers typically use analog representations of problems. An *analog representation* is one that relies on a naïve depiction of something rather than text, numbers, or formulas. These representations are a way of abstracting the problem or issue under study to simplify it and make it easier to solve. In most problem-solving sessions, a designer will use several different representations in quick succession or alternately to study a problem. This is one of the reasons a computer, in the best case, slows the process and, in the worst case, hinders it.

Some of the process tools include the following. A few are illustrated in Figs. 1-2 through 1-5:

- bubble diagrams
- area diagrams
- stacking diagrams

Figure 1-2 Bubble diagram

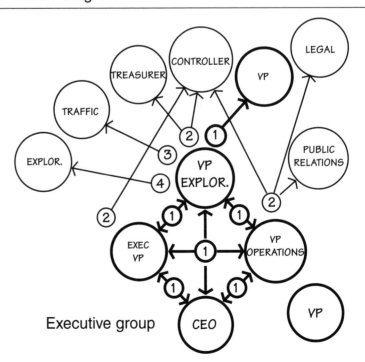

Figure 1-3 Area diagram

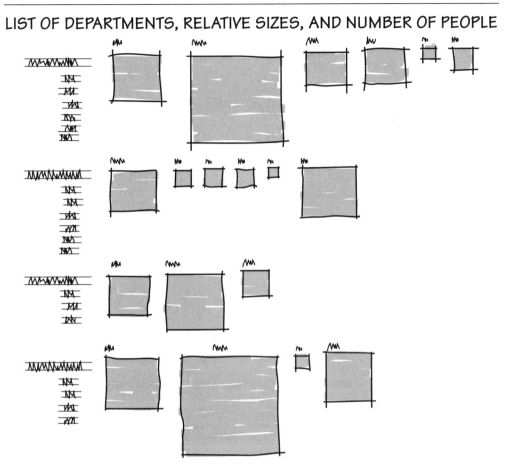

LIST OF DEPARTMENTS, RELATIVE SIZES, AND NUMBER OF PEOPLE

Figure 1-4 Evaluation matrix

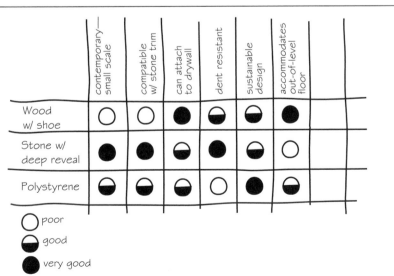

Figure 1-5 Morphological chart

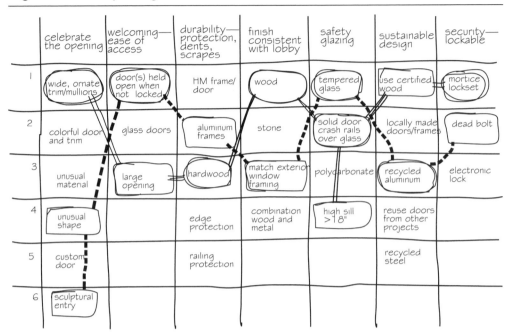

- flow charts and other network diagrams
- matrices
- morphological charts
- comparison charts
- two-dimensional drawings such as plans, elevations, and sections
- three-dimensional sketches including isometrics, perspectives, and others
- bar charts and other intensity diagrams
- graphs

Practical Tips

Although every designer has a unique way of working, and every detailing problem is a little different, here are some practical techniques that can focus efforts and speed the process. Some of the following suggestions assume that the designer's preliminary work is done with marker on paper as described above.

- Use the right marker. The type of marker used affects thinking. A hard, thin pencil will generally lead to precise, detailed thinking too early in the process. A soft, thick marker, on the other hand, will make it impossible to explore smaller scale ideas or details.
- Use markers that are permanent, not a pencil. This makes it impossible to erase. Because every line on paper represents a valuable thought (although not necessarily a correct one), nothing should be lost. If a line needs to be eliminated or modified, use tracing paper to work on a new drawing. Dark, permanent marks also have a practical advantage because they reproduce well on copying machines and scanners and are easy to see.
- Draw a line only once; do not scribble. Scribbling suggests uncertainty and although working through uncertainty is part of the process, it can be done by trying one line in one position and reviewing it. If it is not correct, use another layer of tracing paper to modify the line. Every line is important and records a thought.

- Use color sparingly, if at all. This, of course, depends on the type of problem and the type of drawing. The practical reason for limiting color is to reduce the number of markers on the table and the time it takes to move from one to another. However, in some cases color is useful to differentiate different parts of a very complex detail or to represent grouped parts of sketches such as bubble or flow diagrams. Used sparingly, it is also a useful way to use hierarchy in context as described below. Shading or hatching is another way to differentiate parts of the drawing without having to change markers.

Generally, a medium to thin, black felt-tip marker works well. If a combination of rough sketches and more detailed drawings is being completed, the designer may want to use two or three different marker thicknesses at most.

- Use a small paper size. Large sizes of paper encourage the designer to fill them up with images. Although there is nothing inherently wrong with this, the drawing-thinking-drawing cycle is more useful when the *number* of explorations is more important than their size. Of course, large floor plans may need a large paper size, but most early sketching and problem solving can be accomplished on small paper. A 14-inch (356-mm) roll of inexpensive tracing paper is ideal (12-inch [305-mm] rolls are often a little too small). Fourteen inches is large enough for most sketches, details, and floor plan studies but small enough to easily fit on any desk or drafting table. Smaller pieces of paper have the added advantage of being easier to file, organize, and reproduce on copy machines and scanners.

- Draw images relatively small. Drawings should, for the most part, be small enough to be totally visible without too much shifting of the eyes. Early graphic problem solving and detailing relies on exploring many ideas and variations. Using a small paper size helps encourage this practice. Small images are also faster to complete.

- Use scale early on. Of course, diagrams like bubble diagrams and flow charts are without scale, but when a section or elevation is being sketched, using scale can help keep the various parts in realistic relationship to each other. The drawing does not have to be hardlined or perfect just because scale is being used, but if one part is three times the length of another part, it should look that way on the drawing. For smaller drawings, keeping a 6-in. architect's scale in one hand while drawing with the other hand is a convenient way to accomplish this.

- Limit time spent with each drawing. In general, it is better to produce more drawings than highly complex ones, if not necessary. It is also important not to overwork one drawing that is not advancing the process. Of course, the type of drawing will suggest the amount of time spent; bubble diagrams take less time than a complex section detail. Even isometric or perspective drawings should be completed with a quick sketch technique.

- When possible, keep diagrams simple. One of the most valuable uses of diagrams is to reduce complex problems or issues to their essence so that they can be analyzed. For example, in a bubble diagram, rather than trying to show every room, use one bubble to represent an entire department or group of spaces. If further complexity is required, use another drawing.

- Use hierarchy in context. Hierarchy in context means that within one drawing certain areas may be more important than others and should be highlighted to focus attention on them, while still giving overall context to the detail. Some of the ways to do this include using line weight, shading, color, composition, or a greater number of lines in one area. See Fig. 1-6.

Figure 1-6 Hierarchy in context

- Explore alternatives. Solving design and detailing problems is largely a matter of exploring alternatives. During the early stages of detailing, various broad approaches to the problem should be investigated quickly. It generally becomes apparent that some of the alternatives will not work and that others are worth developing in more detail. For example, Fig. 1-7 shows six alternative concepts for creating an entry into a bar from a hotel lobby. These were quick to develop but expanded the designer's thinking in exploring ways to detail this design element.

- Know when to stop. This is often the most difficult part of the process because there is usually more that the designer feels can be done. However, if a deadline does not stop the process in itself, the designer must keep time spent within the budget.

If a problem is especially difficult and it is unclear where to start, the following additional suggestions may help. All of these are related to each other in the process.

- Go with what you know. Very little creative thinking happens without the designer seeing something on paper. In nearly all detailing situations, there are some givens or

Figure 1-7 Concept alternatives

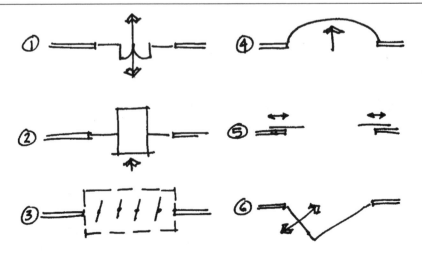

constraints that can be represented on paper. For example, even something as simple as using a horizontal line to represent the floor is a starting point. A vertical line representing a wall immediately suggests the possibility of a sloped orientation instead, a material thickness required, and the connection necessary between horizontal and vertical.

- Draw first, think later. The drawing-thinking-drawing cycle does not work unless there is something on paper to view and respond to. Drawing something that may not be right is better than drawing nothing at all.
- Trace, don't erase. As previously discussed, every line is important, even if it is incorrect because it represents a thought and something learned about the problem. Lines that do not work can be traced over and refined.
- Succeed by failing. A wrong turn may lead to the right path. Part of the drawing-thinking-drawing cycle is learning something with each cycle. Making mistakes is part of this process.

1-5 DETAILING COMPONENTS AND PROCESS

The Four Aspects of Detailing

All detailing is a way to satisfy requirements in four areas: design intent, constraints, function, and constructability. *Design intent* is the requirement produced by the aesthetic needs of the project, including the basic design elements and principles the designer is using. For example, horizontal line may be an important part of the designer's approach to the problem. *Constraints* are the given conditions within which the detail must perform and over which the designer has little or no control. For example, building code requirements and material availability are constraints. *Function* is the requirement the detail must meet based on its basic purpose. For example, a stairway must provide safety, durability, and a good anthropometric fit to the human body. *Constructability* is the set of requirements produced by the detail itself regardless of design intent or functional needs. Once a detail is developed, it must be buildable, structurally sound, durable, and have all the other qualities of good construction. The relationships among these four aspects of a detail are shown in Fig. 1-8.

Figure 1-8 Four aspects of detailing

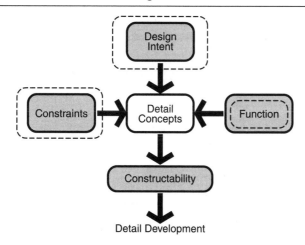

Every detail may have a different emphasis on each of these elements, but they all are always present. For example, some details may be developed primarily to enhance the design intent, while others may be primarily functional requirements to meet given constraints. Constraints, function, and constructability are discussed in more detail in the following chapters.

The Detailing Process

Theoretically the detailing process follows the procedure shown in Fig. 1-9. In most cases, the designer is guided by the design intent and determines the constraints and functional needs of the problem given the particular context of the project. Constraints and functional needs are generally known, but if not, the designer can do any research to resolve the unknowns. The research may be as simple as a quick phone call to the client or as complex as a multiweek investigation of regulatory requirements. From these three aspects of detailing, the designer can develop concept alternatives and, with the help of the client and other stakeholders, select one for final development.

In reality, the process proceeds more like that shown in Fig. 1-10. This is how a designer solves a wicked problem, rarely in a neat, linear process. The starting point may be any of the three aspects of defining the detailing problem, and work may jump into the area of the problem solution to test ideas and then back to problem definition areas again. Figure 1-10 also shows an additional component: social input, including the stakeholders, which may include the client, contractor, subcontractors, suppliers, and regulatory agencies.

During the process, the designer may review previously used details and lessons learned and apply those to either the problem definition or possible solutions to the current problem. Then, at some point, the resources of either time or money, or both, are exhausted and the designer must stop the process and use the best solution developed to date.

Example

The following example illustrates the process of developing a simple detail in which the four aspects of detailing are used in a nonlinear fashion. The detailing problem is to develop a

Figure 1-9 The detailing process

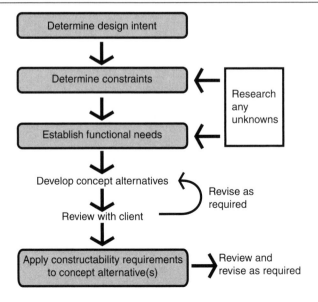

Figure 1-10 Actual detailing process

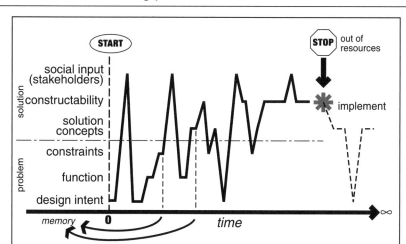

borrowed light in an office partition separating a small conference room from a corridor. The purpose is to bring natural light into the corridor from the exterior windows in the conference room. At the same time, the client wants visual privacy between the corridor and conference room, and the designer wants to use a detail that is sympathetic to the existing window wall and door framing that is being developed for an adjacent wall of the conference room.

To begin, the existing constraints and conditions are sketched as shown in Fig. 1-11(a). This includes the ceiling height and type and the partition construction, which is 5/8-in. (16-mm) gypsum wallboard on 3 5/8-in. (143-mm) metal studs. The ceiling height is noted. In this case, the detail is being sketched at its final scale, and a dashed line is drawn to indicate the drawing module being used for detail placement within the larger-sized sheet.

Next, instead of sketching alternative solutions, the detailer decided to start drawing a standard wood-framed glazed opening to explore the implications of this approach. See Fig. 1-11(b). This was traced over the first sketch, although they are printed separately in the illustration. Assuming that the glass would be clear, an "eye" notation is made to remind the detailer of the constraint of privacy; that is, the sill of the glass should be above eye level. This early sketch also produced some immediate questions to the detailer concerning the size of the casing trim, what kind of glazing rabbet should be used, how the frame should be braced above the ceiling, and what the overall height of the opening should be.

In the third sketch, shown in Fig. 1-11(c), the detailer decided to use the same 3-in. (76-mm) trim used in the other framing in the room and remembered that the change in ceiling height would also have to be considered and coordinated with the wood trim above the adjacent door and full-height glass opening. The detailer also began to question whether the casing trim on the corridor side needed to be the same as the 3-in. trim on the conference room side. In this iteration of the drawing-thinking-drawing cycle, the detailer learned something about the problem and made a decision.

In the fourth sketch, shown in Fig. 1-11(d), the detailer studied the implications of matching the top of the sill trim to the top of the adjacent door trim. If this happened and if the change in ceiling height was taken into consideration, then the overall size of the glass would be too small to make much difference in admitting natural light to the corridor, which was the original purpose of the detail.

Figure 1-11 Development sketches

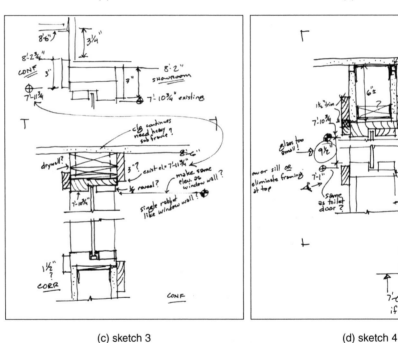

(a) sketch 1   (b) sketch 2

(c) sketch 3   (d) sketch 4

In order to maximize the actual glazed area for the most light, the detailer thought of using a partial or totally frameless glazed system, as shown in Fig. 1-12(a). To study the design implications of these two approaches, the detailer quickly sketched two perspectives, as shown in Figs. 1-12(b) and (c). These raised some additional questions and concerns. The detailer decided the wood frame approach would be more in keeping with the overall design intent of the space and the adjacent construction and decided to try drawing an arbitrary 2'-0'' (610-mm) high glass opening with the head trim positioned to match the adjacent window wall trim.

These assumptions are shown in the final glazing detail illustrated in Fig. 1-13, along with other detailing considerations that are typical for a standard wood-framed, glazed opening. Some quick arithmetic showed that doing this would put the windowsill at an elevation of about 5'-11'' (1803 mm), sufficient to provide the visual privacy the client wanted. In

Figure 1-12 Study sketches

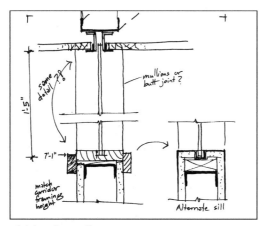

(a) framing options

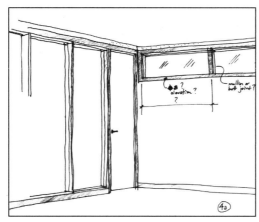

(b) study with framing

(c) study with no frame

addition, the glass would not have to be safety glazing because the sill is more than 60 in. (1525 mm) above the floor. This would minimize the cost of the detail.

Although the final detail would work, additional questions that might be raised include whether to use laminated glass or thicker glass for increased acoustical privacy and whether to use larger areas of obscure glass to increase the light transmission, while still providing privacy. These questions would require more time for study, a cost review, and possibly a longer time

Figure 1-13 Borrowed light final sketch

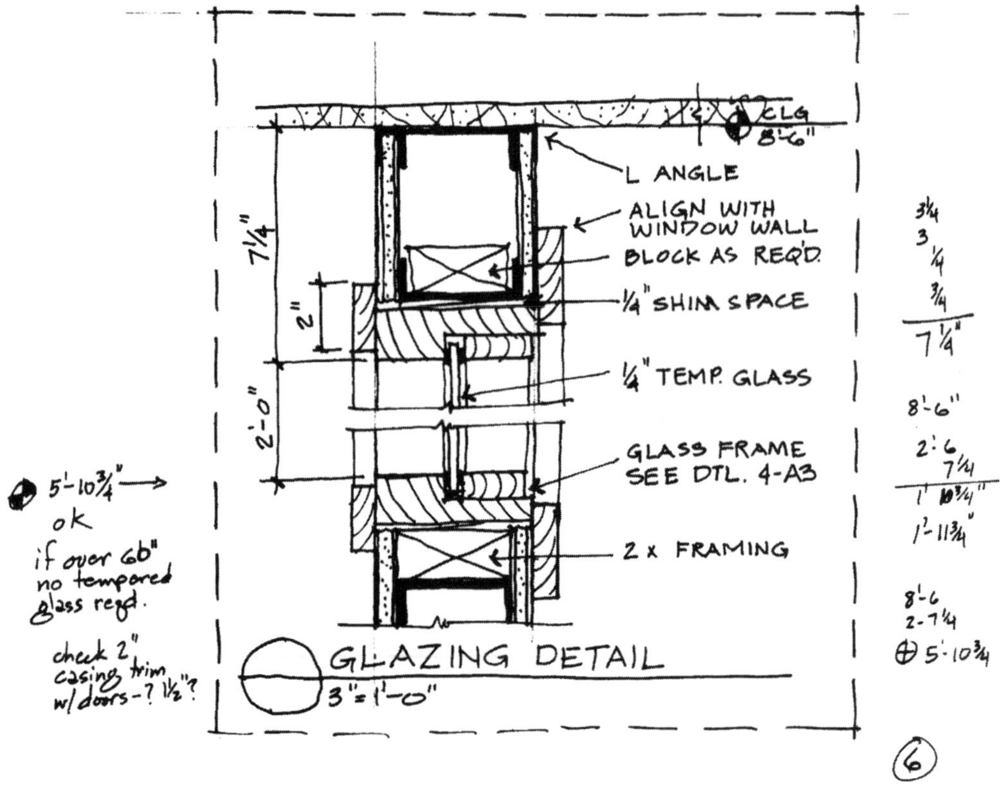

to get glass samples and obtain the client's approval. The designer may decide that in this particular circumstance, the additional time and design costs are not worth the effort for this particular detail.

1-6 THREE PURPOSES OF A DETAIL

As mentioned previously, *design intent* is one of the four aspects of detailing and one of three that defines a detailing problem (as well as any design problem). In many cases, function takes the lead in defining a detailing problem, but when all other factors are equal, design intent is the driving force in determining the final configuration of a detail. Design intent may incorporate many things, but there are basically three design purposes of a detail: to contribute to the overall design concept, to resolve problems of connection or transition, and to coordinate with adjacent construction. These will be discussed here; the aspects of constraints, function, and constructability are reviewed in the next three chapters.

Contributes to Design Concept

Every good design project works as a whole, with every part contributing to the overall concept and look of the space. Details should support the designer's vision, as well as the basic elements and principles of design. A small-scale space, for example, may require small-scale details. In some cases, the designer may choose to design a detail differently to create an eclectic contrast with the rest of the space.

Resolves Problems of Connection or Transition

Details must always resolve the problems of connection or transition of one component to another. This may be done for practical reasons or for purely aesthetic reasons, or for both. For example, a baseboard makes the transition between the floor and the wall and conceals the rough construction joint below the wall finish. It also serves a functional requirement to protect the wall from cleaning equipment and foot scraping. From a strictly design perspective, a baseboard can also modify the scale of the wall or the entire room, create a strong horizontal line, or emphasize the demarcation between architectural planes, depending on how it is detailed.

A connection or transition can be made between different elements, such as between the wall and ceiling plane, or between construction elements that are on or part of other elements, such as door openings as part of a partition. Some of the ways this can be done are discussed in Chapters 10, 11, and 12.

Coordinates with Adjacent Construction

Details also coordinate one construction element with another in terms of connection, structure, and continuity of materials. In some cases, the coordination is strictly functional, as with structural connections. In other cases, the coordination between elements is visual, creating a smooth, coherent transition from one part to another, consistent with the designer's concept.

1-7 PROGRAMMATIC CONCEPTS VERSUS DESIGN CONCEPTS

During the detailing process, the designer must clearly understand the difference between programmatic and design concepts. It is impossible to adequately detail something based only on a programmatic concept. The detailer should have several design concept sketches for each programmatic concept.

A *programmatic concept* is a performance requirement related to methods of solving a problem or satisfying a need without stating a way to achieve it. For example, maintainability is a programmatic concept. Programmatic concepts identify a particular problem or goal in general terms and narrow the focus. They also provide a way to evaluate how well the goal is reached.

A *design concept* is a way to satisfy a programmatic concept that actually has implications for design. Generally, several design concepts are generated as possible ways to satisfy one programmatic concept. These provide guidance for the detailing process.

For example, in the design of a retail store, the owner and designer may agree that one of the programmatic concepts should be the following: *Provide a medium level of security to protect against theft of merchandise without making the security methods obvious.* This statement identifies and responds to a particular problem (security), narrows the problem focus (security of property from theft, as opposed to security of people or from fire), and establishes a way of evaluating how well the goal is reached (Are the security methods obvious or not?). Although a reasonable goal, there is no way a designer can respond directly to this concept. One possible design concept suitable for this programmatic concept might be to provide a central cash/wrap station at the entry and exit point to the store. This way, the clerks could sell merchandise

Figure 1-14 Design concept

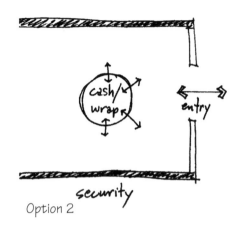

Option 2

medium level of security to protect
against theft without being obvious

and also observe people coming and going. This design concept could be sketched as shown in Fig. 1-14.

This type of sketch is a shorthand way to record a design concept without directly stating how it can be achieved. The designer could use this design concept to design a cash/wrap station that is straight, round, square, or U-shaped and that is placed in the middle of the opening or off to one side. The station could also be located directly at the front of the store so no one could exit without passing through the checkout area, although this response might be considered obvious. It also does not restrict decisions on materials, form, size, or other aspects of the final design.

Additional design concepts could also be generated to satisfy the programmatic concept. For instance, only samples of the merchandise could be displayed, and when the customers wanted to make a purchase they would go to a central point where clerks would retrieve what they wanted. Another way to satisfy the programmatic concept could be to tag all merchandise with electronic identifiers and discreetly incorporate detection devices into the design of the entry.

CHAPTER 2

CONSTRAINTS

2-1   INTRODUCTION

In construction detailing, constraints include any limitation over which the designer has little or no control. In conjunction with design intent and function, determining constraints is part of any problem-solving process because it helps define the problem. This chapter discusses some of the common constraints encountered in interior construction detailing and gives some reference information for common detailing conditions. Not included here are client preferences, which may include a directive to the designer to use a particular material or *not* use a material or construction technique.

Although they are usually fixed, some constraints may be questioned, such as budget, regulatory requirements, industry standards, and local construction practices. For budget, the designer may investigate whether a budget can be reallocated to allow more money for one detail if less money is given to another detail. If a regulatory requirement prevents the use of a particular material, the designer may think it is important enough to explore getting a variance or doing the research necessary to convince the local authority having jurisdiction that the proposed material is equivalent. This can often be done with an IBC evaluation report that manufacturers obtain for new materials not yet in the building code.

Good designers can often turn a constraint into an asset. For example, a limited budget forces the designer to focus on the essential aspects of the problem and may suggest new, innovative ways to solve a problem, which can lead to a unique design solution.

Although constraints may be determined at any time during the detailing process, the detailer should first determine those that are the most restrictive and work toward those that are the least restrictive, as shown in Fig. 2-1.

As the constraints are determined, record them as sketches that can serve as quick reminders during the detailing process. Figure 2-2 shows two quick sketches that consolidate existing conditions and code requirements for an entry into a bar from a hotel lobby. Concept alternatives for this design are shown in Fig. 1-7.

2-2   SUBSTRATES AND ADJACENT CONSTRUCTION

Interior design details are always part of an existing structure. The interior designer is working either within an existing building or on a building being planned or under construction for which architectural plans are available. Basic components, such as floor structure, ceiling

Figure 2-1 Sequence of determining constraints

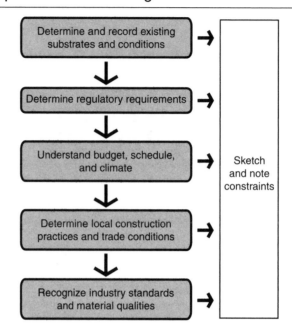

Figure 2-2 Sketch of constraints

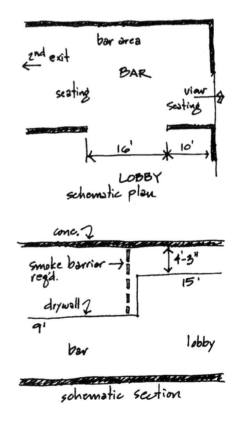

construction, columns, exterior walls, and windows, are all known elements as are the base building mechanical, plumbing, and electrical systems. Unless the interior designer is working with an architect and planning major modifications to an existing building, these elements are generally the basic structural constraints with which the designer must work.

In developing an interior construction detail, the designer may be limited in what is possible because of existing conditions. For example, a relatively thin concrete floor may preclude the use of a floor-mounted door closer, and detailing may require a larger head frame for a concealed overhead closer. In some cases, even existing building services may preclude some design details. An existing main supply air duct, for instance, may prevent making a raised ceiling detail higher than the existing ceiling line.

There are basically four aspects of existing construction that the interior designer must contend with during detailing: substrate material, condition of the substrate, size and position of substrate elements, and available space allowed by the substrates.

Substrate Material

The substrate material refers to the type of material on which or to which the interior detail is attached or touches. Different substrate materials may require different responses. For example, attachment of ornamental metal to an existing steel structural member must take into account possible galvanic action when different metals are in contact with each other. The metals may need to be separated with a plastic or neoprene spacer to prevent direct contact. Some of the common substrate materials and their basic characteristics are shown in Table 2-1.

Some substrate materials may also be limited in their inherent strength. For example, it may be more difficult to attach wall-mounted items to a partition framed with metal studs than one with wood studs. See Table 5-4 for load capacities of some common fasteners in studs.

Substrate Condition

Substrate condition is the strength and appearance of the base material to which the interior detail is attached. In most cases, the strength is the most important characteristic because if affects the ability of the new detail to be adequately supported without additional construction. For example, existing, spalling concrete in an old building may not provide the required strength for anchoring a bolt as well as new concrete. If the strength of any component or connection is a concern, a structural engineer or architect should be consulted for recommendations.

In some detailing situations, the substrate material may be fully or partially visible, in which case its appearance may also be of concern. It may have to be cleaned, painted, refinished, or otherwise modified to make it suitable for the new detail.

Substrate Size and Position

The size and/or position of the substrate may affect how a detail is designed. The thickness of wood subflooring, for example, may dictate how new flooring is anchored or the spacing of floor joists may influence how partitions are anchored to the structure above.

Substrate Space

Substrate space is space available for a portion of the new detail or for its attachment, including clearances required for tools and workspace. This is typically stud depth and spacing, floor or ceiling joint depth and spacing, or clearance around structural beams and columns. It can also

Table 2-1 Substrates for Interior Details

Substrate Material	Characteristics	Typical Sizes/Thicknesses	Fasteners Used	Other Concerns
Concrete	Hard and dense with high strength	Floors typically 4 in. to 6 in. (102 mm to 152 mm) thick; walls 8 in. to 12 in. (203 mm to 305 mm) thick	Power actuated fasteners, expansion bolts, adhesive for lightweight products	Floors and walls contain reinforcing steel; however, most fasteners for interior detail anchoring do not conflict.
Masonry	Hard and brittle; typically not used for interior work except for fire-rated or security partitions	8 in. x 8 in. x 16 in. (200 × 200 × 400 mm) blocks	Power-actuated fasteners, molly bolts, and adhesive for panel products	Generally requires wood or metal furring to attach wallboard or other finishes
Solid wood	Relatively strong and most softwoods used for framing have good holding power for nails and screws	Standard 2 × 4 (1-1/2 in. x 3-1/2 in. [38 mm x 89 mm]; others 2 in. x 6 in., 2 in. x 8 in., 2 in. x 10 in.	Nails, power staples, screws, through-bolts	May shrink; nails may pop out
Panel products	Particleboard, oriented strand board, medium-density fiberboard	Thicknesses from 1/4 in. to 1-1/4 (6.4 mm to 32 mm) with 3/4 in. (19 mm) most common	Screws, bolts, mastic, nails,	Strong material but with low pullout resistance for some fasteners
Aluminum	Lightweight; can be used structurally or as a finish material; many extruded shapes or can be custom extruded; accepts a wide variety of finishes	Extruded shapes vary by manufacturer; available in tubes, angles, bars, and channel shapes as well as sheets	Screws, bolts, mastic for lightweight material; heavier aluminum can be welded and bolted	Galvanic action is a concern with fasteners and other metals touching the aluminum
Steel, structural	Very strong with high strength-to-weight ratio	Sizes based on type; available in bars, tubes, pipes, angles; Z bars, H-shapes, lightweight I beams	Welding, power-actuated fasteners, through bolting, drill and tap for screws	Galvanic action is a concern with fasteners and other metals touching the steel.
Steel, light gage	Very flexible for wall and ceiling framing, as well as soffits and other constructions; noncombustible	1-5/8 in., 2-1/2 in., 3-5/8 in., 4 in., and 6 in. deep studs; runners, J-shapes, angles, and various other specialty shapes for wall framing	Self-tapping screws, through bolts, molly bolts	Galvanic action is a concern with fasteners and other metals touching the steel
Gypsum wallboard	Good wall finish material for painting and other finishes; excellent sound attenuation and fire resistance; easy to attach fasteners	1/4 in., 3/8 in., 1/2 in., 5/8 in., 3/4 in. (6.4 mm, 10 mm, 13 mm, 16 mm, 19 mm) thick boards, 4 in. wide sheets 8 ft, 10 ft, 12 ft, and 14 ft long	Plastic anchors, molly bolts, hollow wall anchors, toggle bolts, various proprietary fasteners; screws directly into studs	Wallboard by itself cannot hold large loads (see Table 5-4); may need wood blocking in metal stud walls for support

include space in architectural woodwork, above ceilings, in mechanical chases, and around the exterior cladding of buildings. The designer must understand tools and construction processes to provide sufficient space to allow a worker to build the detail.

2-3 REGULATORY REQUIREMENTS

Regulatory requirements usually affect detailing in terms of a material's quality, strength, and flammability. Accessibility laws may also affect how materials are selected for some details and how they are sized and configured.

Tables 2–2 and 2–3 summarize some of the regulatory requirements for interior materials as found in the *International Building Code* (IBC). However, the standards listed in Tables 2–2 and 2–3 are only those to which the IBC refers. There are hundreds of additional ASTM, ANSI, and industry standards that apply to interior construction elements. A partial list of these standards for various products is shown in Appendix A. These standards can be used to

Table 2-2   IBC Requirements for Interior Partition Materials

Construction Element	Agency	Standard Number	Standard Name
Accessories	ASTM	C1047	Specification for Accessories for Gypsum Wallboard and Gypsum Veneer Base
Wall framing	AISI	S211	North American Standard for Cold-formed Steel Framing—Wall Stud Design
Wall framing	AISI	S212	North American Standard for Cold-formed Steel Framing—Header Design
Wall framing	ASTM	C754	Specification for Installation of Steel Framing Members to Receive Screw-attached Gypsum Panel Products
Wall framing	ASTM	C954	Specification for Steel Drill Screws for the Application of Gypsum Panel Products or Metal Plaster Bases to Steel Studs from 0.033 inch (0.84 mm) to 0.112 inch (2.84 mm) in Thickness
Wall framing	ASTM	C955	Standard Specification for Load-bearing Transverse and Axial Steel Studs, Runners Tracks, and Bracing or Bridging, for Screw Application of Gypsum Panel Products and Metal Plaster Bases
Gypsum wallboard	ASTM	C840	Specification for Application and Finishing of Gypsum Board
Gypsum wallboard	ASTM	C960	Specification for Predecorated Gypsum Board
Gypsum wallboard	ASTM	C1002	Specification for Steel Self-piercing Tapping Screws for the Application of Gypsum Panel Products or Metal Plaster Bases to Wood Studs or Steel Studs
Gypsum wallboard	ASTM	C1395	Specification for Gypsum Ceiling Board
Gypsum wallboard	ASTM	C1396	Specification for Gypsum Board
Gypsum wallboard	ASTM	C1629	Standard Classification for Abuse-resistant Nondecorated Interior Gypsum Panel Products and Fiber-reinforced Cement Panels
Gypsum wallboard	ASTM	C1658	Standard Specification for Glass Mat Gypsum Panels
Gypsum wallboard	GA	216	Application and Finishing of Gypsum Panel Products
Gypsum wallboard	GA	600	Fire-resistance Design Manual, 18th ed.
Gypsum plaster	ASTM	C28/C28M	Specification for Gypsum Plasters
Gypsum plaster	ASTM	C587	Specification for Gypsum Veneer Plaster
Gypsum plaster	ASTM	C588	Specification for Gypsum Base for Veneer Plasters
Gypsum plaster	ASTM	C842	Specification for Application of Interior Gypsum Plaster
Gypsum plaster	ASTM	C843	Specification for Application of Gypsum Veneer Plaster
Gypsum plaster	ASTM	C844	Specification for Application of Gypsum Base to Receive Gypsum Veneer Plaster
Gypsum plaster	ASTM	C847-06	Specification for Metal Lath

Agencies:

AISI   American Iron and Steel Institute
ASTM   ASTM International
GA   Gypsum Association

Note: masonry products not included in this table.

evaluate materials and to include when specifying them in the final project documents and are especially useful when evaluating new or innovative products.

Flammability and fire resistance are especially important when selecting materials for details or developing details for construction assemblies such as partitions and openings. Table 2-4 summarizes some of the flammability requirements for interior components and finishes as regulated by the IBC. The following sections describe these in more detail.

Fire Tests for Finish Materials

Flammability tests for finish materials determine the following:

- Whether a material is flammable, and if so, if it simply burns with applied heat or if it supports combustion (adds fuel to the fire)
- The degree of flammability (how fast fire spreads across the material)
- How much smoke and toxic gas the material produces when ignited

Table 2-3 IBC Requirements for Quality of Common Interior Materials Other Than Partitions

Construction Element	Agency	Standard Number	Standard Name
Ceilings			
Acoustical ceilings	ASTM	C635	Specification for the Manufacture, Performance and Testing of Metal Suspension Systems for Acoustical Tile and Lay-in Panel Ceilings
Acoustical ceilings	ASTM	C636	Practice for Installation of Metal Ceiling Suspension Systems for Acoustical Tile and Lay-in Panels
Doors			
Doors	WDMA	101/I.S.2/A440	Specifications for Windows, Doors, and Unit Skylights
Fire doors	NFPA	80	Fire Doors and Other Opening Protectives
Hardware	UL	305	Panic Hardware
Hardware	UL	325	Door, Drapery, Gate, Louver and Window Operations and Systems
Power-operated	BHMA	A156.10	Power Operated Pedestrian Doors
Power-operated	BHMA	A156.19	Standard for Power Assist and Low Energy Operated Doors
Glazing/windows			
Glass	ASTM	E1300	Practice for Determining Load Resistance of Glass in Buildings
Safety glazing	CPSC	16 CFR 1201	Safety Standard for Architectural Glazing Material
Windows	ASTM	F2090	Specification for Window Fall Prevention Devices with Emergency Escape (Egress) Release Mechanisms
Tile			
Ceramic tile	ANSI	A108 series	Installation of Ceramic Tile (various methods in this series)
Ceramic tile	ANSI	A118 series	Standards for Mortar and Grout (various types in this series)
Ceramic tile	ANSI	A136.1	American National Standard for Organic Adhesives for Installation of Ceramic Tile
Ceramic tile	ANSI	A137.1	American National Standard Specifications for Ceramic Tile
Wood			
Glulam construction	AITC	AITC 104	Typical Construction Details
Hardboard	ANSI	A135.4	Basic Hardboard
Panels	DOC	PS-2	Performance Standard for Wood-based Structural Panels
Particleboard	ANSI	A208.1	Particleboard
Plywood	DOC	PS-1	Structural Plywood
Plywood	HPVA	HP-1	Standard for Hardwood and Decorative Plywood
Wood framing	DOC	PS-20	American Softwood Lumber Standard

Agencies:

AITC	American Institute of Timber Construction
ANSI	American National Standards Institute
ASTM	ASTM International
BHMA	Builders Hardware Manufacturers' Association
CPSC	Consumer Product Safety Commission
DOC	U.S. Department of Commerce
HPVA	Hardwood Plywood Veneer Association
NFPA	National Fire Protection Association
UL	Underwriters Laboratories
WDMA	Window and Door Manufacturers Association

Note: masonry and metal products not included in this table

Several tests are typically used for building and interior construction as briefly described in the following list.

ASTM E84

ASTM E84, *Standard Test Method for Surface Burning Characteristics of Building Materials,* is one of the most common fire-testing standards. It is also known as the *Steiner tunnel test* and rates the surface burning characteristics of interior finishes and other building materials by testing, in a narrow test chamber, a sample piece with a controlled flame at one end. The primary

Table 2-4 Summary of Tests for Flammability of Interior Design Components

Common Name	Application	Test Number(s)
Floor finishes		
Flooring radiant panel test	Carpet, resilient floors, and other floor coverings in corridors	NFPA 253 (ASTM E648)
Methenamine pill test	Carpets and rugs	16 CFR 1630 (ASTM D2859)
Floor/ceiling construction		
Wall and floor/ceiling assembly test	Fire ratings of walls, structure, and floor construction assemblies	ASTM E119
Wall finishes		
Steiner tunnel test	Flame-spread rating of finishes	ASTM E84
Room corner test	Evaluates extent to which wall and ceiling finish (other than textiles) contributes to fire growth	NFPA 286
Room corner test for textiles	Contribution of textile wall finish to fire growth in full-scale mockup	NFPA 265
Wall construction		
Wall and floor/ceiling assembly test	Fire ratings of walls, structure, and floor construction assemblies	ASTM E119
Ceiling finish		
Steiner tunnel test	Flame-spread rating of finishes	ASTM E84
Alternate to E84	Evaluates extent to which wall and ceiling finish (other than textiles) contributes to fire growth	NFPA 286
Door/glass openings		
Fire tests of door assemblies	Endurance test of doors to flame and heat transfer	NFPA 252 (UL 10C)
Fire tests of window assemblies	Endurance of glazing for 45 minutes to flame and heat transfer, including glass block	NFPA 257
Fire tests of fire-resistance-rated glazing	Endurance of glazing when tested as a transparent wall	ASTM E119
Trim and decorative materials		
Decorative materials	Draperies, curtains, and other window treatment as well as banners, awnings, and fabric structures	NFPA 701
Foam plastic used as trim	Maximum flame spread index of 75 with limitations on density, thickness, and total area within a room	ASTM E84
Trim such as baseboards, chair rails, picture molds, door and window frames	Flame-spread rating with minimum Class C, excluding handrails and guardrails	ASTM E84
Window coverings		
Vertical ignition test	Draperies, curtains, and other window treatment as well as banners, awnings, and fabric structures	NFPA 701

Requirements based on 2009 International Building Code

result is a material's flame-spread rating compared to glass-reinforced cement board (with a rating of 0) and red oak flooring (with an arbitrary rating of 100). ASTM E84 can also be used to generate a *smoke developed index*, which is a number representing the amount of smoke generated as a material burns in the test chamber.

With this test, materials are classified into one of three groups. A, B, or C, based on their tested flame-spread characteristics. These groups and their flame-spread indexes are given in Table 2-5.

Table 2-5 Flame-Spread Ratings

Class	Flame-Spread Rating
A (I)	0–25
B (II)	26–75
C (III)	76–200

Class A is the most fire resistant. Product literature generally indicates the flame spread of the material, either by class (indicated with a letter, A, B, or C) or by numerical value of I, II, or III. The IBC then specifies the minimum flame-spread requirements for various occupancies in specific areas of the building.

Traditionally, the E84 test was used exclusively for interior finishes, but the IBC also allows the use of finish materials other than textiles if they meet requirements set forth in the IBC when tested in accordance with NFPA 286 and when a Class A finish would otherwise be required.

NFPA 253

NFPA 253, *Standard Method of Test for Critical Radiant Flux for Floor Covering Systems Using a Radiant Heat Energy Source*. Also called the Flooring Radiant Panel Test, this procedure tests a sample of floor covering mounted on a typical substrate in the normal horizontal position and measures the flame spread in a corridor or exitway that is under the influence of a fully developed fire in an adjacent space. The resulting test numbers are measured in watts per square centimeter; the higher the number, the more resistant the material is to flame propagation. This is the same test as ASTM E648.

Two material classes are defined by NFPA 253: Class I and Class II. Class I materials have a critical radiant flux of 0.45 W/cm^2 or greater, and Class II materials have a critical radiant flux of 0.22 W/cm^2 or greater. Class I finishes are typically required in corridors and exitways of hospitals, nursing homes, and detention facilities. Class II flooring is typically required in corridors and exitways of other occupancies, except one- and two-family dwellings. The IBC establishes criteria that limit the critical radiant flux of flooring material for textile coverings or coverings composed of fibers. The IBC specifically excludes traditional flooring types such as wood, vinyl, linoleum, and terrazzo. It also allows Class II materials in sprinklered buildings where Class I materials might otherwise be required.

NFPA 265

NFPA 265 is the *Method of Fire Tests for Evaluating Room Fire Growth Contribution of Textile Wall Coverings on Full Height Panels and Walls*. Also called the Room Corner Test for Textile Wall Coverings, this test determines the contribution of interior wall and ceiling textile coverings to room fire growth. It attempts to simulate real-world conditions by testing the material in the corner of a full-sized test room. It was developed as an alternate to the ASTM E84 Steiner tunnel test.

NFPA 286

NFPA 286 is the *Standard Methods of Fire Test for Evaluating Contribution of Wall and Ceiling Interior Finish to Room Fire Growth*. Also called the Room Corner Test, this standard was developed to address concerns with interior finishes that do not remain in place during testing according to the E84 tunnel test. It is sometimes required in addition to or instead of an ASTM E84 rating for interior finishes. The 286 test evaluates materials other than textiles. It is similar to NFPA 265 in that materials are mounted on the walls or ceilings inside a room, but more of the test room wall surfaces are covered, and ceiling materials can be tested. This test evaluates the extent to which finishes contribute to fire growth in a room, assessing factors such as heat and smoke released, combustion products released, and the potential for fire spread beyond the room.

NFPA 701

NFPA 701 is the *Standard Methods of Fire Tests for Flame Propagation of Textiles and Films*. This test, also called the Vertical Ignition Test, establishes two procedures for testing the flammability of draperies, curtains, or other window treatments. Test 1 provides a procedure for assessing the response of fabrics lighter than 21 oz/yd^2 individually and in multilayer composites used as curtains, draperies, and other window treatments. Test 2 is for fabrics weighing more than 21 oz/yd^2, such as fabric blackout linings, awnings, and similar architectural fabric structures and banners. NFPA 701 is appropriate for testing materials that are exposed to air on both sides. A sample either passes or fails the test.

16 CFR 1630

Another test for carpet flammability is the *Code of Federal Regulations*, 16 CFR Part 1630 (also ASTM D2859, *Standard Test Method for Ignition Characteristics of Finished Textile Floor Covering Materials*), also known as the Methenamine Pill Test, which is required for all carpet sold and manufactured in the United States. A test sample of the carpet is placed in a draft-protected cube and held in place with a metal plate with an 8-in. (203-mm) diameter hole. A timed methenamine pill is placed in the center and lighted. If the sample burns to within 1 in. (25 mm) of the metal plate, it fails the test. This is also sometimes called by an older designation, DOC FF-1.

Fire Tests for Construction Assemblies

The following summaries include fire testing for building *assemblies* such as partitions, door openings, and ceiling/floor assemblies.

ASTM E119

One of the most commonly used tests for fire resistance of construction assemblies is ASTM E119, *Standard Test Methods for Fire Tests of Building Construction and Materials*. This test involves building a sample of the wall or floor/ceiling assembly in the laboratory and burning a controlled fire on one side. Monitoring devices measure temperature and other aspects of the test as it proceeds.

There are two parts to the E119 test. The first measures heat transfer through the assembly. The goal of this test is to determine the temperature at which the surface or adjacent materials on the side of the assembly not exposed to the heat source will combust. The second is the *hose stream test*, which uses a high-pressure fire hose stream to simulate an impact from falling debris to evaluate how well the assembly stands up to it and the cooling and eroding effects of water. Overall, the test evaluates an assembly's ability to prevent the passage of fire, heat, and hot gases for a given amount of time.

For construction assembly testing according to ASTM E119, a time-based rating is given to the assembly. In general terms, this rating is the amount of time an assembly can resist a standard test fire without failing. The ratings are 1 hour, 2 hours, 3 hours, and 4 hours. Doors and other opening assemblies can also be given 20-minute, 30-minute, and 45-minute ratings.

NFPA 252

NFPA 252, *Standard Methods for Fire Tests of Door Assemblies*, evaluates the ability of a door assembly to resist the passage of flame, heat, and gases. It establishes a time-endurance rating for the door assembly, and the hose stream part of the test determines if the door will stay within its frame when subjected to a standard blast from a fire hose after the door has been subjected to the fire-endurance part of the test. Similar tests include UL10B, UL10C, and UBC 7-2.

NFPA 257

NFPA 257, *Standard for Fire Test for Window and Glass Block Assemblies*, prescribes specific fire and hose stream test procedures to establish a degree of fire protection, in units of time, for window openings in fire-resistive walls. It determines the degree of protection from the spread of fire, including flame, heat, and hot gasses.

2-4 BUDGET

The budget for an interiors project is usually fixed and, in the designer's mind, never enough to do the job adequately. However, like other constraints, the budget can be a generator of design ideas and solutions whether is it low *or* high. A low budget may force the designer to explore new ways of using inexpensive materials and construction processes, while a generous budget may encourage exploration into materials and solutions that the designer might otherwise not investigate.

Even though a budget is fixed there are three ways to use it: by reallocation, phasing, and life-cycle costing. Reallocation is simply setting priorities concerning what is most important in the overall design and using more of the budget in those areas and less where it may not be as important. For example, in an office design, it may be more important to spend more of the budget in the public reception and conference areas than in private offices. The designer may even suggest forgoing private offices for systems furniture to reduce construction costs and where the purchase may have beneficial tax advantages for the client.

Phasing is the postponement of building a portion of the interior until more money is available. The designer may feel it is critical for the success of the project to put the available budget into certain areas, while waiting to complete other portions of the project. For example, basic partition and ceiling finishes can be used until money is available for more decorative treatments and improved functionality. Of course, the reality of this approach is that more money is seldom available or the client will elect never to make the additional improvements.

Life-cycle costing is more than examining just the first costs of construction. Instead, it determines what the cost is over the life of the product or material, including the maintenance costs of a material, its expected service life, its replacement costs, disposal costs, and the value of money over time. Although not technically a way to use an existing budget, the technique may be used to convince a client it is in their economic interest to budget more money initially. For example, one flooring material may have a higher first cost than another but will last longer and require lower maintenance and disposal costs over its service life and, in the long run, be less expensive for the client.

Whether or not life-cycle costing is important depends on the type of client. If the client will the owner of the facility and be responsible for its maintenance, then long-terms costs are important. If the client is a tenant and expects only short-term use and will not be responsible for maintenance and replacement, then only first costs are likely to be important. It is beyond the scope of this book to discuss the methods in detail but one good resource is *Life Cycle Costing for Facilities* by Alphonse J. Dell'Isola (Reed Construction Data, 2003).

In the detailing process the designer can most affect the cost of construction in material selection and the complexity of details. In many cases, a less expensive finish material can achieve the same goals as a more expensive material without compromising the look and overall effect of the design. As discussed in Chapter 4, the designer can also minimize costs by developing a detail with the least number of components and connections, and by minimizing the number of construction trades involved and the time it takes to build the detail.

2-5 TIME

In the construction industry, time is always a constraint. It is closely related to budget in that the longer it takes to design and build generally the more money it takes, unless the contractor is working on a strictly fixed price basis. The interior designer is usually under constant pressure to produce the design and construction documentation as fast as possible. In turn, accurate, innovative, and efficient details must be completed as quickly as possible. If time is limited, the designer may decide to use simple, standard details that can be developed quickly without excessive research, development, review, and documentation. In turn, standard details generally require less time to build than custom details.

When selecting materials, availability is an important criterion as it relates to how easily a product can be obtained and if it can be delivered to the job site in time to maintain the overall project schedule. Some specialty products can require six months or more to get. Other products are in stock for immediate delivery but may only be available in a limited choice of colors or finishes. Some products are specifically available in "quick ship" programs to meet tight schedules.

2-6 CLIMATE

Although climate does not influence interior design nearly as much as architectural design, it can nonetheless affect some material and detailing decisions. The orientation of windows and sun angle can influence the type of window coverings and selection of materials that may fade in the sunlight. Hard, durable, easy-to-clean flooring materials near entrances may be warranted in climates where snow, rain, and mud are tracked into the building. In very dry climates, wood should be detailed differently than in humid climates to conceal the inevitable shrinkage. If the building in which the interior project is located was built to use passive solar design, the choice of interior materials and construction should not compromise this intent.

2-7 LOCAL LABOR CONDITIONS AND TRADE PRACTICES

The local labor market for an interior design project can affect the selection of materials and construction techniques in four ways. These include the availability of skilled labor, the common trade divisions of labor, the use of union or nonunion workers, and the preferred local materials and construction methods.

First, every interior design project, residential or commercial, requires some type of skilled labor, whether it is as simple as painting or as complex as installing a custom stair involving steel, glass, stone, and other materials. Most large urban markets have an abundance of skilled labor in all trades, while smaller cities and rural areas may not. If cost and time are important constraints, the detailer may want to select materials and develop details that the local labor market can readily construct. The alternate is to have skilled labor brought in from other areas, usually at a significant cost. Even for projects in large cities, some specialty product manufacturers often insist on using their own installers or approved installers, who may be far removed from the project locale.

Second, the construction industry has developed commonly accepted divisions of labor; that is, one type of worker will only do particular work. A plumber, for example, does not install gypsum wallboard. For every trade worker involved in a detail, the cost increases. The best approach to detailing is to design the detail to minimize the number of separate trades that must work on it.

A related factor is the sequence of labor. In most cases, tradespeople do not want to be working in the same area of the project as other trades and generally only want to come on a job site once. A detail that requires a trade to do one portion of a job, leave the job site, and come back later to do additional work will cost more, and such a detail runs the risk of slowing the job if the trade cannot come back at the appropriate time to finish its work. For example, a complex partition detail should not require drywall finishers to finish part of their work before the carpenters can place additional framing, which then requires the finishers to return to complete their work. This type of detail would only be efficient if the drywall finishers could be working on another part of the job while the carpenters prepared the framing for them. Table 2-6 lists some of the common trade names and the type of work they do as well as the unions that represent the workers when union labor is involved.

The third way labor can affect detailing is whether or not union or nonunion workers will be involved. Again, if cost is a consideration, union work on a detail may be slightly more expensive than having it built by nonunion workers. The robustness of the local labor market may also affect the cost of building. When business is good and competition low, price estimates are usually higher than in sluggish markets. Both of these factors may suggest how complex a detail should be given the client's budget. Refer to the various union web sites given in Table 2-6 for more information.

Finally, any given labor market has preferred materials and methods of building. For example, in the northeast part of the United States, it is common for gypsum veneer plaster to be used whereas in the Midwest, gypsum wallboard is only finished at the joints and fastener locations. When working in a new or unfamiliar market, the interior designer should talk with local designers and contractors to determine local trade practices.

2-8 INDUSTRY STANDARDS

Three of the basic constraints for detailing are industry standards for sizes, material quality, and configuration of details. Common materials such as lumber, steel studs, panel products, and metal shapes are manufactured to standard sizes and shapes. In nearly all cases, these should be used as is, although some materials can be modified more easily than others. For example, it is a fairly simple matter to trim a piece of lumber to a custom size but not possible to manufacture nonstandard metal studs. It may be possible to have a metal

Table 2-6 Trade Divisions of Labor

Trade Name	Work Performed	Trade Union
Carpenter, residential carpenter	Residential rough and finish carpentry, residential flooring	UBC
Carpenter, interior systems carpenter	Metal studs and framing, suspended ceiling systems, wood trim, specialty interior products	UBC
Carpenter, lather/drywaller	Lath for plaster	UBC
Carpenter, cabinet maker/millworker	Architectural woodwork, store fixtures, furniture	UBC
Carpenter, floorlayer	Carpet, hardwood flooring, resilient flooring	UBC
Drywall finisher	Drywall taping and finishing	IUPAT
Plasterer	Plastering, concrete construction, cement finishing	OPCMIA
Flooring installer	Carpet, resilient flooring, prefinished hardwood, Laminate flooring, seamless flooring, flooring trim and accessories, underlayment	IUPAT
Mason	Stone and marble masonry, tile setting, terrazzo and mosaic	BAC
Painter	Painting, wallcovering, stretched fabric systems, plastic wallcoverings, wall accessories and trim	IUPAT
Glazier	Glass, mirrors, decorative glass, glass handrails, shower enclosures, aluminum storefront frames, suspended glass systems, column covers, glass doors	IUPAT
Ornamental iron worker (finisher)	Ornamental metal, metal stairs, gratings and ladders, railings, elevator fronts, metal screens	IABSORIW
Sheet metal worker	Architectural sheet metal work, HVAC, heating and air conditioning ducts	SMWIA
Sign and display worker	Signage, trade show decorators, metal polishing	IUPAT
Electrician (inside wireman)	Electrical, computer cabling, telecommunications	IBEW
Plumber	Plumbing	UA
Sprinkler fitter	Sprinkler systems	UA
Elevator contractor	Elevator installation and remodeling	IUEC
Steel worker (steel fixer)	Reinforcing bar for concrete	IABSORIW

BAC	International Union of Bricklayers and Allied Craftworkers bacweb.org
IABSORIW	International Association of Bridge, Structural, Ornamental and Reinforcing Iron Workers ironworkers.org
IBEW	International Brotherhood of Electrical Workers ibew.org
IUEC	International Union of Elevator Contractors iuec.org
IUPAT	International Union of Painters and Allied Trades iupat.org
OPCMIA	Operative Plasterers' and Cement Masons' International Association opcmia.org
SMWIA	Sheet Metal Workers International Association smwia.org
UA	United Association of Journeymen and Apprentices of the Plumbing and Pipe Fitting Industry of the United States and Canada ua.org
UBC	United Brotherhood of Carpenters and Joiners of America carpenters.org

shop custom-fabricate a unique size of brass angle, but it is less costly and faster to use a standard brass angle size. Proprietary products are often manufactured to fixed sizes, and these sizes are usually the basis for developing a detail that incorporates them into the design. Standard methods of detailing can be found in references such as *Interior Graphic Standards* and *Architectural Graphic Standards*. Refer to Appendix A for a list of industry standards for material qualities.

Some common sizes of substrates are given in Table 2-1. In addition, limiting sizes of metal partition framing, glass, and ornamental metal are often constraints when developing custom details. The sizes and shapes of common metal framing components are shown in Fig. 2-3.

Constraints of glass detailing are shown in Fig. 2-4, and values are given in Tables 2-7, 2-8, and 2-9.

Details utilizing ornamental metal are least costly and most efficient if standard shapes and sizes are used. Some of these for stainless steel and brass and copper alloys are shown in Figs. 2-5 and 2-6, and sizes given in Tables 2-10 and 2-11.

Figure 2-3 Common metal framing components

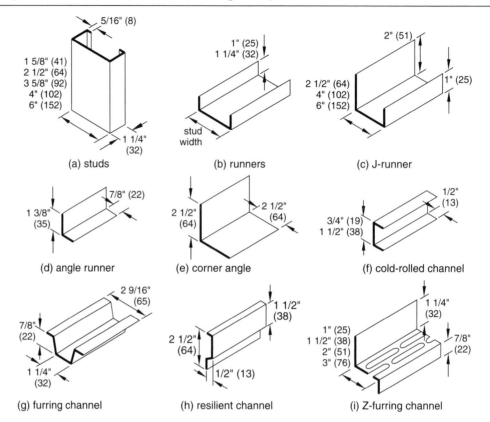

(a) studs

(b) runners

(c) J-runner

(d) angle runner

(e) corner angle

(f) cold-rolled channel

(g) furring channel

(h) resilient channel

(i) Z-furring channel

Figure 2-4 Glazing framing dimensions

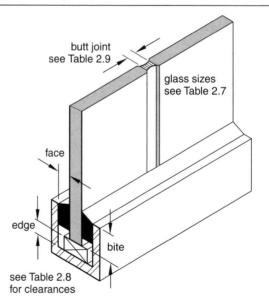

butt joint
see Table 2.9

glass sizes
see Table 2.7

face

edge

bite

see Table 2.8
for clearances

Table 2-7 Approximate Maximum Glass Sizes Based on Type and Thickness

Glass Type	Thickness, in. (mm)	Maximum Size, in. (mm)
Float glass	1/8 (3)	102 × 130 (2590 × 3300)
	1/4 (6)	130 × 200 (3300 × 5080)
Tempered glass	1/8 (3)	42 × 84 (1067 × 2134)
	3/16 (5)	78 × 102 (2000 × 2600)
	1/4 (6)	78 × 165 (2000 × 4200)
	3/8 (10)	78 × 165 (2000 × 4200)
	1/2 (12)	78 × 165 (2000 × 4200)
	3/4 (19)	71 × 158 (1800 × 4000)
Laminated glass	13/64 (5.2)	84 × 130 (2134 × 3300)
	9/32 (7.1)	84 × 144 (2134 × 3658)
	1/2 (13)	84 × 180 (2134 × 4570)
Bent glass, tempered	1/4 (6)	130 × 72 (curve) (3300 × 1830)
	1/2 (12)	130 × 84 (curve) (3300 × 2134)
Fire-resistant rated (requires manufacturer's special framing)	45 min., 3/4 (19)	95 × 95 (2413 × 2413)
	60 min., 15/16 (23)	95 × 95 (2413 × 2413)
	90 min., 1-7/16 (37)	90 × 90 (2286 × 2286)

Source: manufacturers' catalogs. Sizes are only approximate; consult individual manufacturers for specific limits on size based on glass type and thickness.

Table 2-8 Recommended Face and Edge Clearance for Interior Glass

Glass Thickness, in. (mm)	Minimum Clearance, in. (mm)		
	Face	Edge	Bite
1/8 (3)	1/8 (3.2)	1/4 (6.4)	3/8 (9.5)
3/16 (5)	1/8 (3.2)	1/4 (6.4)	3/8 (9.5)
1/4 (6)	1/8 (3.2)	1/4 (6.4)	3/8 (9.5)
5/16 (8)	3/16 (4.8)	5/16 (7.9)	7/16 (11.1)
3/8 (10)	3/16 (4.8)	3/16 (4.8)	7/16 (11.1)
1/2 (12)	1/4 (6.4)	3/8 (9.5)	7/16 (11.1)
3/4 (19)	1/4 (6.4)	1/2 (12.7)	5/8 (15.9)

Source: GANA Glazing Manual

Table 2-9 Recommended Joint Width for Butt-joint Glazing

Glass Thickness, in. (mm)	Joint Width, Min., in. (mm)	Joint Width, Max., in. (mm)
3/8 (10)	3/8 (10)	7/16 (11)
1/2 (12)	3/8 (10)	7/16 (11)
5/8 (16)	3/8 (10)	1/2 (12)
3/4 (19)	1/2 (12)	5/8 (16)
7/8 (22)	1/2 (12)	5/8 (16)

Source: GANA Glazing Manual

Figure 2-5 Standard stainless steel shapes

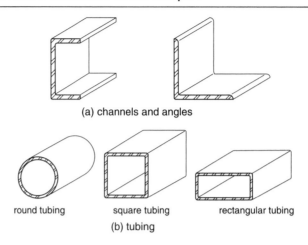

(a) channels and angles

round tubing   square tubing   rectangular tubing

(b) tubing

2-9   MATERIALS

Although an almost unlimited number of details can be developed using standard materials, each does have its own advantages and disadvantages that the detailer must understand to use them effectively. Many products have withstood the test of time, and their quality and characteristics are well known and documented. Newer materials should be reviewed carefully and their qualities documented with standardized tests or individual manufacturer's tests to verify that they will serve the intended purpose. The manufacturer is the best source for detailed information on any particular product. However, for a more objective evaluation, trade associations and designers who have already used a new material are good sources to consult. When determining which materials or products to use in a detail, the following criteria should be reviewed.

Figure 2-6 Standard brass shapes

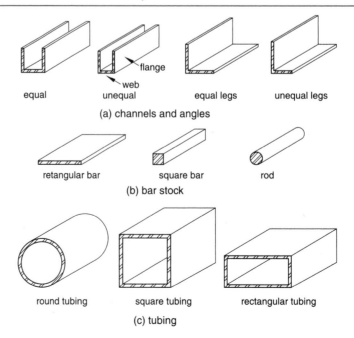

equal   unequal   equal legs   unequal legs

flange
web

(a) channels and angles

retangular bar   square bar   rod

(b) bar stock

round tubing   square tubing   rectangular tubing

(c) tubing

Table 2-10 Standard Sizes of Common Stainless Steel Shapes

Channels, in. (mm)				Square Tubing, in. (mm)		Tubing, in. (mm)	
Flange	Web	Thickness	Angles, in. (mm)	Size	Thickness	Rectangular	Round[a]
1 (25.4)	2 (50.8)	1/4 (6.4)	3/4 × 3/4 × 1/8 (19.1 × 19.1 × 3.2)	5/8 × 5/8 (15.9 × 15.9)	0.060 (1.52)	1/2 × 1 × 0.060 (12.7 × 25.4 × 1.52)	1 (25.4)
1-1/2 (38.1)	3 (76.2)	3/16 (4.8)	1 × 1 × 1/8 (25.4 × 25.4 × 3.2)	3/4 × 3/4 (19.1 × 19.1)	0.060 (1.52)	3/4 × 1 × 0.060 (19.1 × 25.4 × 1.52)	1-1/4 (31.8)
1-1/2 (38.1)	3 (76.2)	1/4 (6.4)	1-1/4 × 1-1/4 × 1/8 (31.8 × 31.8 × 3.2)	1 × 1 (25.4 × 25.4)	0.060 (1.52)	1 × 2 × 0.060 (25.4 × 50.8 × 1.52)	1-1/2 (38.1)
1-3/4 (44.5)	4 (101.6)	1/4 (6.4)	1-1/4 × 1-1/4 × 3/16 (31.8 × 31.8 × 4.8)	1 × 1 (25.4 × 25.4)	0.083 (2.11)	1 × 2 × 0.120 (25.4 × 50.8 × 3.05)	1-5/8 (41.3)
2 (50.8)	4 (101.6)	1/4 (6.4)	1-1/2 × 1-1/2 × 1/8 (38.1 × 38.1 × 3.2)	1-1/4 × 1-1/4 (31.8 × 31.8)	0.060 (1.52)	1 × 3 × 0.120 (25.4 × 76.2 × 3.05)	1-3/4 (44.5)
2-1/2 (63.5)	5 (127)	1/4 (6.4)	1-1/2 × 1-1/2 × 3/16 (38.1 × 38.1 × 4.8)	1-1/4 × 1-1/4 (31.8 × 31.8)	0.120 (3.05)	1-1/2 × 2-1/2 × 0.120 (38.1 × 63.5 × 3.05)	2 (50.8)
3 (76.2)	6 (152.4)	1/4 (6.4)	2 × 2 × 1/8 (50.8 × 50.8 × 3.2)	1-1/2 × 1-1/2 (38.1 × 38.1)	0.049 (1.24)	2 × 3 × 0.060 (50.8 × 76.2 × 1.52)	2-1/2 (63.5)
3 (76.2)	6 (152.4)	3/8 (9.5)	2 × 2 × 3/16 (50.8 × 50.8 × 4.8)	1-1/2 × 1-1/2 (38.1 × 38.1)	0.060 (1.52)	2 × 3 × 0.120 (50.8 × 76.2 × 3.05)	3 (76.2)
			2-1/2 × 2-1/2 × 3/16 (63.5 × 63.5 × 4.8)	1-1/2 × 1-1/2 (38.1 × 38.1)	0.083 (2.11)	2 × 4 × 0.120 (50.8 × 101.6 × 3.05)	
			3 × 3 × 3/16 (76.2 × 76.2 × 4.8)	2 × 2 (50.8 × 50.8)	0.060 (1.52)		
			3-1/2 × 3-1/2 × 1/4 (88.9 × 88.9 × 6.4)	2 × 2 (50.8 × 50.8)	0.083 (2.11)		
			4 × 4 × 1/4 (101.6 × 101.6 × 6.4)	2-1/2 × 2-1/2 (63.5 × 63.5)	0.120 (3.05)		
				3 × 3 (76.2 × 76.2)	0.120 (3.05)		

Source: manufacturers' catalogs. Other sizes, thicknesses, and shapes are available but these are the most common for interior detailing. Verify with manufacturer.
[a]Diameter in. (mm). All round tubing is 0.062 in. (1.58 mm) thick.

Aesthetic Qualities

Aesthetic qualities are the characteristics that contribute to the design intent of the detail, as reviewed in Chapter 1. These qualities either contribute to the overall design concept of the space, resolve problems of connection or transition, visually coordinate with adjacent construction, or fulfill some combination of these three purposes.

Depending on the particular material or product, aesthetic qualities include color, texture, scale, proportion, shape, line, form, light reflectance, and any number of unique qualities specific to the material. The designer must make selections based on aesthetic qualities, while considering the other functional and practical aspects of the material. Some manufacturers or product lines may have a wider range of choice than others, and this fact alone my sway the decision to use a particular company or material.

Function

Acoustic qualities of a material relate to the material's ability to absorb sound or to block the transmission of sound. For most finish materials, sound absorption is the more important criterion and is typically measured with the sound absorption average (SAA) or the previously used noise reduction coefficient (NRC). For open-plan office design, the articulation class of

Table 2-11 Standard Sizes of Brass Shapes

Channels[a]			Angles[b]			
	Unequal Legs					Square Bars
Equal Legs	Flange	Web	Equal Legs	Unequal Legs	Rectangular Bars[c]	and Rods
1/4 × 1/4 (6.4 × 6.4)	1/2 (12.7)	3/8 (9.5)	3/8 × 3/8 (9.5 × 9.5)	3/8 × 3/4 (9.5 × 19.1)	1/8 × 1/2 (3.2 × 12.7)	1/4 (6.4)
3/8 × 3/8 (9.5 × 9.5)	1/2 (12.7)	3/4 (19.1)	1/2 × 1/2 (12.7 × 12.7)	1/2 × 3/4 (12.7 × 19.1)	1/8 × 5/8 (3.2 × 15.9)	5/16 (7.9)
1/2 × 1/2 (12.7 × 12.7)	1/2 (12.7)	1 (25.4)	5/8 × 5/8 (15.9 × 15.9)	1/2 × 1 (12.7 × 25.4)	1/8 × 3/4 (3.2 × 19.1)	3/8 (9.5)
5/8 × 5/8 (15.9 × 15.9)	1/2 (12.7)	1-1/4 (31.8)	3/4 × 3/4 (19.1 × 19.1)	1/2 × 1-1/2 (12.7 × 38.1)	1/8 × 1 (3.2 × 25.4)	1/2 (12.7)
3/4 × 3/4 (19.1 × 19.1)	1/2 (12.7)	1-1/2 (38.1)	1 × 1 (25.4 × 25.4)	1/2 × 2 (12.7 × 50.8)	1/8 × 1-1/4 (3.2 × 31.8)	5/8 (15.9)
1 × 1 (25.4 × 25.4)	5/8 (15.9)	1-1/4 (31.8)	1-1/4 × 1-1/4 (31.8 × 31.8)	3/4 × 1 (19.1 × 25.4)	1/8 × 1-1/2 (3.2 × 38.1)	3/4 (19.1)
1-1/4 × 1-1/4 (31.8 × 31.8)	5/8 (15.9)	1-1/2 (38.1)	1-1/2 × 1-1/2 (38.1 × 38.1)	3/4 × 1-1/4 (19.1 × 31.8)	1/8 × 2 (3.2 × 50.8)	1 (25.4)
1-1/2 × 1-1/2 (38.1 × 38.1)	3/4 (19.1)	1/2 (12.7)	2 × 2 (50.8 × 50.8)	3/4 × 1-1/2 (19.1 × 38.1)	3/16 × 3/8 (4.8 × 9.5)	1-1/4 (31.8)
2 × 2 (50.8 × 50.8)	3/4 (19.1)	1 (25.4)	2-1/2 × 2-1/2 (63.5 × 63.5)	1 × 1-1/2 (25.4 × 38.1)	3/16 × 1/2 (4.8 × 12.7)	
	3/4 (19.1)	2 (50.8)	3 × 3 (76.2 × 76.2)	1 × 2 (25.4 × 50.8)	3/16 × 3/4 (4.8 × 19.1)	
	1 (25.4)	3/4 (19.1)			3/16 × 1 (4.8 × 25.4)	
	1 (25.4)	1-1/2 (38.1)			1/4 × 1/2 (6.4 × 12.7)	
	1 (25.4)	2 (50.8)			1/4 × 3/4 (6.4 × 19.1)	
	1 (25.4)	2-1/2 (63.5)			1/4 × 1 (6.4 × 25.4)	
	1-1/2 (38.1)	2-1/2 (63.5)			1/4 × 1-1/4 (6.4 × 31.8)	
					1/4 × 1-1/2 (6.4 × 38.1)	
					1/4 × 1-3/4 (6.4 × 44.5)	
					1/4 × 2 (6.4 × 50.8)	

Source: manufacturers' catalogs. Verify available sizes with manufacturer. Other sizes are available but these are the most common for interior detailing.
[a]channel thickness varies with size ranging from 0.062 in (1.58 mm) to 0.125 in (3.18 mm).
[b]angles are typically 1/8 in (3.2 mm) thick.
[c]rectangular bars are also available in 3/8 in., 1/2 in., and 3/4 in (9.5 mm, 12.7 mm, and 19.1 mm) thicknesses.

ceilings may also be important. For details of barriers, such as partitions, doors, glazing, and ceiling assemblies, sound transmission is important and may factor into the configuration of the detail.

Installation method is the precise sequence of steps needed to place the material or product into the work. Installation method can affect the cost and scheduling of a material and whether skilled workers will be required or not. In most cases, installation methods for the same types of materials will be very similar. However, some specialty items may require a particular method using factory-approved installers.

Refer to Chapter 3 for a full discussion of functional requirements of details.

Safety and Health

Safety relates to the prevention of accidental harm to people, as well as to security from intentional harm. Health covers a wide variety of topics, from mold resistance to indoor air quality.

Finish safety relates to the surface and edge condition of products. There should be no sharp projections, edges, or surfaces rough enough to cut or abrade people when they come in contact with the exposed portions of the detail.

Flammability, the likelihood that a material will combust, is one of the most important criteria for material and finish selection. Regulatory requirements for flammability is discussed in a separate section of this chapter.

Mold and mildew resistance of a material is important to prevent the growth of these microscopic organisms. Many materials are inherently susceptible to the growth of mold or mildew because they provide an organic nutrient that, when combined with moisture and a suitable temperature, will provide a growing medium for these biological contaminants. Most materials can be treated to resist the growth of mold and mildew.

Outgassing is the release of toxic gasses from materials, most commonly after the material has been installed. These gasses include formaldehyde, chlorofluorocarbons (CFCs), and others listed on the Environmental Protection Agency's list of hazardous substances. Outgassing is one of the important components of indoor air quality. Refer to Chapter 3 for a discussion of sustainability issues.

Security is providing protection against theft, vandalism, intentional physical harm, or a combination of all three. If security is an important aspect of a design, material and product selection can be evaluated in terms of this. Doors, glazing, and hardware are common products that are available with various levels of security.

Slip resistance is the ability of a flooring material to help prevent accidental slipping. It is commonly measured with the coefficient of friction (COF). The COF is a measurement of the degree of slip resistance of a floor surface and ranges from 0 to 1. The higher the COF, the less slippery the surface. Although both the International Building Code and the Americans with Disabilities Act require flooring to be slip resistant, there are no specific requirements for the COF.

Many variables affect slip resistance, including wet versus dry conditions, shoe material, a person's weight, the angle of impact, stride length, and floor contamination. Numerous tests have been developed to measure the COF accurately and consistently, while accounting for the slip-resistance variables. These ASTM tests are listed in Appendix A. One of the most commonly used tests is ASTM D2047, *Standard Test Method for Static Coefficient of Friction of Polish-Coated Floor Surfaces as Measured by the James Machine.* This test is considered by many to be the most accurate and reliable measurement of slip resistance. However, it can only be performed in the laboratory on smooth, dry surfaces. It should not be used for wet or rough surfaces.

When using the James Machine test, a COF of 0.5 has generally been considered the minimum required for a slip-resistant floor. Underwriters Laboratories requires a level of 0.5 or higher as a minimum safety level based on the ASTM C1028 standard. The Occupational Safety and Health Administration (OSHA) also recommends a COF of 0.5 as a minimum. Some have suggested a level of 0.6 for a good slip-resistant floor. In any case, when developing flooring details and specifying slip resistance, the designer must refer to the specific test being used.

As stated earlier, the Americans with Disabilities Act requires that a floor surface be slip resistant, but it does not give any specific test values. However, an appendix in a handbook

Table 2-12 VOC Limits for Interior Materials

Material	Volume Limits, g/L (lb/gal)		
	EPA Limits	California Limits[a]	Green Seal Limits
Flat, interior paint	250 (2.1)	50 (0.42)	100 (0.84)[b]
Nonflat, interior paint	380 (3.2)	50 (0.42)	150 (1.26)[b]
Interior stains	550 (4.6)[c]	100 (0.84)	250 (2.10)
Clear wood finishes, varnish	450 (3.8)	275 (2.31)	350 (2.94)
Clear wood finish, lacquer	680 (5.7)	275 (2.31)	550 (4.62)
Multicolored coatings	580 (4.8)	250 (2.1)	
Carpet adhesives		50 (0.42)	150 (1.26)[d]
Wood flooring adhesives		100 (0.84)	150 (1.26)
Ceramic tile adhesives		65 (0.55)	130 (1.09)
Drywall and panel adhesives		50 (0.42)	
Multipurpose construction adhesives		70 (0.59)	200 (1.68)

[a]South Coast Air Quality Management District (SCAQMD) Rules 1113 and 1168.
[b]Effective 1/1/10 with colorant added at the point-of-sale.
[c]EPA limits for clear and semitransparent stains. Opaque stain limits are 350 g/L (2.9 lb/gal).
[d]For carpet pad only.
In California the Collaborative for High Performance Schools (CHPS) maintains a low-emitting material list at www.chps.net/manual/lem_table.htm.

for the ADA recommends a static coefficient of friction of 0.6 for accessible routes and 0.8 for ramps.

Until specific, uniform criteria are established, the designer should take into account the conditions under which flooring materials will be used before selecting a particular type of floor and incorporating it into a detail. For example, a public lobby where snow and rain may be tracked in may need to be more slip resistant than a residential bathroom, where people are taking smaller strides without slippery shoe material.

Volatile organic compound (VOC) emissions result when chemicals that contain carbon and hydrogen vaporize at room temperature and pressure. VOCs are found in many indoor sources such as paint, sealants, and carpeting as well as many cleaning products. When selecting a material, its VOC content must be limited to the applicable standards. Table 2-12 gives some VOC standards from various organizations. Refer to Chapter 3 for a discussion of VOCs.

Durability

Durability relates to the serviceability of the product or material when in use. There are many aspects of durability, and one or more of these may apply to a particular detail. The following list gives some of the more common aspects of durability. Most of them have associated ASTM or other recognized standards that describe how they are measured and applied to products. Some standards are specific to a particular type of test, while others apply to a particular type of material. For example, durability standards for wall coverings are covered in ASTM F793, *Standard Classification of Wallcovering by Durability Characteristics*.

Abrasion resistance is the ability of a material or finish to resist being worn away or to maintain its original appearance when rubbed with another object. Abrasion resistance can be measured according to several standard test methods.

Attachment is the method by which one material is connected to another. This criterion can have a significant influence on product selection, depending on the substrate. Some products or materials cannot be attached to other materials or can only be attached with significant expense or extra effort. Attachment is one criterion that applies to nearly all materials and that must be reviewed as part of a systematic view of the entire detail of which the material is a part. Connection methods are discussed in more detail in Chapter 4.

Breaking strength refers to the load that, when placed on a material, is just great enough to break the material. In interior design, it typically refers to fabrics and other textiles where the load is applied in the plane of the material, with the material laid flat. It may also apply to tile, stone, and other materials subjected to a localized load.

Chemical resistance is a material's resistance to damage, change of finish, or other deleterious changes resulting from exposure to chemicals. Because there are so many possible combinations of chemicals and finishes, most manufacturers specifically state which chemicals their products are resistant to.

Coating adhesion refers to the ability of a thin coating, like wall covering or paint, to adhere to its substrate.

Colorfastness is the resistance of a finish to change or loss of color when exposed to light, most commonly the ultraviolet light of the sun.

Corrosion resistance is a product's resistance to deterioration by a chemical or electrochemical reaction resulting from exposure to moisture, chemicals, or other elements. Corrosion is typically a problem when metal products are exposed to moisture.

Fabrication quality is the measure of how well a product is assembled in the factory. Each industry establishes measures of fabrication quality. For example, woodwork is measured according to three grades—economy, custom, and premium—as established by the Architectural Woodwork Institute's (AWI's) *Architectural Woodwork Standards*.

Heat-aging resistance is a wall covering's resistance to the deterioration caused by high temperatures over an extended time.

Scrubbability is a material's ability to be cleaned repeatedly with a brush and detergent.

Stain resistance is a material's resistance to a change in appearance after the application and removal of another material. As with chemical resistance, all products are resistant to some staining agents more than others, so the manufacturer's literature should be consulted to verify if a material is resistant to staining agents likely to be present in a particular application.

Maintainability

Maintainablity is an important quality for finish materials, products, and details that experience wear and tear through the life of a building. All buildings and interior finishes need to be maintained to preserve their appearance and service life. Many durability criteria directly relate to maintainability; the more durable a material is, the less maintenance is required.

Cleanability refers to the ease with which a material can be cleaned using whatever methods are appropriate for the material. For example, carpet must be easy to vacuum, while wall finishes in a restaurant should be easy to wash. Because all materials in all types of buildings get dirty with time, cleanability is one of the most important criteria to consider when selecting finishes and incorporating them into a detail.

Repairability is a product or material's ability to be repaired when damaged. The ability to replace damaged components of a detail may also be evaluated when selecting a product. The designer should avoid details that make it difficult or expensive to repair or replace one of the component parts.

Resilience is a material's capacity to recover its original size and shape after deformation caused by some load. Resilience is typically applied to soft floor covering material, such as vinyl tile but may also be an important consideration for wall details that incorporate soft covering materials.

Self-healing quality is a material's ability to return to its original configuration after it has been deformed or temporarily changed. It is similar to resilience but may apply to any type of product. For example, the holes in a corkboard should be self-healing after pins have been removed.

Cost and Delivery Time

Cost of a detail, as it relates to overall project budget, was discussed in a previous section. However, when looking at a detail individually, it is important to look at the cost of the detail in proportion to the total cost of the project. If the entire project is going to cost $3 million, it does not make sense to spend a great deal of time and worry over saving $100 on one detail. On the other hand, if research and study on a typical wall detail of the same building can save $30,000, then it is reasonable to make the effort. In another situation, saving a little money on quantity items is desirable. If just $100 can be trimmed from the construction cost of one door detail that occurs three hundred times, then saving this amount will add up to $30,000.

Also, as previously discussed, the availability and delivery time of components of a detail may affect how the designer develops a detail.

Sustainability

Sustainability can be viewed as a constraint if there are local, state, or federal regulations concerning aspects such as energy use, volatile organic compounds, indoor air quality, and the like. For example, California has very strict regulations on VOCs, lighting, and other aspects of energy conservation. However, in most cases, sustainability should be viewed as a basic function of any detail, even absent governmental regulations. Refer to Chapter 3 for a discussion of sustainability issues as a functional requirement.

CHAPTER 3

FUNCTION

3-1 INTRODUCTION

Function is the requirement or set of requirements a detail must meet based on its basic purpose. For example, a doorframe must provide support for the door, conceal the rough opening, provide a way to stop the door swing, and provide a way to latch or lock the door. If the opening is fire rated, the frame must also be rated along with the other components of the opening. Although related, function is most often independent of design intent, constraints, and constructability issues. In the case of a doorframe, the door must be supported by the frame regardless of the design of the opening or constraints such as local regulatory requirements or the project budget. This chapter reviews some of the common functional requirements of details and how they can be met.

3-2 CONCEALMENT AND FINISH

Details are often used to conceal other construction or simply as a decorative surface. For example, a wood base hides the joint between the partition and the floor. A coat of plaster provides a smooth finish over a rough concrete masonry wall.

In many cases, a concealing or finishing detail is simple, with few requirements other than direct application. In other situations, the concealing detail may be an integral part of the detail it covers, requiring the detailer to consider requirements such as fire resistance, durability, connections, movement, and tolerances. There are three variations of concealment and finish: covering substrates, covering joints or connections, and hiding mechanical and electrical services.

Covering Substrates

Covering a substrate is the simplest type of concealment and finish detail. It can be as straightforward as painting, applying wallpaper, and laying carpet, or more complex such as hanging thick stone panels on a high partition. However, even the simplest material application must take into account concerns such as the limitations of the material, the proper type and preparation of the substrate, and material durability.

Most designers and architects consider the requirements of applied materials to be specification items. Although they are communicated in writing in the specifications, they are best dealt with during the early stages of detail design and development. By reviewing applied materials early in the process, the designer can prevent problems, develop useful information for the specification writer, and coordinate the efforts of the design team.

There are two detailing responses for *covering substrates*.

MINIMIZE THE NUMBER OF CONSTRUCTION STEPS

To minimize costs and speed construction the number of individual steps required to apply a finish should be kept to a minimum. For example, if a rough plaster finish is desired, it may be possible to achieve it with veneer plaster construction rather than a more complex three-coat plaster application. If the right paint is specified in the correct dry-film thickness one coat can be used instead of two coats.

MINIMIZE THE WEIGHT/THICKNESS/SIZE OF THE COVERING, WHEN APPROPRIATE

In most situations, minimizing the weight, thickness, or size of the covering saves money, simplifies installation, and minimizes structural problems. For example, using thin veneer stone as a wall covering requires a less rigid substrate than a traditional full-thickness stone application. It is also faster and costs less. See Fig. 3-1. Thick stone would only have to be used if the substrate was significantly out of plumb or if large, individual stone panels were required.

However, minimizing thickness and weight is not always desirable. When the functions of fire resistance, acoustics, durability, maintainability, and security are considered, a heavier or thicker covering may be required. The desired weight and thickness of the covering should be matched to the functional needs and approved by the client before detailing begins.

Covering Joints and Connections

In many details, there are rough joining methods or mechanical connections that should not be visible, either for strictly aesthetic reasons or for reasons of safety, security, or maintainability. For instance, the joint between a carpet and adjacent tile flooring can be made without any covering, as shown in Fig. 3-2(a), if the installer correctly turns the edge. However, it is likely that the joint will collect dirt, the carpet edge will fray, and the edge of the tile will chip. Two simple solutions are to use a metal edge or cover the joint with a metal strip, as shown in Figs. 3-2(b) and (c). Although other solutions are possible, these are two of the simplest.

In some cases, however, the designer may decide to emphasize the joints or connections, making them a prominent design feature. While this may contribute to the overall design concept, it can create other problems. Complex and intricate details can collect dirt, dust, and debris and may require greater maintenance than construction where complex joining is covered.

There are three detailing responses for *covering joints and connections*.

COORDINATE WITH OTHER FUNCTIONAL NEEDS

The strictly functional needs of a detail must be considered when deciding how to cover a joint or connection. These include the functions of fire resistance, acoustics, water and moisture control, durability, maintainability, and safety.

Figure 3-1 Minimize weight/thickness of covering

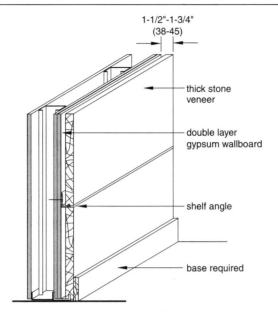

1-1/2"-1-3/4"
(38-45)

— thick stone veneer

— double layer gypsum wallboard

— shelf angle

— base required

(a) full thickness stone application

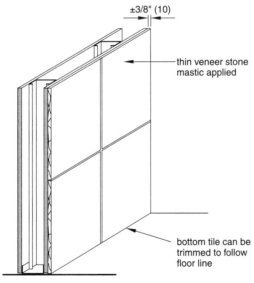

±3/8" (10)

— thin veneer stone mastic applied

— bottom tile can be trimmed to follow floor line

(b) thin veneer stone application

If fire resistance is required, the covering, in most cases, must have the same fire rating or flame spread rating as the construction or it must be part of a tested assembly, such as a premanufactured, fire-rated access panel. For example, a reveal joint in a fire-rated partition would have to be detailed in such a way that the approved fire-resistant construction was not compromised. One way of doing this is shown in Fig. 3-3, where an extra layer of gypsum wallboard provides the continuity of the fire rating while a standard reveal joint is mounted in a second layer of wallboard. Unfortunately, this detail requires the entire partition to be covered with an additional layer of gypsum wallboard, increasing cost and construction time.

Joints in construction assemblies that are designed to reduce sound transmission must be given special attention because even very small cracks in an otherwise well-detailed and constructed assembly can ruin its sound rating. Small joints and cracks can only be sealed

Figure 3-2 Covering joints

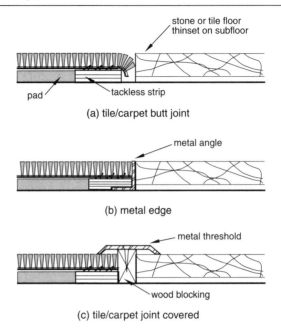

(a) tile/carpet butt joint

(b) metal edge

(c) tile/carpet joint covered

easily and effectively with acoustical sealant, so any finish covering only conceals the sealant rather than providing the acoustical seal itself.

A covering in a wet area must be sealed against water penetration and itself be resistant to damage from moisture. In most cases, water-resistant covering materials include ceramic tile for continuously and intermittently wet areas, such as bathrooms and shower rooms. Materials such as high-pressure decorative laminate and solid surfacing are also used for occasionally wet areas such as countertops. In either situation, joints must be sealed against water because even small amounts of moisture can damage wood, finishes, and other construction.

Concealing joints and connections should be also made with a material that is both durable and easily maintained. Materials should be at least as durable as the surrounding construction, and the covering should be replaceable if it wears or gets damaged.

Finally, a detail should be covered or otherwise designed to reduce the likelihood that people will be injured. For instance, a handrail prominently fastened to a wall in a corridor with exposed bolts may create an interesting detail but poses both safety problems as well as maintenance problems. The detail shown in Fig. 3-4(a) could result in cut fingers and torn clothing.

Figure 3-3 Reveal joint covering fire-rated partition

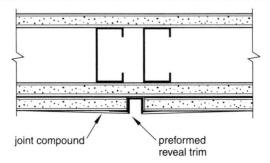

Figure 3-4 Covering connections for safety

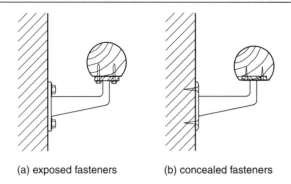

(a) exposed fasteners   (b) concealed fasteners

The detail is improved by concealing the fastening with the handrail itself, recessing the screws, as shown in Fig. 3-4(b). Rounding the edges of the wall bracket also minimizes dirt and dust collection and makes maintenance easier.

COORDINATE WITH OTHER CONSTRUCTABILITY NEEDS

Once a method of covering a joint or connection has been selected, it presents its own problems of fabrication, including those related to the functions of connection, structure, movement, tolerances, and construction. For example, a designer may want to use wood wainscoting and trim on a fire-rated partition that requires control joints. The detail must allow for movement of the partition as well as for the attachment of trim. One way to do this is shown in Fig. 3-5. In this example, a piece of wood trim is screwed to only one side of the joint, providing a sliding joint. Deep rabbets in the trim allow the paneling to move with the partition, while the joint still provides the continuity of fire rating. In this detail, the paneling must met flame-spread ratings of the applicable building code.

MAKE COVERING REMOVABLE IF REQUIRED

In many situations, the underlying joint or construction must be accessible for repair or replacement. Coverings should be detailed so that they are easily removable with simple tools and in such a way that soiling and physical damage are avoided or minimized. Making coverings removable also makes it easier to deconstruct the project to recycle or reuse individual materials.

Figure 3-6(a) shows a removable covering for a backlighted panel so that lamps and other electrical components can be serviced. The cover is hung with Z-clips at the top and fixed

Figure 3-5 Trim covering an expansion joint

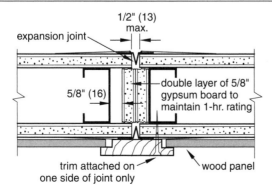

Figure 3-6 Use removable coverings

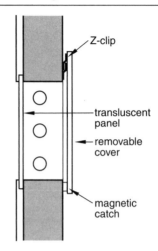

Z-clip

transluscent panel

removable cover

magnetic catch

(a) access to equipment

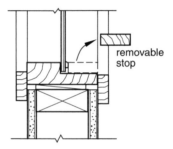

removable stop

(b) access for repair and replacement

with a magnetic catch at the bottom. This cover is easily removed without the need for tools or special knowledge. Figure 3-6(b) shows a typical removable stop for replacing broken glass.

Hiding Mechanical and Electrical Services

One of the most common reasons to use a concealment detail is to hide building services, including mechanical ductwork, plumbing pipes and fittings, electrical conduits and wiring, light fixtures, and sprinkler piping. In addition to simply concealing the services, certain mechanical and electrical equipment must be accessible. This is particularly true for control devices such as fire dampers, fans, heating and air conditioning units, valves, electrical junction boxes, control panels, and similar equipment.

There are three detailing responses for hiding mechanical and electrical services.

INCREASE PARTITION OR CEILING THICKNESS

If a service does not fit into a particular partition or ceiling construction being used the building assembly can simply be made thicker or larger as required to accommodate the service. The assembly can be made larger in just the area where the increased size is needed or the entire partition or ceiling can be enlarged so there is a smooth surface.

The amount of size increase required is dependent, of course, on the service or services to be accommodated. Where space is limited, the exact sizes of equipment should be verified with the consulting engineers, contractors, or suppliers. Some of the clearance requirements for common mechanical and electrical services are shown in Figs. 3-7 through 3-11. Actual

Figure 3-7 Clearances for HVAC distribution equipment

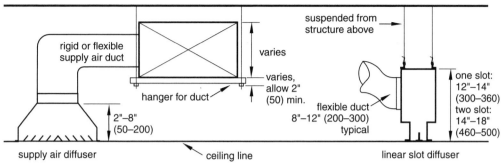

sizes of common plumbing piping is given in Table 3-1. These clearances are approximate for preliminary detailing purposes. Exact clearances should be verified once specific fixtures or services are specified.

USE SEPARATE CHASES

When several services must be accommodated near each other or when increasing a partition thickness is not practical a separate chase can be constructed. A chase wall between two back-to-back restrooms is one example of this detailing technique. Two rows of studs are used, separated by enough space to accommodate all the plumbing pipes and fixture hangers used for both restrooms. Another common example is a ceiling plenum, where enough space is provided between the structural floor above and a suspended ceiling to conceal all the

Figure 3-8 Actual pipe sizes

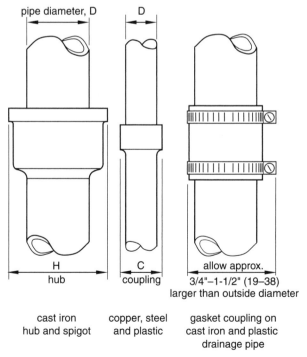

see Table 3.1 for sizes

Figure 3-9 Sprinkler piping clearances

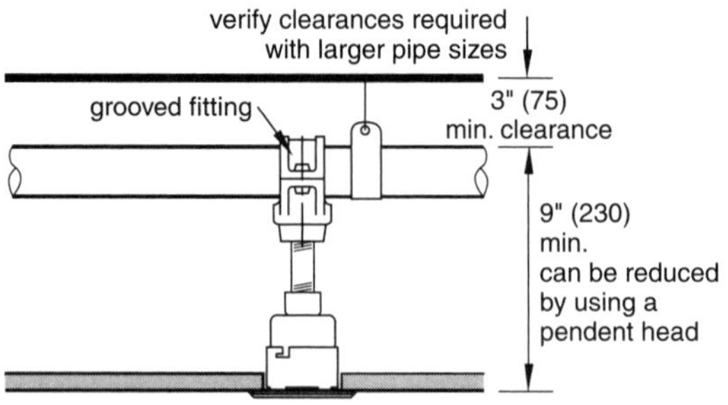

verify clearances required
with larger pipe sizes

grooved fitting

3" (75)
min. clearance

9" (230)
min.
can be reduced
by using a
pendent head

(a) concealed head drop from 2" main

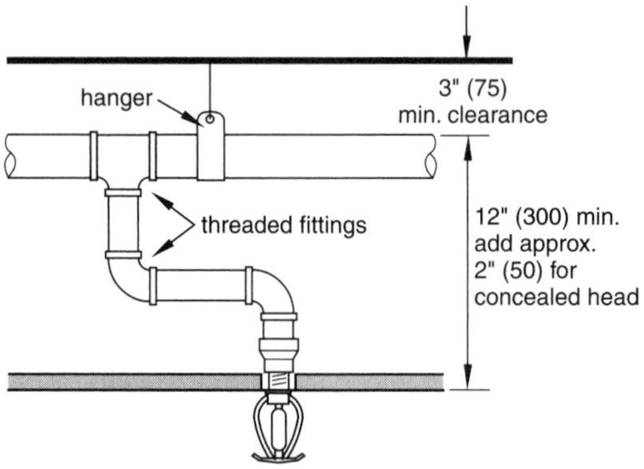

hanger

3" (75)
min. clearance

threaded fittings

12" (300) min.
add approx.
2" (50) for
concealed head

(b) pendent head offset drop from 1-1/4" main

note: all dimensions approximate depending
on pipe sizes, coupling types, head types, and
installation methods

necessary services. Some of the common alternatives to using separate chases are shown in Figs. 3-12(a) and (b). Solutions for horizontal services are shown in Figs. 3-12(c) and (d).

EXPOSE SERVICES

In some situations, the best approach is not to conceal services at all but to leave them exposed. This generally only works for services in the horizontal plane above where a suspended ceiling would normally be. At this location, the services are safely out of reach and do not interfere with the function of the space. If exposing ductwork, piping, and light fixtures is consistent with the overall design concept, this approach often reduces both cost and construction time, as well as minimizes the need for new materials and their embodied energy that would otherwise be added to the project. The services can be left in their natural state, painted black to minimize their appearance, painted bright colors to make them a design feature, or partially deemphasized by suspending an open grid as an open ceiling. One popular technique is to use a standard T-bar suspended acoustical ceiling grid without using any acoustical tiles and paint all the services above the grid black. The effect for people at eye level is that of a normal ceiling plane with everything below it lighted, while the exposed services are less visible in darkness.

If the mechanical services are a major design feature, exposing them can sometimes cost more than concealing them. This is because of the additional expenses of carefully planning their layout, accurate and neat installation, and additional finishing, such as painting.

Figure 3-10 Clearances for electrical conduit and boxes

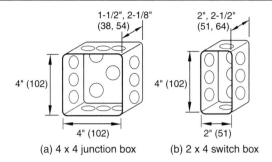

(a) 4 x 4 junction box	(b) 2 x 4 switch box

Approximate outside diameter of conduit	
EMT or IMC size in. (mm)	Approx. diam. D, in. (mm)
1/2 (13)	7/8 (22)
3/4 (19)	1-1/16 (27)
1 (25)	1-5/16 (33)
1-1/4 (32)	1-7/8 (48)
1-1/2 (38)	2-3/8 (60)

EMT: electrical metallic conduit
IMC: intermediate metal conduit

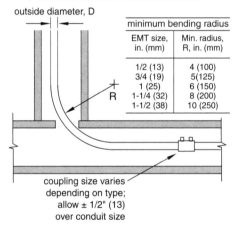

minimum bending radius	
EMT size, in. (mm)	Min. radius, R, in. (mm)
1/2 (13)	4 (100)
3/4 (19)	5 (125)
1 (25)	6 (150)
1-1/4 (32)	8 (200)
1-1/2 (38)	10 (250)

coupling size varies
depending on type;
allow ± 1/2" (13)
over conduit size

(c) electrical metallic conduit sizes and minimum bends

3-3 HUMAN FIT/OBJECT FIT

One of the most basic design and detailing parameters is responding to the basic size and movement capabilities of human beings or for the objects the environment serves. In most cases, human beings are the primary users of interior space but interior design may also be concerned with accommodating such nonhuman elements or scale such as factory processes, automobiles, animals, or sports stadia.

There are four detailing responses for *human and object fit*.

Base Dimensions on Human Size and Reach or Object Size

The size, form, and movement capabilities of humans have been extensively studied and published by both the military and private sectors. Two good reference books for interior designers are *Human Dimension & Interior Space* and *The Measure of Man and Woman: Human Factors in Design*. Refer to the sources at the end of this book for complete bibliographic

Figure 3-11 Typical clearances for recessed luminaires

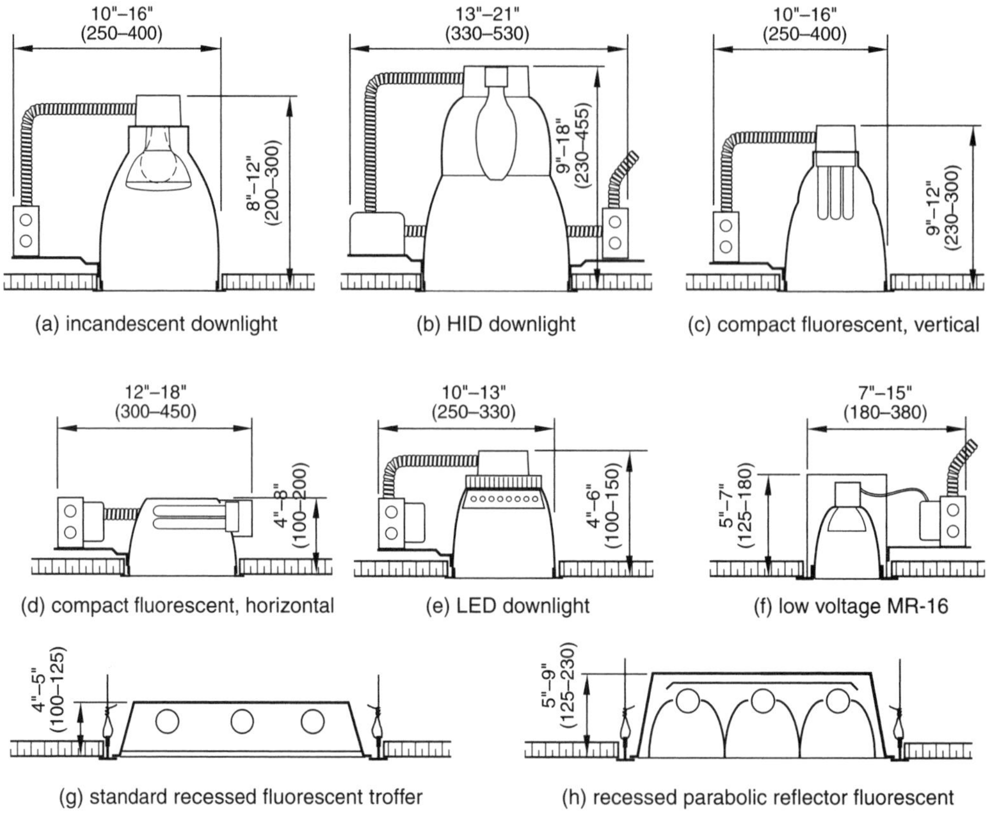
10"–16"
(250–400)
8"–12"
(200–300)
(a) incandescent downlight
13"–21"
(330–530)
9"–18"
(230–455)
(b) HID downlight
10"–16"
(250–400)
9"–12"
(230–300)
(c) compact fluorescent, vertical
12"–18"
(300–450)
4"–8"
(100–200)
(d) compact fluorescent, horizontal
10"–13"
(250–330)
4"–6"
(100–150)
(e) LED downlight
7"–15"
(180–380)
5"–7"
(125–180)
(f) low voltage MR-16
4"–5"
(100–125)
(g) standard recessed fluorescent troffer
5"–9"
(125–230)
(h) recessed parabolic reflector fluorescent

Note: when space is limited, verify sizes based on specific luminaires specified

Table 3-1 Plumbing Pipe and Coupling Sizes

	Type L Copper		Steel Pipe		Plastic, PVC, Sch. 40		Cast Iron Hub and Spigot	
Nominal Size	Pipe, D	Coupling, C	Pipe, D	Coupling, C, Threaded	Pipe, D	Coupling, C	Pipe, D	Hub, H
in. (mm)	in. (mm)	in. (mm)	in. (mm)	in. (mm)	in. (mm)	in. (mm)	in. (mm)	in. (mm)
1/4 (6)	.37 (9.4)	0.43 (10.9)						
3/8 (10)	0.50 (12.7)	0.56 (14.2)	0.675 (17.1)		0.675 (17.1)			
1/2 (13)	0.62 (15.7)	0.70 (17.8)	0.840 (21.3)	1.30 (33.0)	0.840 (21.3)	1.30 (33.0)		
3/4 (19)	0.87 (22.1)	1.00 (25.4)	1.050 (26.7)	1.50 (38.1)	1.050 (26.7)	1.50 (38.1)		
1 (25)	1.13 (28.7)	1.40 (35.6)	1.315 (33.4)	1.80 (45.7)	1.315 (33.4)	1.80 (45.7)		
1-1.4 (32)	1.34 (34.0)	1.50 (38.1)	1.660 (42.2)	2.30 (58.4)	1.660 (42.2)	2.40 (61.0)		
1-1/2 (38)	1.62 (41.1)	1.80 (45.7)	1.900 (48.3)	2.50 (63.5)	1.900 (48.3)	2.70 (68.6)	1.90 (48.3)	3.00 (76.2)
2 (51)	2.10 (53.3)	2.30 (58.4)	2.375 (60.3)	3.00 (76.2)	2.375 (60.3)	3.20 (81.3)	2.40 (61.0)	4.00 (101.6)
2-1/2 (64)	2.60 (66.0)	2.80 (71.1)	2.875 (73.0)	3.50 (88.9)	2.875 (73.0)	3.90 (99.1)		
3 (76)	3.10 (78.7)	3.40 (86.4)	3.500 (88.9)	4.30 (109.2)	3.500 (88.9)	4.60 (116.8)	3.5 (88.9)	5.30 (134.6)
4 (102)	4.10 (104.1)	4.30 (109.2)	4.500 (114.3)	5.40 (137.2)	4.500 (114.3)	5.80 (147.3)	4.5 (114.3)	6.30 (160.0)
5 (127)	5.10 (129.5)	5.40 (137.2)	5.563 (141.3)	6.60 (167.6)	5.563 (141.3)	7.00 (177.8)	5.5 (139.7)	7.30 (185.4)
6 (152)	6.10 (154.9)	6.30 (160.0)	6.625 (168.3)	8.00 (203.2)	6.625 (168.3)	8.00 (203.2)	6.5 (165.1)	8.30 (210.8)
8 (204)	8.10 (205.7)	8.50 (215.9)	8.625 (219.1)	10.60 (269.2)	8.625 (219.1)	9.40 (238.8)	8.8 (223.5)	11.0 (279.4)

Source: ANSI B16.3, ANSI B16.18, manufacturer's data

Figure 3-12 Use separate chases

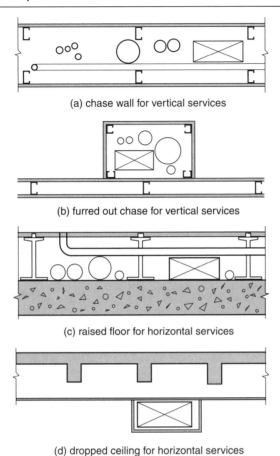

(a) chase wall for vertical services

(b) furred out chase for vertical services

(c) raised floor for horizontal services

(d) dropped ceiling for horizontal services

information. These sources, as well as others, document the wide range of human dimensions both as averages and relative to percentile data. Other reference sources, such as *Interior Graphic Standards*, give similar, condensed data and suggested sizes for spaces and objects designed for human use.

Designing details for human use must take anthropometric requirements into account for construction such as cabinets, work surfaces, storage units, built-in seating, doors, kitchens, and stairs. Although many dimensional standards have been developed for most of these items based on average human size, many of them may not be the best for current human usage. For example, the standard heights of vanities and kitchen countertops are generally too low for most users.

Designing for objects or processes in addition to human beings can be a challenge because of the often conflicting requirements of scale or environmental requirements.

Recognize Differences in Age, Height, Abilities

Most standard dimensions for details are based on the average, adult, able-bodied human. In many cases, an interior detail must accommodate a wide range of users who may differ in age, size, and physical abilities. For example, a stairway intended for use by both adults and children should have two handrails at different heights. A detail with operating devices should be accessible to the disabled as well as others.

Provide Adjustable Details

When possible, design details so that there is adjustability for different people who may use the detail at different times during its life cycle. Adjustable shelving, tilting surfaces, and movable partitions are examples of adjustable details. Because of the added cost, adjustable details are not always possible unless the convenience, use, or number of people involved justify such a detail.

Provide Alternate Fits

When it is not possible to provide adjustability in a detail, two or more options may be given to the users. For example, providing two different service counter heights is a common way to allow access to both standing and wheelchair users.

3-4 SAFETY: PROTECTION FROM ACCIDENTAL HARM

There are two different types of safety. One is safety from accidental harm, such as trips, cuts, scraps, and falls, and the other is safety from intentionally harm, such as robbery, shootings, and terrorism. In many cases, safety from accidental harm is important enough that requirements have been codified in building codes and other regulations, as discussed in Chapter 2. This section highlights some of those and provides additional information on basic safety parameters for all details.

There are eight detailing responses for *protection from accidental harm*.

Use Nonslip Flooring

Some of the most common accidents in the environment involve slipping on stairs and ramps, as well as on flat surfaces. Details that involve flooring should use material that provides an adequate degree of slip resistance for the intended use. Tile, stone, terrazzo, and other smooth surfaces can be potentially dangerous, especially when wet or covered with grease or other slippery substances.

As discussed in Chapter 2, slip resistance is evaluated and specified with the coefficient of friction (COF). A COF of 0.5 is generally considered a minimum value, with a minimum value of 0.6 for accessible routes and 0.8 for ramps.

Avoid Sharp Edges Close to Human Contact

Many details and standard methods of construction result in sharp edges and corners. These are unnecessary hazards to human safety and are easily preventable. Consider the height and typical movement of human beings near counters, work surfaces, upper cabinets, shelving, and other woodwork. Also treat corners near circulation spaces where people are likely to cut a corner. Corners can be rounded, chamfered, or otherwise detailed to minimize injury on contact. See Fig. 3-13(a).

Hardware and exposed fasteners should also be selected and detailed to minimize sharp edges and places where people could catch clothing or scrape their hands or other parts of their body. See Fig. 3-13(b).

Figure 3-13 Avoiding sharp edges

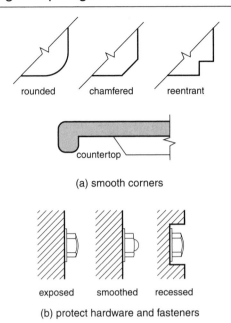

rounded   chamfered   reentrant

(a) smooth corners

exposed   smoothed   recessed

(b) protect hardware and fasteners

For finish materials, carefully consider avoiding the use of rough finishes close to where people may scrape their body against them.

Provide Handrails and Guards When Necessary

Handrails and guards are required by both building codes and ADA regulations in most of the common hazardous locations, such as stairs, ramps, and elevated platforms more than 30 in. (762 mm) above the adjacent floor surface. However, the designer should consider detailing handrails and guards when they may not be necessary by regulation, such as corridors, low platforms, or near three or fewer rises in dwelling units and sleeping units in Group R-2 and R-3 occupancies, and in corridors.

When handrails are used, they must be easily graspable and mounted far enough away from a wall to allow gripping. The IBC and ADA/ABA guidelines limit the size and shape of handrails. These are shown in Fig. 3-14. In addition to a standard Type I handrail, the IBC now allows a Type II handrail where the perimeter is greater than 6-1/4 in. (160 mm). These are allowed in group R-3 (residential) occupancies, within dwelling units in Group R-2 occupancies (apartments, condominiums), and in Group U occupancies that are accessory to a Group R-3 occupancy or accessory to individual dwellings in Group R-2 occupancies.

Design Stairs Correctly

A large number of accidental falls occur on stairs in both residential and commercial construction. As with handrails, stair design is largely governed by code and accessibility requirements, but these are minimum acceptable limits. The designer can improve on stair design by following several guidelines.

- When possible, use riser heights slightly less than code maximums. A riser height of 6-1/4 in. to 6-1/2 in. (159 mm to 165 mm) is easier to traverse, especially for older people, and reduces fatigue on long flights of stairs. Do not use risers less than 4 in. (102 mm) high.

Figure 3-14 Handrail configurations

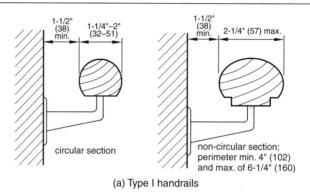

(a) Type I handrails

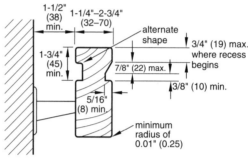

If handrails have a perimeter greater than 6-1/4" (160 mm), they must have a graspable finger recess as shown or a similar profile.

(b) Type II handrail

- Increase the depth of the tread beyond the minimum of 11 in. (279 mm). In addition to matching a corresponding decrease in riser height, a deeper tread accommodates larger foot and shoe sizes and gives firmer footing and a greater allowance for missteps. A depth of 12 in. (305 mm) is good with a riser height of 6-1/2 in. (165 mm).
- Do not use nosings with sharp edges underneath as required by code, and limit nosing projection to 1 in. (25 mm) instead of the 1-1/4 in. (32 mm) allowed by the IBC. Limit the radius of the leading edge of nosings to 1/2 in. (12.7 mm) as required by the IBC.
- Do not use open risers, even if they are allowed by the local building code or occupancy type.
- Maintain consistency in riser height from one riser to the next. Although the IBC allows up to 3/8 in. (9.5 mm) variation between the largest and smallest riser height or tread depth in any flight of stairs, keep the variation to a maximum of 3/16 in. (5 mm) between adjacent riser heights.
- Provide a stairway width to accommodate the volume of people using it. For monumental stairs that are not part of the required width of egress, a minimum width for two people walking abreast or passing is about 60 in. (1525 mm). When wider than 60 in., monumental stairs that are not part of the required means of egress should have a handrail for each 60 in. of width, even if they are not required by the local code. Provide handrails for both sides of narrow stairs, even if they are not required by the local building code.
- For hard surface floors on stairs, use nonslip nosings and contrasting colors or materials so that the nosing is clearly visible. Avoid carpet or flooring patterns that may be confusing and make it difficult to discern the edge of the nosing.

- Provide a second handrail about 24 in. (610 mm) above the nosing line if children will frequently be using the stair.
- Extend handrails beyond the top and bottom risers in residential applications where they might not otherwise be required, just as they are for commercial construction.
- Avoid sharp edges in handrails, balusters, and walls along stairways.

Mark Full-Height Glass

Although the IBC allows the use of full-height glass adjacent to walking surfaces if it is safety glazing, consider using a horizontal mullion, crash bar, or other clearly visible markings on the glass at eye level to prevent accidental collisions with the glass. If clear views are not required, textured or art glass can also be used to transmit light, while making the barrier obvious.

Avoid Single Steps

Single steps can be unsafe. However, if one or two steps are used, they should be clearly marked with distinctive risers, treads, or nosings and provided with handrails. Consider using a ramp instead or adjust the change in levels to accommodate a minimum of three risers.

Avoid Slight Change of Level

Changes in level, no matter how slight, pose a tripping risk. This is especially true for children and the elderly. A change as small at 1/2 in. (13 mm) can be enough to trip someone. In most cases, accessibility regulations limit a vertical change in level to 1/4 in. (6 mm). Changes in level of 1/2 in. (13 mm) may be made but only with a bevel of one vertical unit to two horizontal units. If possible, make changes in level less than these maximums where they are required and use the same guidelines for residential occupancies and other locations where they might not otherwise be required by accessibility regulations.

Use Nontoxic Materials

Many materials used in detailing may contain harmful chemicals such as formaldehyde and volatile organic compounds (VOCs), as well as others. Adhesives, particleboard, and other panel products may contain formaldehyde and adhesives, and other finishes may contain VOCs. Refer to the section on sustainability later in this chapter.

3-5 SECURITY: PROTECTION FROM INTENTIONAL HARM

All interior design projects require some type of security, whether as simple as a lock on the front door of a house or as complex as an alarm system and security barriers for a bank or government installation. In most cases, the designer or detailer does not develop security systems but may work closely with an architect or consultant to incorporate security measures into partitions, door opening assemblies, glazing systems, reception stations, security stations, display cases, and support for wall- and ceiling-mounted equipment. Before beginning the details, the designer should gather and understand all the requirements including the type of equipment that must be incorporated into the detail, and any electrical, communication, and data cabling requirements.

There are five detailing responses for *protection from intentional harm.*

Use Locks, Detection, and Intrusion Alarms as Appropriate

Locks and alarms are the simplest types of standard security measures to control access, protect property, and secure rooms or entire areas of a building. Locks can be as simple as a cabinet lock on a drawer or as complex as a system of card-reader-controlled doors monitored at a central supervision station. With information provided by the security consultant, owner, or architect, the interior designer can plan ahead to accommodate security devices and hardware to minimize their visual impact.

Design Physical Barriers for the Level of Security Required

Although standard interior partitions provide little protection from break-in or firearms, when combined with intrusion alarms they are often enough for most uses. If more security is required gypsum wallboard partitions can be reinforced or other types of partitions constructed. Figure 3-15 shows some possible security partitions.

As shown in Fig. 3-15(a), heavy-gauge steel studs can be used with security mesh to create a partition that appears to be like any other wallboard construction, with about the same thickness. Solid plaster partitions, shown in Fig. 3-15(b), can be used, but they are more difficult to construct. For very high-security partitions, reinforced masonry may be needed, as shown in Fig. 3-15(c). In any case, the owner must inform the interior designer of the desired level of security before design and detailing begin.

Use Electronic Surveillance When Required

Electronic surveillance is the interception of sound and electromagnetic signals with remote sensing devices. When an owner requires security from this type of intrusion, a variety of methods can be used, which basically require building a "cage" of continuously conductive material that catches signals and conducts them to the ground. For most corporate needs copper foil or nonwoven fabric with electronically conductive metallic coatings can be used. This is placed behind the finished wall surface so that it is not noticeable. For windows, fine metal screens can be used, but special shielded glass is also available that looks like normal glass. Doors designed for radio frequency or electromagnetic shielding are also required to seal a room. In all cases, a security expert should be consulted for specific product specifications and detailing requirements.

Use Ballistic-Resistant Assemblies

If security from a ballistic attack rather than a physical break-in is required, ballistic armor can be used, as shown in Fig. 3-16. This is fiberglass-reinforced composite material available in rigid sheets like plywood, in thicknesses from 1/4 in. to 1/2 in. (6 mm to 13 mm). It can be covered with various finishes or simply painted. Flexible ballistic armor is also available, which is covered with gypsum wallboard.

Figure 3-15 Security partitions

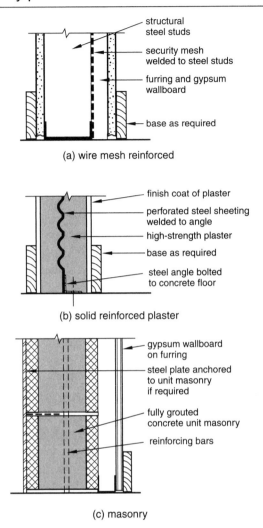

structural
steel studs

security mesh
welded to steel studs

furring and gypsum
wallboard

base as required

(a) wire mesh reinforced

finish coat of plaster

perforated steel sheeting
welded to angle

high-strength plaster

base as required

steel angle bolted
to concrete floor

(b) solid reinforced plaster

gypsum wallboard
on furring

steel plate anchored
to unit masonry
if required

fully grouted
concrete unit masonry

reinforcing bars

(c) masonry

Devise Space Plan for Supervision

Although not strictly a part of detailing, space planning can aid in a good overall security plan. For example, spaces with similar security needs should be located together, if possible. This makes it easier to enclose the area with physical barriers and well as minimizing the number of electronic devices required. Also, security personnel can be located in a central

Figure 3-16 Ballistic protection partition

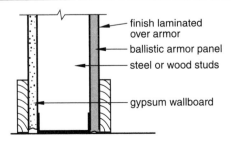

finish laminated
over armor

ballistic armor panel

steel or wood studs

gypsum wallboard

position with a clear line of sight to as many secure areas as possible. For minimal security, store clerks, receptionists, and other normal users can be located where they can supervise much of the space.

3-6   SUSTAINABILITY

As discussed in Chapter 2, sustainability can be treated as a constraint if there are local or state regulations concerning materials, energy use, VOCs, and the like. In most cases, however, creating sustainable interiors should be considered an opportunity to create a functional, healthy, responsible environment. In this way, sustainability should be considered one of the basic *functions* that all details fulfill. Even if the owner of the facility is interested in applying for LEED certification, sustainability should be viewed as an opportunity rather than a constraint.

Sustainability, as a broad term, means meeting the needs and wants of the present generation without harming or compromising the ability of future generations to meet their needs. Sustainable design involves the design, operation, and reuse concepts that together can create functional, healthy, nonpolluting, and environmentally friendly buildings without compromising practical requirements or human comfort. When evaluating details and products for sustainability, the designer should consider many individual criteria, including recycled content, recyclability, energy consumption, and life-cycle assessment, among others as described below.

Some of the criteria for evaluating how sustainable a detail or product is include the following. Of course, not all of the criteria apply to every detail. In addition, the designer must make informed judgments because some criteria conflict. For example, aluminum has a very high embodied energy, but recycled aluminum has about one third the embodied energy, is plentiful, and the material can be recycled again after its useful life. The value of a lightweight, extruded aluminum section may outweigh the fact that it takes large amounts of energy to produce aluminum and it may not be a locally produced product. The amount of aluminum in a detail may also be so small in proportion to all the material in a building that the question is less important than other sustainability concerns.

There are 12 detailing responses for *sustainability*.

Detail with Materials That Incorporate as Little Embodied Energy as Possible

The material or product in a detail or used as a finish should require as little energy as possible for its extraction as a raw material, initial processing, and subsequent manufacture or fabrication into a finished building product. This includes the energy required for transportation of the materials and products during their life cycle. The production of the material should also generate as little waste or pollution as possible. Table 3-2 gives some of the embodied energy requirements of some common building materials. When comparing proprietary products, the manufacturers may be able to provide information on the embodied energy of their products. Generally, products that are produced near the building site require less embodied energy because of transportation issues. However, the embodied energy in materials accounts for a very small percentage (some estimate about 2%) of the total energy requirement of a building's design and long-term operation.

Table 3-2 Embodied Energy in Common Interior Detailing Materials

Material	Embodied energy Btu/lb.	Embodied energy MJ/kg
Detail elements		
lumber	1080	2.5
gypsum wallboard	2630	6.1
particleboard	3450	8.0
aluminum (recycled)	3490	8.1
steel (recycled)	3830	8.9
plywood	4480	10.4
glass	6850	15.9
steel	13,790	32.0
PVC	30,170	70.0
aluminum	97,840	227
Finishes		
stone (local)	340	0.79
clay brick	1,080	2.5
zinc	21,980	51.0
brass	26,720	62.0
copper	30,430	70.6
paint	40,210	93.3
linoleum	49,990	116
synthetic carpet	63,790	148

Source: Environmental Resource Guide
To convert MJ/kg to Btu/lb, multiply by 431

Use Renewable Materials

A material is sustainable if it comes from sources that can renew themselves within a fairly short time. Some examples of products that meet this criterion include wool carpets, bamboo flooring and paneling, straw board, linoleum flooring, poplar oriented strand board (OSB), sunflower seed board, and wheatgrass cabinetry. However, as with all sustainability issues choices must often be made between conflicting facts. For example, bamboo is a very renewable resource, but it must be transported long distances to the United States. However, bamboo so quickly renews itself that the transportation issue may not be as important as not using other hardwoods for flooring.

Use Materials with High Recycled Content

The more recycled content a material has, the less raw materials and energy are required to process the raw materials into a final product. Each of the three types of recycled content should be considered: postconsumer materials, postindustrial materials, and recovered materials. *Postconsumer materials* are those referring to a material or product that has served its intended use and has been diverted or recovered from waste designed for disposal, having completed its life as a consumer item. *Postindustrial materials* refer to materials generated in the manufacturing process that have been recovered or diverted from solid waste. *Recovered materials* are waste or byproducts that have been recovered or diverted from solid-waste disposal. Using recycled content products has two advantages. First, it reduces the need for the production of new materials. Second, greater use creates a better market for recycled products and encourages others to recycle, while lowering the cost.

When Possible, Use Products or Design Details That Can Reduce Energy Consumption

In addition to using materials with low embodied energy, some materials and details may help reduce the energy consumption of building operation. For example, intelligent use of glazing can improve daylighting and reduce lighting energy requirements, as can the use of light-reflective materials. If a building has been designed for natural ventilation or solar energy, interior partitions, openings, and other finishes and details should not defeat the heating and ventilating systems designed by the architect and mechanical engineer. Although there are limited opportunities with detailing to affect the overall energy use of a building, the designer should consider the possibilities whenever possible.

Use Local Materials

Using locally produced materials reduces transportation costs and can add to the regional character of a design. Generally, local materials are considered those that are extracted, harvested, recovered, or manufactured within a radius of 500 mi (804 km) of the project. When compared with many traditional interior materials that are sourced from other countries, the use of local material can make a huge difference in the sustainability of a project.

Use Materials with Low or No VOCs

As mentioned in Chapter 2, volatile organic compounds are now regulated by the EPA as well as some states, notably California, which has strict limits on the VOC content of building materials and cleaning products, among others. VOCs are found in many indoor sources, including building materials and common household products. Common sources of VOCs in building materials and details include paint, stains, adhesives, sealants, water repellents and sealers, particleboard, furniture, upholstery, and carpeting. Other sources include copy machines, cleaning agents, and pesticides. Any detail should minimize or eliminate the use of materials with VOCs. The designer may even want to use materials that have a lower VOC content than required by EPA or local regulations. Refer to Table 2-12 for a listing of some of the VOC limits on finishes and adhesives.

Use Materials with Low Toxicity

In addition to limiting VOC-containing products, materials should be selected that emit few or no harmful gases such as chlorofluorocarbons (CFCs), formaldehyde, and others. There are potentially hundreds of organic and inorganic chemicals that may be harmful to humans. The California Office of Environmental Health Hazard Assessment has a list of 76 chemicals (current at the time of this writing) that the state regulates along with the chronic inhalation reference exposure level (REL) for each, in micrograms per cubic meter ($\mu g/m^3$). These were developed as a result of California's Proposition 65, which was passed in 1986.

The Greenguard Environmental Institute also produces a list of products, chemicals in those products, and allowable maximum emission levels. Some of the common chemicals include VOCs, formaldehyde, aldehydes, 4-phenylcyclohexene, and styrene, as well as particulates and biological contaminates. In order to be certified by Greenguard, a product must meet the Greenguard standards after being tested according to ASTM D5116 and D6670, the state of Washington's protocol for interior furnishings and construction materials, and the EPA's testing protocol for furniture.

Design Details and Select Materials to Minimize Moisture Problems

If possible, materials should be selected that prevent or resist the growth of biological contaminants, mainly mold and mildew. Molds and mildew are microscopic organisms, a type of fungi, that produce enzymes to digest organic matter. Their reproductive spores are present nearly everywhere.

Mold spores require three conditions to grow: moisture, a nutrient, and a temperature range from 40°F to 100°F (4°C to 38°C). Nutrients are simply organic materials, which can include wood, carpet, the paper coating of gypsum wallboard, paint, wallpaper, insulation, and ceiling tile, among others, that serve as a nourishing food source for organisms. Because nutrients and a suitable temperature are always present in buildings, the only ways to prevent and control mold are to prevent and control moisture in places where it should not be, or to use a material that does not provide a nutrient. For most details this is not a problem unless the detail is near a water or moisture source, such as a kitchen or bathroom cabinet, millwork in humid areas, or materials in pool and spa areas.

Use Durable Materials and Details

Materials that have a long life span contribute to sustainability in two ways. First, durable materials obviate the need to create new materials, reducing energy consumption and resource depletion. Second, durable materials need to be replaced less often, reducing waste problems. As an added benefit, durable materials generally require less maintenance over the life of a product or building. Even though initial costs may be higher, the life-cycle costs may be less.

Design Details to Simplify Maintenance

Details that degrade or break need to be maintained or parts need to be replaced, and as with durability, this creates the requirement for more materials and waste disposal issues. Details should also be designed to only require nontoxic and low-VOC cleaners.

Specify Materials and Design Details to Maximize Recycling Potential

Some materials and products are more readily recycled than others. Steel and aluminum, for example, can usually be separated from other materials and melted down to make new products, reducing the embodied energy in the new products. On the other hand, plastics used in construction details are difficult to remove and separate. Details should be designed to allow them to be dissembled easily for recycling, if possible.

Table 3-3 Sustainable Product Certification Programs

Program	Description
BIFMA International www.bifma.org	Develops two standards for VOC emissions from office furniture systems and seating as well as a furniture sustainability standard.
FloorScore of the Resilient Floor Covering Institute www.rfci.com	FloorScore program tests and certifies flooring products for compliance with strict indoor air quality requirements in California and that qualify for use in high-performance schools and office building in California.
Forest Stewardship Council (FSC) www.fsc.org	International body that oversees the development of national and regional standards based on basic forest management principles and criteria. It accredits certifying organizations that comply with its principles. The FSC logo ensures that materials have come from well-managed forests and have followed the other FSC principles.
Greenguard Environmental Institute (GEI) www.greenguard.org	Nonprofit, industry-independent organization that oversees the Greenguard Certification Program that tests indoor products for emissions to ensure acceptable indoor air quality.
Green Label Plus program of the Carpet and Rug Institute (CRI) www.carpet-rug.org	The Green Label Plus program is a voluntary testing program for carpet, cushion, and adhesive that conforms to California's high performance schools program. Carpet carrying the Green Label Plus mark is certified as being low-emitting.
Green Seal www.greenseal.org	Independent, nonprofit organization that develops standards for products in specific categories and certifies products that meet the high standards of the program.
Institute for Market Transformation to Sustainability (MTS) www.mts.sustainableproducts.com	MTS is an organization that oversees the SMaRT (Sustainable Materials Rating Technology) program, which identifies sustainable products based on awarding points in the areas of (1) safe for public health and environment, (2) energy reduction and renewable energy materials, (3) company and facility requirements, including social equity, and (4) reuse and reclamation. Products are certified at one of three levels: silver, gold, and platinum.
MBDC Cradle to Cradle (C2C) www.mbdc.com	The C2C certification program offers two types of product certification: C2C technical/biological nutrient certification that certifies that a material can be continually reused as either a biological or technical nutrient or a C2C product certification, which is a three-tiered classification of silver, gold, or platinum, based on the criteria of materials, nutrient reutilization, energy, water, and social responsibility.
Scientific Certification Systems (SCS) www.scscertified.com	Under its Environmental Claims Certification program, SCS certifies specific product attributes such as biodegradability and recycled content. It also certifies environmentally preferable products (EPP). Another program is Indoor Advantage, which covers nonfloor interior products. SCS also certifies well-managed forests under its Forest Certification Program.
Sustainable Forestry Initiative (SFI) www.sfiprogram.org	The SFI program gives four different product labels to participating companies that meet the SFI requirements based on both environmental and market demands.

Design Details for Reusability

A product should be reusable after it has served its purpose in the original building. The product may become a salvaged material that can be reused in another project, such as a door assembly, or the component parts should be easily separated for recycling as discussed above. For example, details that can easily be dismantled with mechanical fasteners are often better than those that may require adhesive for connection that can destroy the component parts when disassembled or make it too difficult to deconstruct.

For more information on sustainable materials and certification programs refer to Table 3–3.

Sustainability Issues Related to the Detailing Parameter *Function*

- Question if covering a detail is really necessary. This minimizes the need for materials, avoids possible toxic materials, and makes it easier to deconstruct the detail for reuse or recycling.
- Question the need to hide building services for the same reasons.
- If coverings are used, make them easily removable for reuse or recycling.

- Think "end-of-life" product responsibility from the start of design and detailing. This includes thinking of how the materials in the detail will be disposed of or recycled or reused.
- Use nontoxic materials in details such as formaldehyde-free panel products, adhesives with volatile organic compounds, or plastics that may outgas harmful chemicals. Limit toxic fire-retardant materials.
- Use materials that minimize organic material that could support mold or mildew if they got wet. If this is not possible, detail to control moisture penetration into the construction assembly.
- Provide for multiple uses of the same construction element. Cabinetry, movable partitions, and similar elements can be designed for different purposes to limit the need for disposal of existing products and creation of new products.

3-7 CHANGE AND RELOCATABILITY

The use of a buildings or leased interior seldom stays the same. If possible, details should adapt to the possibility for change over the life cycle of their use. In many cases, a detail may be so specific to a particular user or function that, when the use changes, the detail must be removed. In this case, the responses to the sustainability function of recycling and reuse apply. For example, a serving line in a cafeteria would work for little else if the space were remodeled into a bank. However, in many cases the designer can anticipate change and design accordingly.

There are three detailing responses for change and relocatability.

Design for Relocating the Detail with the Same User

In many situations, the same user may occupy the same space for a long time but may need to make occasional (or frequent) changes to continue the business. This is one of the easiest responses to implement because the basic physical environmental requirements usually stay more or less the same with the same user. Business offices are a common example of this situation, where changes to business needs, methods of operating, or personnel require a new arrangement of offices and support facilities. Movable partitions or demountable partitions are one of the common design responses to this type of need. Cabinets, workstations, storage units, and doorframes can be designed and detailed to make modification and relocation possible. Other details, such as glazing, gypsum wallboard, or ceilings may not be easily relocated but may be designed to be simple, low cost, and easy to deconstruct.

Detail for the Same Function but with a Change in Users

Many times an owner or tenant will move and a similar user will occupy the same space for the same purpose. The existing physical configuration may work for the new user with only minor modifications or just significant modifications to one part of the space. This happens often with apartments, condominiums, offices, retail stores, and even some restaurants. In these cases, basic details can be designed to remain structurally the same with the potential for easy modification of finishes. For example, built-in display cases for a retail store can remain the same size and shape with lighting and adjustability but allow for a simple replacement of new shelves with a different finish for different merchandise.

As the needs and design requirements of a future user can only be roughly anticipated at the time of the original design, the detailer must make a best judgment concerning what may change.

Detail for a Change of Function of the Space with Different Users

This type of response is more difficult to respond to because a change in user with a different function usually means a completely different environmental response. For example, changing from a restaurant to a retail store requires a wide difference in design, detail types, construction, and finishes. In reality, the most the designer can do is detail common building element, such as door openings, storage cabinets, suspended ceiling systems, stairways, and the like so that they can be reused as much as possible.

3-8   FIRE RESISTANCE

In most cases, fire resistance is generally viewed as a constraint, as discussed in Chapter 2. Unless otherwise required by the client, the designer seldom builds in more fire resistance than is required by the building code or the local fire marshal. However, for general safety of an interior, fire resistance can also be viewed as a basic function. As stated in Chapter 2, there are two basic concerns with fire resistance, the surface burning characteristics of finishes and the fire resistance of an entire assembly.

There are five detailing responses for creating *fire resistance*.

Use Noncombustible Materials in Details

A basic material is considered to be noncombustible when it meets the requirements of ASTM E136. For composite materials, the structural base must be noncombustible and the surfacing can be no more than 1/8 in. (3.18 mm) thick with a maximum flame spread of 50 when tested in accordance with ASTM E84 or UL 723. Even if the building code does not require a portion or all of a detail to be fire-resistance-rated, consider using noncombustible materials. For example, if wood blocking is allowed, metal framing may be used instead.

Limit the Amount of Flammable Materials

The simplest way to create a fire-resistant surface is to specify a material that that has a flame spread rating below 25 (Class A) when tested in accordance with ASTM E84. Most commercial interior finish manufacturers provide materials that have a Class A flame spread rating. If not, consider applying a fire-retardant coating as described below.

Use Applied Fire Retardants When Required

When required in a detail, applied fire retardants may take four basic forms: encasement with a fire-resistant material, spray-applied fire-resistive coatings, intumescent materials, or coatings. Encasement is generally with one or more layers of gypsum wallboard used to give a steel column or beam a one-, two-, or three-hour fire resistance rating. Approved methods of doing

Figure 3-17 Two-hour rated steel column enclosure

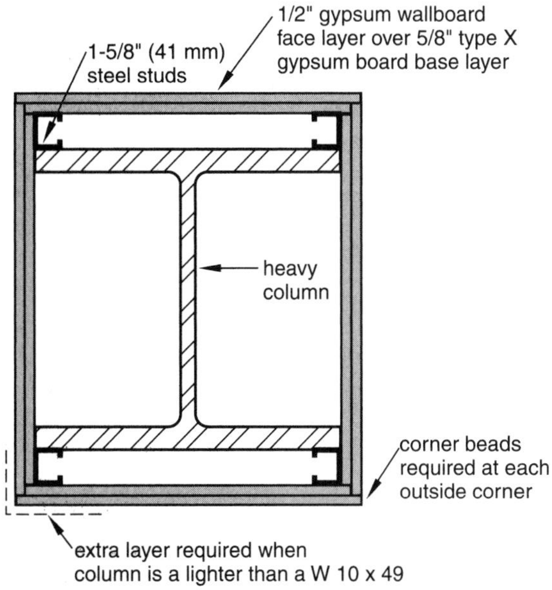

1-5/8" (41 mm) steel studs

1/2" gypsum wallboard face layer over 5/8" type X gypsum board base layer

heavy column

corner beads required at each outside corner

extra layer required when column is a lighter than a W 10 x 49

this are given in the *Building Material Directory* published by Underwriters Laboratories, the *Fire Resistance Design Manual* published by the Gypsum Association, or other reference books. Figure 3-17 shows a typical two-hour rated steel column encased in gypsum wallboard.

Spray-applied fire-resistive coatings are typically applied to structural steel framing during the construction of a building and are seldom specified by the interior designer. However, if such fireproofing is removed or damaged during interior construction, it must be patched by a qualified worker.

Intumescent materials are commonly used in fire-resistive-rated doors, fire-stopping penetrations through fire-rated walls and floors, and for applied coatings. An *intumescent material* is one that swells and chars to form a smoke and fire barrier when exposed to heat. Intumescent materials for details may take the form of sealants, gasketing, and coatings. These are generally not specified by the interior designer but may be used in door details where a positive pressure fire-rated door assembly is required. When a door must meet the requirement of positive-pressure fire testing, it must have approved gasketing or intumescent material along its edge or on the frame. The material can be placed in a small dado along the edge of the door or in a reveal in the frame.

Fire-retardant coatings may also be applied to wood panel products, finish paneling, metal, fabrics, and other materials to give then a Class A flame spread rating. However, the available colors and textures may be limited, depending on the product and manufacturer, and may affect the final, finished appearance.

Use Only Tested and Rated Assemblies and Materials

Fire-resistance rated assemblies, such as partitions, doors, and glazing, need to be tested according to industry standards to be approved for use in buildings. For example, partitions and some glazing systems must meet the requirements of ASTM E119, *Standard Test Methods for Fire Tests of Building Construction and Materials* and doors must be tested in accordance with NFPA 252, *Fire Tests of Door Assemblies*. Refer to Table 2-4 for a summary of fire testing required for various interior components. The interior designer must verify with the manufacturer that a product or assembly meets the requirements of the local building code.

Use Listed or Labeled Components

For individual components, such as electrical devices, lighting fixtures, doors, hardware, and other building products, an independent testing laboratory may be required to verify that the component meets the requirements of a standard. One of the best-known testing laboratories is Underwriters Laboratories (UL). When a product successfully passes the prescribed test, it is given a UL label. There are several types of UL labels, and each means something different. When a complete and total product is successfully tested, it receives a *listed label*. This means that the product passed the safety test and is manufactured under the UL follow-up services program. A *classified label* means that samples of the product were tested for certain types of uses only. In addition to the classified label, the product must also carry a statement specifying the conditions that were tested for. The detailer should verify that required products, such as electrical devices, are UL listed or labeled or that other approved testing agencies have tested the product.

3-9   ACOUSTICAL CONTROL

Not all details must provide acoustical control, but when it is important the design responses listed in this section may be considered. For interior design, there are three types of conditions that require acoustical control. These are controlling sound within a room, controlling the transmission of sound between spaces, and controlling the transmission of vibration throughout a space or building. For many designs, the interior designer can apply these design responses directly. For critical applications, such as recording studios, concert halls, large lecture halls, and spaces close to unusually loud noise-producing sources (like train tracks or highways), an acoustical consultant should be employed.

Noise Control and Reverberation

Controlling sound within a space may either involve trying to minimize unwanted sound (noise) or trying to enhance reflection and reverberation, for example, in a classroom or concert hall.

There are four detailing responses for *noise control*.

CONTROL OR ISOLATE SOURCE

Removing or controlling the source is the simplest way to control noise within a room. However, this is not always possible if the noise is created by a fixed piece of machinery outside of the room or normal human activity within the room. If a single piece of machinery is producing the noise, it can often be enclosed or modified to reduce it noise output.

AVOID ROOM SHAPES THAT CONCENTRATE NOISE

Barrel vaulted hallways or circular rooms produce undesirable focused sounds if they are finished with a hard surface such as gypsum wallboard. Use these shapes carefully and only where the focused sound may not be annoying or disruptive. Alternately, they can be covered with sound-absorbent material. Rooms that focus sound in some places and not others may also deprive some listeners of useful reflections.

CONTROL THE POSITION OF REFLECTIVE SURFACES

A highly reflective surface, such as glass, can reflect a noise-producing source into another area. For point sources, the angle of incidence is equal to the angle of reflection so that this simple geometry can be used to estimate how to orient a finished surface. In other situations, it may be desirable to reflect the sound, as in a lecture or concert hall.

INCREASE ABSORPTION

One of the best and most common methods of controlling noise within a space is to add absorptive materials. Sound absorption is used to reduce the intensity level of sound within a space, to control unwanted sound reflections, to improve speech privacy, and to decrease reverberation. A detailed discussion of acoustics and sound absorption is beyond the scope of this book; however, keep the following points in mind:

- The absorption of a material is defined by the coefficient of absorption, α, which is the ratio of the sound intensity absorbed by the material to the total intensity reaching the material. The maximum absorption possible, therefore, is 1, that of free space. Generally, a material with a coefficient below 0.2 is considered to be reflective and one with a coefficient above 0.2 is considered sound absorbing. These coefficients are published in manufacturers' technical literature.
- The coefficient of absorption varies with the frequency of the sound, and some materials are better at absorbing some frequencies than others. For critical applications, all frequencies must be checked, but for convenience the single-number *noise reduction coefficient* (NRC) is used. The NRC is the average of a material's absorption coefficients at the four frequencies of 250, 500, 1000, and 2000 Hz, rounded to the nearest multiple of 0.05. Some typical NRC ratings are shown in Table 3-4. The higher the number, the better the material is in absorbing sound at most frequencies encountered in interior design.

Table 3-4 Noise Reduction Coefficients	
Material	NRC
Marble or glazed tile	0.00
Gypsum wallboard	0.05
Vinyl tile on concrete	0.05
Heavy glass	0.05
Wood strip flooring	0.10
Plywood paneling	0.15
Carpet, direct glue to concrete	0.30
Carpet, 1/2 in. pile on concrete	0.50
Heavy velour fabric (18 oz.)	0.60
Suspended acoustic tile, 5/8 in.	0.60
Fiberglass wall panel, 1 in.	0.80
Suspended acoustic tile, 1 in.	0.90

Note: These are representative of various materials based on the older NRC ratings. The Sound Absorption Average (SAA) is the current method of rating the average noise reduction of materials over several frequency bands.

Although most product literature still gives NRC ratings, the NRC has been superseded by the sound absorption average (SAA), although both are similar and provide a single number rating. The SAA is the average of the absorption coefficients for the 12 one-third octave bands from 200 to 2500 Hz when tested in accordance with ASTM C423.

- The total absorption of a material depends on the material's coefficient of absorption and area. The unit used for this quantity is called the *sabin*, which is the absorption value of 1 ft^2 of material with a perfect absorption of 1.0 (An SI sabin equals 10.76 U.S. sabins). The total absorption in a room is the sum of the various individual material absorptions. Finishes and construction detailing should be balanced to provide the best overall room absorption.
- The average absorption coefficient of a room should be at least 0.20. An average absorption above 0.50 is usually not desirable, nor is it economically justified. A lower value is suitable for large rooms, while larger values are suitable for small or noisy rooms.
- Although absorptive materials can be placed anywhere, ceiling treatment for sound absorption is more effective in large rooms, while wall treatment is more effective in small rooms.
- Generally, absorption increases with an increase in thickness of a porous absorber, except for low-frequency sounds that require special design treatment.
- The amount of absorption of a porous type of sound absorber, such as fiberglass or mineral wool, depends on (1) material thickness, (2) material density, (3) material porosity, and (4) the orientation of the material's fibers.

Transmission Control

Controlling sound transmission is a different problem than controlling sound within a room. For interior designers, the most common situation is detailing partitions to control sound, but it may also include detailing ceilings within an existing building to decrease sound transmission between floors.

To simplify the selection of partitions and other building components, such as doors, a single-number rating called the *sound transmission class* (STC) is often used to rate the transmission loss of construction. The higher the STC rating, the better the barrier is (theoretically) in stopping sound. Table 3-5 lists some STC ratings, in decibels (dB) and their subjective effects on hearing. Manufacturers' literature, testing laboratories, and reference literature typically give the transmission loss at different frequencies.

STC ratings represent the ideal loss through a barrier under laboratory conditions. Partitions, floors, and other construction components built in the field are seldom constructed as well as those in the laboratory. Also, breaks in the barrier such as cracks, electrical outlets, doors, and the like will significantly lessen overall noise reduction. Because of this, a published rating for a barrier should be at least 2 to 3 dB higher than the rating actually wanted.

Table 3-5	Effect of Barrier STC Ratings on Hearing
STC	**Subjective effect**
25	Normal speech can be clearly heard through the barrier.
30	Loud speech can be heard and understood fairly well.
35	Loud speech is not intelligible but can be heard.
42–45	Loud speech can only be faintly heard, and normal speech cannot be heard.
46–50	Loud speech not audible and loud sounds other than speech can only be heard faintly, if at all.

Table 3-6 Sound Isolation Criteria of Dwelling Units

Partition Function between Dwellings		STC Ratings, dB		
Apartment A	Apartment B	Grade I, Luxury	Grade II, Average	Grade III, Minimum
bedroom	bedroom	55	52	48
living room	bedroom[a, b]	57	54	50
kitchen[c]	bedroom[a, b]	58	55	52
bathroom	bedroom[a, b]	59	56	52
corridor	bedroom[b, d]	55	52	48
living room	living room	55	52	48
kitchen[c]	living room[a, b]	55	52	48
bathroom	living room[a]	57	54	50
corridor	living room[b, d, e]	55	52	48
kitchen	kitchen[f, g]	52	50	46
bathroom	kitchen[a, g]	55	52	48
corridor	kitchen[b, d, e]	55	52	48
bathroom	bathroom[g]	52	50	46
corridor	bathroom[b, d]	50	48	46
Partition function within a dwelling unit				
bedroom	bedroom[a, b]	48	44	40
living room	bedroom[h, i]	50	46	42
bathroom	bedroom[g, h, i]	52	48	45
kitchen	bedroom[g, h, i]	52	48	45
bathroom	living room[h, i]	52	48	45
mechanical room	sensitive areas	65	62	58
mechanical room	less sensitive areas	60	58	54

[a]The most desirable plan is to have the partition separating spaces with equivalent function; for example, living room opposite living room.
[b]Whenever a partition wall might serve to separate several functional spaces, the highest criterion must prevail.
[c]Or dining, or family, or recreation room.
[d]Assuming that there is no entrance door leading from corridor to living unit.
[e]If a door is part of the corridor partition, it must have the same rating as the corridor. The most desirable arrangement has the entrance door leading from the corridor to a partially enclosed vestibule or foyer in the living unit.
[f]Double-wall construction is recommended to provide, in addition to airborne sound insulation, isolation from impact noises generated by the placement of articles on pantry shelves or the slamming of cabinet doors.
[g]Special detailing is required for vibration isolation of plumbing in kitchens and bathrooms.
[h]Closets may be used as buffer zones, provided that unlouvered doors are used.
[i]Doors leading to bedrooms and bathrooms preferably should be of solid-core construction and gasketed to ensure a comfortable degree of privacy.
Source: A Guide to Airborne, Impact, and Structure Borne Noise Control in Multifamily Dwellings. U.S. Dept. of Housing and Urban Development, HUD-TS-24 (1974)

Minimum STC ratings are required by the IBC as well as various government agencies for residential construction. Table 3-6 provides a summary of some common STC requirements.

In critical situations, transmission loss and selection of barriers should be calculated using the values for various frequencies rather than the single STC average value. Some materials may allow an acoustic "hole," stopping most frequencies but allowing transmission of a certain range of frequencies. However, for preliminary design purposes the STC value is adequate.

Although there are several ways to minimize problems with sound transmission, including space planning and controlling the source, there are six detailing responses for noise transmission control.

USE MASS

Because sound energy must be transmitted through a material to be heard in an adjacent space, it must overcome the inertia of the material. The heavier or more massive the material, the less sound transmitted. For example, a thin piece of glass will not reduce sound transmission as much as a gypsum wallboard partition. A double layer of wallboard is better than a single layer.

MAKE MASS FLEXIBLE

Although the transmission of sound is primarily retarded by the mass of the partition, the stiffness, or rigidity, of the partition is also important. Given two partitions of the same weight per square foot, the one with less stiffness will perform better than the other. Using resilient channels or proprietary products to support one or more layers of gypsum wallboard can reduce partition stiffness. The channels or resilient products "float" the wallboard to dampen sound striking it rather than allowing it to be transmitted to the stud and then through the partition.

PLACE SOUND-ABSORBING MATERIALS IN BARRIER CAVITIES

As sound energy is transmitted through one layer of material into a partition or ceiling cavity, it sets the air in motion, which, in turn, causes the second layer to vibrate, transmitting the sound energy. By placing absorbing material in the cavity this energy is further reduced. This is most often done with acoustic insulation or simple fiberglass insulation. In ceiling plenums, acoustical batts can be placed on top of the suspended ceiling tiles.

Figure 3-18 shows the combined use of the three design responses discussed above.

ELIMINATE GAPS IN THE BARRIER AND SEAL OPENINGS

In addition to the construction of the barrier itself, other variables are critical to the control of sound transmission. Gaps in the barrier must be sealed. Edges at the floor, ceiling, and intersecting walls must be caulked. Penetrations of the barrier should be avoided, but if absolutely necessary, they should be sealed as well. For example, electrical outlets should not be placed back to back but should be staggered in separate stud spaces and caulked. Pipes, ducts, and similar penetrations provide a path for both airborne sound and mechanical vibration and should not be rigidly connected to the barrier. Any gaps between ducts, pipes, and a partition should be sealed.

Typical openings, such as doors and glazed openings, must be detailed to seal around the edges and prevent rigid connections. Figure 3-19 shows one type of acoustical seal around a door opening.

Interior-glazed openings require a combination of approaches to minimize sound transmission. First, the glazing should be set in resilient gaskets to minimize movement between the glazing and the frame. Second, laminated glass should be used to provide additional mass

Figure 3-18 Sound attenuation partition components

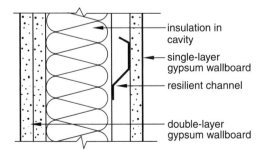

insulation in
cavity

single-layer
gypsum wallboard

resilient channel

double-layer
gypsum wallboard

Figure 3-19 Acoustical principles for doors

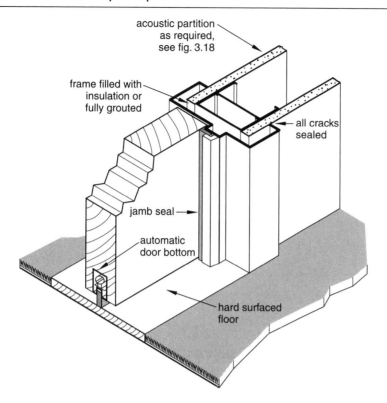

as well as the damping effect created by the plastic interlayer. If a higher STC rating is needed, a double-glazing system can be used as shown in Fig. 3-20.

Avoid Sound Travel through Plenums

One of the most common problems in offices and other commercial construction is the transmission of sound from one space to another in the ceiling plenum if partitions are terminated at the suspended ceiling. The best way to avoid this is to carry partitions from floor to the structural slab above, sealing all penetrations and joints. However, when this is not possible, plenum barriers should be detailed. Two ways of doing this are shown in

Figure 3-20 Glazing detail for acoustical control

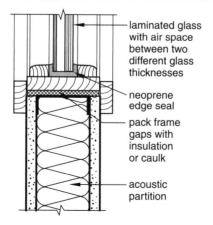

Figure 3-21 Plenum sound barriers

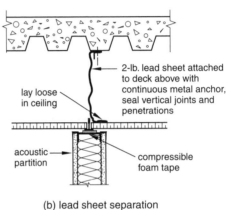

(a) suspended wallboard separation

(b) lead sheet separation

Fig. 3-21. With either approach, any penetrations with pipes, ducts, or conduit must be adequately sealed.

REDUCE SOUND TRAVEL THROUGH DUCTWORK

Ductwork provides a clear path for sound. Ducts should be lined with sound-absorbent material, and connections between vibrating equipment and the ducts attached to it should not be rigid. If ductwork connects two adjacent rooms, it can be laid out in a Z- or U-pattern to increase the length and avoid straight paths for sound. These requirements should be coordinated with the mechanical consultant.

Vibration and Impact Noise Control

In addition to traveling through air, noise can also be transmitted by a source directly through the structure of a building. Dropped objects and footfalls on hard-surfaced floors are a common problem, but machines, HVAC systems, plumbing fixtures, and water flowing through pipes can also create structure-borne noises.

Impact noise, or sound resulting from direct contact of an object with a sound barrier, can occur on any surface, but it generally occurs on a floor and ceiling assembly. It is usually caused by footfall, shuffled furniture, and dropped objects.

Impact noise control is quantified by the *impact insulation class* (IIC) number, a single-number rating of a floor/ceiling's impact sound performance. The higher the IIC rating, the better the floor performs in reducing impact sounds in the test frequency range. Minimum

Table 3-7 Impact Insulation Class between Dwelling Units

Floor Function between Dwellings		IIC Ratings, dB		
Apartment A Above	Apartment B	Grade I, Luxury	Grade II, Average	Grade III, Minimum
bedroom	bedroom	55	52	48
living room	bedroom[a, b]	60	57	53
kitchen[c]	bedroom[a, b, d]	65	62	58
family room	bedroom[a, b]	65	62	58
corridor	bedroom[a, b]	65	62	58
bedroom	living room[e]	55	52	48
living room	living room	55	52	48
kitchen	living room[a, b, d]	60	57	53
family room	living room[a, b]	62	60	56
corridor	living room[a, b]	60	57	53
bedroom	kitchen[a, d, e]	55	50	46
living room	kitchen[a, d, e]	55	52	48
kitchen	kitchen[d]	55	52	48
bathroom	kitchen[a, b, d]	55	52	48
family room	kitchen[a, b, d]	60	58	54
corridor	kitchen [a, b, d]	55	52	48
bedroom	family room[a, e]	50	48	46
living room	family room[a, e]	52	50	48
kitchen	family room[a, e]	55	52	50
bathroom	bathroom[d]	52	50	48
corridor	corridor[f]	50	48	46

[a]The most desirable plan is to have the floor-ceiling assembly separating spaces with equivalent function; for example, living room above living room.
[b]This arrangement requires greater impact sound insulation than the converse, where a sensitive area is above a less sensitive area.
[c]Or dining, or family, or recreation room.
[d]Special detailing is required for vibration isolation of plumbing in kitchens and bathrooms.
[e]This arrangement requires equivalent airborne sound insulation and perhaps less impact sound insulation than the converse.
[f]Special detailing is required for proper treatment of staircase halls and corridors.
Source: A Guide to Airborne, Impact, and Structure Borne Noise Control in Multifamily Dwellings. U.S. Dept. of Housing and Urban Development, HUD-TS-24 (1974)

ICC ratings are required by the IBC, as well as various government agencies for residential construction. For example, the IBC requires floor/ceiling assemblies between dwelling units or between a dwelling unit and a public or service area to have a minimum IIC rating of 50 dB (or 45 dB if field tested) when tested in accordance with ASTM E492. Table 3-7 provides a summary of some common IIC requirements.

The IIC value of a floor can most easily be increased by adding carpet. It can also be improved by providing a resiliently suspended ceiling below, floating a finished floor on resilient pads over the structural floor, or providing sound-absorbing material (insulation) in the air space between the floor and the finished ceiling below.

There are three detailing responses for vibration and impact noise control.

PROVIDE FLEXIBLE CONNECTIONS

Flexible connections can be used to isolate noise-producing construction elements. Flexible connectors are available to join ductwork as well as pipes. Rubber or steel spring mounts can be used for machinery. Plumbing pipes can be suspended with wire or attached to the structure with plastic or rubber clamps and hangers to avoid noise caused by expansion and contraction and by the noise of running water.

Figure 3-22 Proprietary acoustic clip

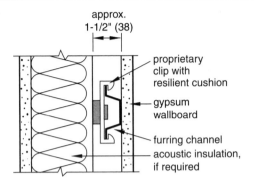

approx.
1-1/2" (38)

proprietary
clip with
resilient cushion

gypsum
wallboard

furring channel
acoustic insulation,
if required

USE DAMPING DEVICES

One of the most effective ways to minimize structure-borne sound is to cushion the source of the noise from the rest of the structure. Using pads on a doorframe is a simple example of this principle. For floors, sound deadening underlayment can be used for hard-surfaced flooring as well as carpeting.

For partitions, one of the most common detailing elements is the resilient channel, as shown in Fig. 3-18. An alternate to this is a proprietary device that attaches to the stud and uses a resilient material to hold standard furring channels. Two types are manufactured; one is shown in Fig. 3-22. The device can be used on metal or wood studs or under a roof or floor structure. The manufacturers claim that the STC rating of a partition using this type of device is better than resilient channels.

MAXIMIZE DISTANCE

If possible, locate mechanical rooms, service areas, and other sources of structure-borne noise together and plan to maximize the distance between them and the areas intended to be quiet.

3-10 MOISTURE/WATER RESISTANCE

Whenever water or moisture may be present in or near an interior detail, the designer must take every precaution to prevent moisture intrusion. Moisture can rust unprotected ferrous metal, warp wood, expand absorbent materials, create stains, damage adjacent construction, degrade insulation, and create an environment for mold and mildew. Although resisting moisture intrusion in many interior details is not as difficult as preventing it in the exterior envelope of a building, it is no less important.

There are six detailing responses for control of moisture and water resistance.

Use Nonabsorbent Materials

When moisture may be present, the detail should not have any absorbent materials, such as unprotected wood, or fabrics not designed to repel water. Wood may be covered with a waterproof material, painted, or otherwise sealed, but this can create a maintenance problem if exposed. Even countertops covered with plastic laminate may be damaged if water seeps behind the laminate.

Use Nonferrous Metals

Unprotected steel will rust in the presence of moisture. Structural supports, fasteners, or other ferrous components should be avoided if water intrusion is expected in the detail. If steel is used it should be stainless steel, galvanized, or given some other protective coating.

Eliminate or Minimize Joints

One of the easiest ways to keep water out of a detail is to minimize the number and location of joints where small cracks may develop, allowing water to seep in. For example, it is easy to detail a continuous cove between a countertop and the backsplash instead of using two separate pieces. Joints are better located on vertical services where water is likely to run off instead of on horizontal surfaces where standing water may be a problem. For continuously wet areas, such as shower rooms, reducing the number of joints reduces the likelihood of leaks.

Employ Overlap

Where water will be splashed on two or more separate pieces of material on vertical or sloped surfaces, they should be lapped like the shingles on a roof instead of being connected with a butt joint. Even if small cracks develop, the shingle effect will prevent water from running behind the finish material.

Use Drips

As with overlaps, drips use gravity to force water to drop away from a construction element instead of running back into the construction by capillary action or surface tension. A drip is simply a groove or sharp edge under a material that forces water flowing vertically down the side of a material to drip away instead of running horizontally back to the main structure (see Fig. 3-23). Drips are commonly used on architectural elements, such as the lowest course of lap siding, under windowsills, and at building overhangs. They can also be used on interior details where large quantities of water may be present, such as in commercial washrooms, showers, pools, kitchens, and the like.

Use the Correct Sealant and Joint Design

Sealants are commonly used to close small joints where water may be present. They may also allow minor movement of the joint while maintaining a seal. In interior construction, there are two types of joints: nonmovement joints and movement joints. Nonmovement joints

Figure 3-23 Drips to shed moisture

without drip   groove drip   angle drip

Figure 3-24 Movement joint with thin-set tile

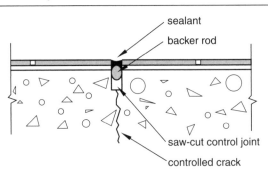

are those where the two adjacent materials are not expected to move relative to each other. An inside joint in a tile shower is an example of a nonmovement joint because the tile is rigidly attached to the backup walls, which will not move during the life of the installation. Nonmovement joints in wet areas can usually be sealed with an acrylic or silicone sealant.

Movement joints are those designed to accommodate expected movement because of expansion and contraction of materials, movement of the building, or movement of individual parts of the building. For example, movement joints are required for ceramic tile floors where there are control joints in the concrete floor or where there are large expanses of tile flooring. See Fig. 3-24.

Verify the required joint size and location with the manufacturer of the material. The recommended joint widths and sizes for ceramic tile are shown in Table 3-8.

Movement joints in wet interior areas are usually sealed with a silicone sealant, which has good movement capabilities and is impervious to water.

Table 3-8 Recommended Ceramic Tile Expansion Joint Width and Spacing

	Interior		Exposed to Direct Sunlight or Moisture
	Ceramic Mosaic and Glazed Wall Tile	Quarry and Paver tile	
Spacing, ft. (m)	20–25 (6.10–7.62)	20–25 (6.10–7.62)	8–12 (2.59–3.66)
Width, in. (mm)	1/8–1/4[a] (3–6)	1/4[b] (6)	1/4 (6)

[a] 1/4 in. (6 mm) is the preferred minimum, but the joint should never be less than 1/8 in. (3 mm).
[b] same as grout joint but not less than 1/4 in. (6 mm).

CHAPTER 4

CONSTRUCTABILITY

4-1 INTRODUCTION

Constructability is the sum of the requirements produced by a detail itself, independent of the basic function or aesthetic needs of the detail. For example, every detail must be structurally sound, use appropriate connections, accommodate tolerances, and be durable enough to suit its intended life cycle. This chapter discusses these and other aspects of constructability and offers some ways to address these universal concerns found in all detailing problems.

Although constructability issues are a part of all detailing problems, the methods by which they are satisfied may conflict with design intent, constraints, or function. It is the designer's task to resolve these conflicts in the best way possible. For example, the design intent of a service counter in a restaurant may suggest a highly articulated assembly of countertop, opening framing, and overhead lighting, while the basic constructability issues of cleanability, durability, and ease of construction may require a simpler assemblage of materials and connections.

4-2 STRUCTURAL REQUIREMENTS

Strength and structure are terms referring to the inherent ability of a material, product, or assembly to withstand any loads that may be placed on it. This may be as simple as the ability of one part of a detail to support the weight of another part of a detail, or as complex as the ability of an assembly to withstand complex gravity and wind loads that would require a structural engineer to calculate.

For many interior details structural requirements are not critical; the ability of one component to support another and common loads placed on the detail are satisfied by standard methods of construction. For example, the typical methods by which a hollow metal door frame is anchored to metal studs is sufficient to hold the frame in place, support the door, withstand the forces of opening and closing the door, and resist the occasional impact on the frame caused by people or objects moving through the opening. However, if the door is detailed as wider, higher, or heavier, or if a custom frame configuration is developed the required structural connections will need to be examined and designed to support the detail's unique loading.

In other cases, the particular function and constraints of the detail require the designer to develop a unique solution to the problem. For example, a countertop spanning two supporting cabinets will require structural support sufficient to hold any equipment or materials placed on it, while accounting for the possibility that someone might lean or sit on the countertop. These loads must be resisted by materials and configurations based on the material and span of the countertop, how much deflection is allowable, and required knee space below the countertop.

Basic Concepts of Structure

Although complex details with unique structural requirements must be designed by a structural engineer, the interior designer can develop many light-loading details with an understanding of some basic structural concepts. With this knowledge, the designer can make decisions regarding the basic configuration of a detail, the types of connections required, and the size of the components. If required, a structural engineer can then verify the adequacy of the structural portions of the detail.

There are several basis types of loads that building elements must resist. These are shown diagrammatically in Fig. 4-1.

Compression loads push the elements of a material together. These loads are resisted by making the structural element sufficiently large and/or by using a material that is sufficiently strong. Every material has a particular ability to resist loading per unit area. For example, steel can resist more compressive force per square inch than wood. Compressive loads are typically the easiest to resist with a variety of materials. Wood, steel, aluminum, brass, stone, concrete, and even plastic are all good choices for interior details with compressive loads.

In addition to simple compression there is another aspect of materials resisting compressive loads that must be considered. This is called the buckling load and is the point at which compressive forces in a column or other vertical member cause the member to bend outward (and break, if the load is sufficiently large), even though it is capable of resisting the basic compressive load. Buckling commonly happens when the vertical element is long relative to its thickness. For example, very thin legs on a tall table or countertop supporting a heavy weight could be subject to buckling loads. In most cases, however, the commonly used materials and sizes of most interior details eliminate problems with buckling loads.

Tension loads tend to pull the elements of a material apart. A wire supporting a suspended weight is in tension. Some materials, such as concrete or masonry, are good at resisting compressive loads, while very poor at resisting tensile forces. Steel, on the other hand, has great strength in both compression and tension and is typically used for wire supports.

When a material is subject to tensile loads, it becomes longer, or stretches. The amount of stretch depends on the weight being supported or force being applied, as well as the strength and size of the supporting member. For most interior design and detailing applications, the

Figure 4-1 Basis structural loads

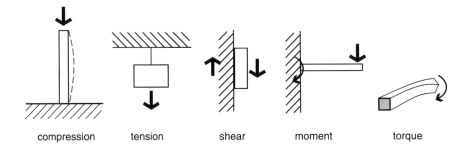

compression   tension   shear   moment   torque

change in length is not significant, but if heavy loads are anticipated, this elongation must be taken into account and calculated by a structural engineer.

Shear loads tend to cause the elements of a material to slide relative to each other. While shear stress is always present in large structural members, such as a beam supporting a load, for interior details shear stresses are also commonly present in smaller elements, such as a screw supporting a wall panel or cabinet.

Moment is a property by which a force applied to an element tends to cause the element to rotate about a point or line. The amount of moment is proportional to the amount of load applied and the distance from the line of action of the load and the point of rotation. In building construction, moment is most often found in cantilevered beams where the beam is supported at only one end or a shelf is supported along only one edge. When one material is connected to another material and the connection must resist moment forces, the connection must be carefully considered and designed. Even if the connection is sufficient to support the load, the cantilevered element may deflect by an unacceptable amount. The configuration of interior details can be simplified by avoiding situations where moment loads are present.

Torque is the result of a force tending to produce a rotation. A very simple example of torque is using a wrench to tighten a bolt. For most interior details, torque forces are not present or are of magnitudes small enough not to be problematic.

The following suggestions include approaches to dealing with structural issues in interior details.

Use Simple Direct Bearing Connections Whenever Possible

In most cases, resting one material directly on another can easily accommodate weight or applied load in a detail. This sets up simple compressive forces that nearly any material can resist and simplifies any connection required. For example, setting a privacy partition directly on the floor is an easier structural connection to make than hanging it from the wall. In the first case, the weight of the partition rests directly on the floor, while in the second case the weight must be transferred with moment connections or with fasteners loaded in shear and tension, in which case both the fasteners and the substrate to which they are applied must be adequate to support the weight.

Incorporate Beam Action

Beams are the most basic type of structure in which a horizontal element rests on two or more vertical elements. Uniform or concentrated loads on the beam are transferred through bending action to the supports. As diagrammed in Fig. 4-2(a), when a load is applied to a simple rectangular beam, the beam bends with portions of the beam above the centerline, called the neutral axis, tending to shorten, while the portions below the centerline tend to lengthen. Thus, the top of the beam is in compression and the bottom of the beam is in tension, with the maximum stresses being at the extreme distances from the neutral axis.

Because of the way beams resist loads, it is most efficient to locate as much of the area of the beam as far away from the neutral axis as possible. This is why steel beams are formed in an I- or H-shape and some manufactured wood joists use a thin plywood web with thicker, solid members at the top and bottom of the web to form an I-shaped assembly.

For simple rectangular shapes, beam action can be most efficient and result in a stiffer and stronger beam if the rectangle is placed such that the orientation is vertical rather than

Figure 4-2 Beam action

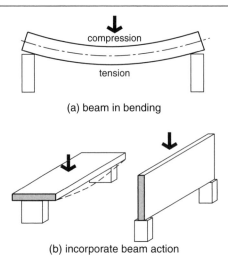

(a) beam in bending

(b) incorporate beam action

horizontal. See Fig. 4-2(b). In practical terms, for example, if a 1 × 2 piece of wood is being used to support a countertop, it is better to orient it vertically rather than horizontally. This principle can be used with wood, aluminum, steel, or any other material. When space is limited for a detail incorporating beam action, steel or aluminum strips or angles can be used instead of wood.

Use the Simplest Connections Possible

Because the forces acting on most interior details are minimal, connections can be kept as simple as possible to minimize cost and shorten construction time. As long as the individual components are sufficiently supported and attached to each other, the most direct method of making connections should be used. For example, adhesives may be used in place of screws or clips can be used instead of ledgers.

Use Redundant Connections or Bearing When Required

If the structural integrity of the detail is critical consider using redundant connections in case one weakens or fails. For example, three bolts may be used instead of two or one detail component may be placed directly on top of another for a simple gravity bearing connection, while using fasteners to secure the two elements in place.

The decision to use redundant connections, however, must be balanced with the goal of using simple structural connections and as few as possible, as suggested below. The designer must weigh the need for ensuring that the detail is structurally sound against the requirements of cost, construction time, aesthetics, and ease of assembly.

Use Structural Connections Approved by the Manufacturer

For details that use premanufactured components, the recommendations provided by the manufacturer should be used. Manufacturers often provide instructions for installing their products on a variety of substrates and give recommendations on the types of fasteners to use.

However, if the manufactured item is being used in a manner that is different than intended, the connections should be reviewed by a structural engineer.

Use Removable Connections for Reuse Potential

Although not typically considered with current construction methods, a building or detail can be designed for disassembly. This allows the building component to be taken apart for reuse, recycling, or proper disposal as part of a larger program of sustainable design. Designing for disassembly must be considered during detailing, at the beginning of the building life cycle rather than at the end. Connections are one of the key components in designing for disassembly, because taking apart a building must be reasonably easy or the decision will be made to simply dispose of materials rather than reusing or recycling them.

Connections can be made for disassembly in a variety of ways. For example, screws or bolts can be used instead of nails or adhesive. Clips or pressure joints can also be used instead of rigid connections, where appropriate. As part of the disassembly mindset, the fewest number of components should also be used to minimize the time required for taking the detail apart.

As with other aspects of detailing, the designer must balance the practicality of designing for disassembly with the sustainability benefits that may be gained and factors of cost, function, and the many other aspects of detailing.

4-3 CONNECTIONS

Connections are the ways the various parts of a detail are attached to each another and to the substrate to which the detail is anchored. Connections can be made with adhesives, nails, screws, bolts, tape, or Velcro® or by power fastening, crimping, clipping, welding, or soldering. Which method is selected depends, of course, on the materials being fastened, but other factors may include appearance, cost, strength, safety, simplicity, clearance available, adjustability, and the ability to disassemble the detail, as mentioned in the previous section. For example, steel can be welded, bolted, or screwed to other steel members, while it can only be bolted or screwed to wood members. Even if two pieces of steel need to be connected, considerations of safety and the need for a skilled welder may suggest using another method.

Use the Appropriate Method for Rigid Connections

Rigid connections are those that are not intended to move or accommodate incidental movement. Rigid connections include fasteners, such as nails, screws, bolts, and clamps, as well as welding and soldering. Adhesives, tape, and crimping provide a slightly less rigid connection, allowing for very minor movement if the force acting on the two joined materials is great enough. Screws and bolts tend to hold better than nails, adhesives, and clamping and are useful if some amount of adjustability is required. If the designer wants to emphasize the method of connection as part of the aesthetics of the detail, screws or bolts can be used and even oversized. Many types of screws and bolts are available if the designer wants something other than a standard connection. There are available in steel, stainless steel, and some other materials depending on the connector type. Some of these are shown in Fig. 4-3. Most of the screws are available with various types of heads, including slotted, Phillips, square, slotted hex, and one-way tamperproof.

Figure 4-3 Types of bolt and screw heads

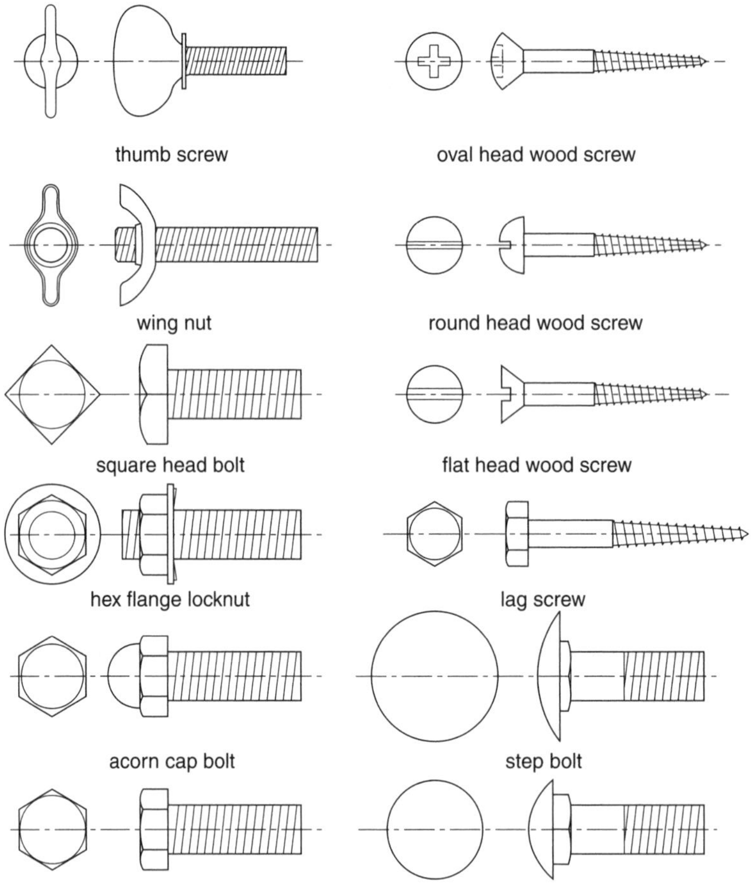

thumb screw

oval head wood screw

wing nut

round head wood screw

square head bolt

flat head wood screw

hex flange locknut

lag screw

acorn cap bolt

step bolt

hex cap bolt

carriage bolt

Determine Movable Connection Type Based on Use

Many times a detail must have moving parts, such as an access panel on a cabinet or a sliding platform in a display case. There are a variety of methods and hardware types of movable connections. Which type is selected depends on whether the movable portion must be completely removable (loose), sliding, swinging, rolling, or some combination. Loose components are a low-cost and simple method of providing a removable panel when only occasional access is required. The panel can be affixed by screws or bolts. For panels, cabinet doors, and other construction elements that must be opened repeatedly, some type of hinge should be used. These may include butts, wraparounds, pivots, continuous hinges, and concealed hinges. Some of the many types of hinges are shown in Fig. 4-4.

Other specialized hardware is available for attaching doors or drawers to cabinets and other millwork. These include flap stays, lid stays, flipper door slides, swing-up fittings, slides, running track, and sliding door hardware.

Minimize Number and Types of Connections

Unless redundant connections are required for safety and in critical circumstances, as mentioned in the previous section, try to minimize the variety and number of connections. For example, use only one size and type of bolt for every connection in a detail, and if possible, in

Figure 4-4 Hinge types

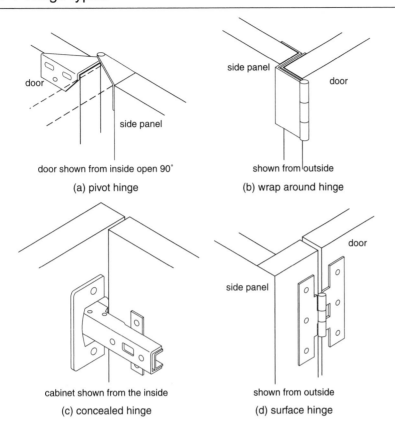

door

door shown from inside open 90°

side panel

(a) pivot hinge

side panel

door

shown from outside

(b) wrap around hinge

cabinet shown from the inside

(c) concealed hinge

door

side panel

shown from outside

(d) surface hinge

all details. This makes it less likely that workers will confuse one type of connector for another in different construction assemblies. Minimizing both number and types also generally reduces construction time and minimizes cost.

Make Connections Accessible

When any type of connection is shown in a detail there must be sufficient clearance to install the connection during initial construction, to replace the connection if necessary, and to disassemble the construction. For instance, there must be room to install and tighten a bolt or screw, to apply adhesive, to solder a connection, or to use a power tool. Space must be provided to both accommodate the worker's hand as well as any tools being used.

4-4 MOVEMENT

Movement is that aspect of a detail that makes provision for any anticipated displacement of the detail itself or its components as well as overall building motion that the detail must accommodate. Buildings move for a variety of reasons, and interior construction must accommodate this movement. Movement can be caused by temperature changes, deflection of the structure, wind-induced sway, seismic motion, building settlement, or warping of wood. The amount of movement expected will determine the detailing response.

Figure 4-5 Recommended average moisture content for interior wood products

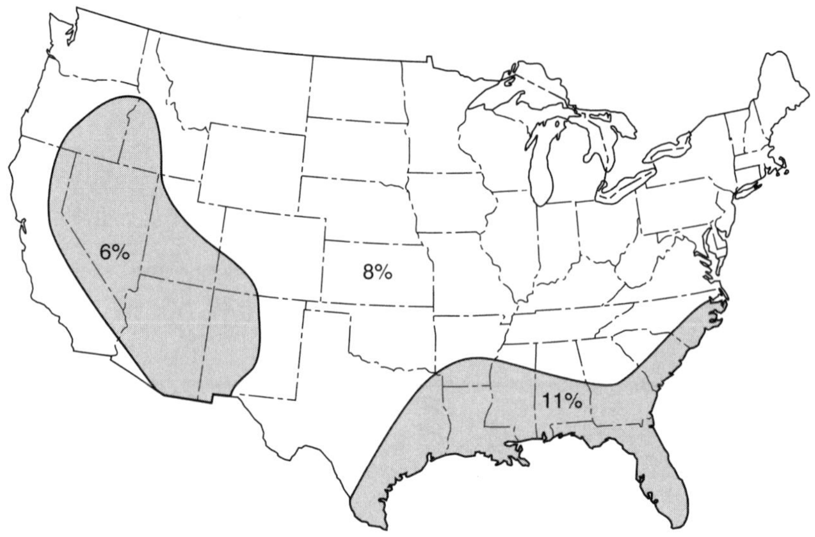

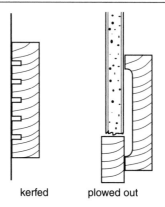

Use Acclimated Materials

Materials that respond to changes in moisture and temperature, such as wood, should be seasoned and installed at approximately the same humidity and temperature levels that will be present during their use. If they come from a climate substantially different than the one in which they will be used they should be stored on site for a period of time as recommended by the manufacturer before installation. Figure 4-5 shows the recommended moisture content levels for woodwork used for interior applications.

Use Relieved Backs on Wood

Flat, solid pieces of wood are subject to cupping distortions caused by differences in shrinkage on opposite sides of the board. This tendency can be minimized by relieving the back, or nonvisible side, of the board, as shown in Fig. 4-6. This can be done by cutting small kerfs in the back of the board or by cutting out a wide portion, which also makes it easier to attach the board to two slightly uneven surfaces. Normally, shop-fabricated wood trim comes

Figure 4-6 Relieved backs

kerfed   plowed out

with relieved backs. Custom-fabricated wood pieces may need to be relieved on site or the requirement clearly stated in the architectural woodwork specifications.

Use Control Joints

Control joints are small joints purposely built into a construction component to cause any incidental cracking that occurs to happen in a predetermined location. For example, control joints are commonly seen in concrete slabs as small grooves. These grooves weaken the concrete slightly so that minor cracking will be concealed within the joint rather than show up as a random crack elsewhere in the slab. In interior construction, control joints, sometimes incorrectly called expansion joints, are used in large expanses of wood paneling or flooring. For flush wood panels, eased joints should be used between two panels. An eased joint is one with the visible corners slightly beveled about 1/16 in. (1.6 mm). See Fig. 4-7(a). Although the joint is visible it looks like a deliberate design decision and is not objectionable and can conceal any slight shrinkage of the wood panels. Without it, any shrinkage at joints would be noticeable. Control joints are also used in terrazzo floors by placing a zinc strip in the floor, which is flush with the floor and may be part of a decorative pattern to separate different colors of terrazzo.

Provide Expansion Joints

Expansion joints provide for greater movement than control joints. They are used in large expanses of gypsum wallboard, plaster, ceramic tile, wood paneling, and other materials that expand or contract or may move slightly from other causes. For example, expansion joints in ceramic tile floors accommodate slight deflection of the supporting slab and expansion and

Figure 4-7 Interior control and expansion joints

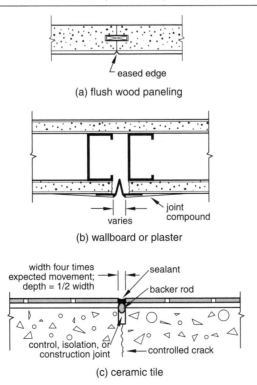

eased edge

(a) flush wood paneling

varies

joint compound

(b) wallboard or plaster

width four times expected movement; depth = 1/2 width

sealant

backer rod

control, isolation, or construction joint

controlled crack

(c) ceramic tile

contraction of the flooring itself. Figures 4-7(b) and (c) show some common control and expansion joints used in interior detailing.

If large movement is expected, then slip joints or building expansion joints should be used, as described below.

Use Sliding/Overlapping Joints

A simple method to accommodate movement, either as a control joint or as an expansion joint is to detail materials that overlap or otherwise allow for sliding movement. See Fig. 4-8. This generic type of detail can be used with wood, metal, plastic, or proprietary products. Sliding joints can be combined with reveals to allow a material to move without the movement being noticeable. For example, as diagrammed in Fig. 4-8(e), wall panels can be mounted flush with each other on wall clips with a reveal space between them. The clips hold the panels in place and take the gravity loads, while allowing horizontal movement. The reveals between the panels effectively conceal any slight movement. As an added benefit, the clips allow the panels to be easily removed for repair or replacement.

Use Slip Joints

When a significant amount of movement is expected in a detail, slip joints should be used to allow the detail to move without damaging the detail or surrounding materials. For example, in covering the joint between a fire-rated partition and the underside of a floor slab the potential deflection of the floor slab must be considered in addition to the requirement for properly sealing the joint against fire and smoke penetration. A typical site-constructed detail is shown in Fig. 4-9. This detail provides a slip joint that creates a fire-rated seal, while allowing the slab to deflect up to approximately 1/2 inch (13 mm) without buckling the partition. Another approach is to use a proprietary product as shown in Fig. 4-10, which does the same job, but allows greater deflection. Several proprietary products are available

Figure 4-8 Sliding joints

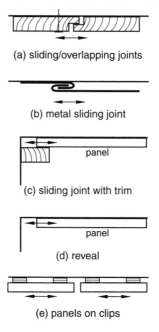

(a) sliding/overlapping joints

(b) metal sliding joint

(c) sliding joint with trim

(d) reveal

(e) panels on clips

Figure 4-9 Site constructed slip joint

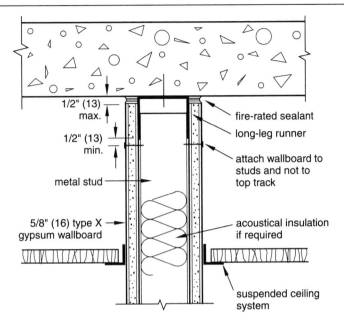

that make constructing partition slip joints easier, while allowing for various amounts of slab deflection.

Significant horizontal movement in high-rise buildings can be caused by wind loading. It an interior partition is detailed against a window mullion with no provision for accommodating the movement, partition cracking or buckling can occur, just as with vertical deflection. A slip joint, such as that shown in Fig. 4–11, should be provided. This can be constructed with

Figure 4-10 Proprietary fire-rated slip joint

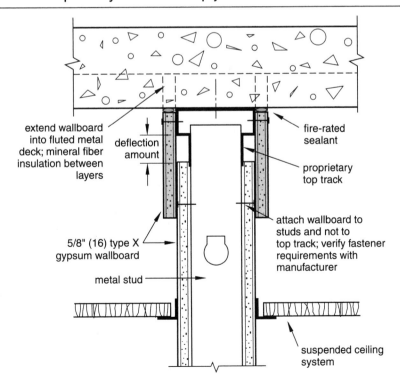

Figure 4-11 Relief joints at perimeter walls

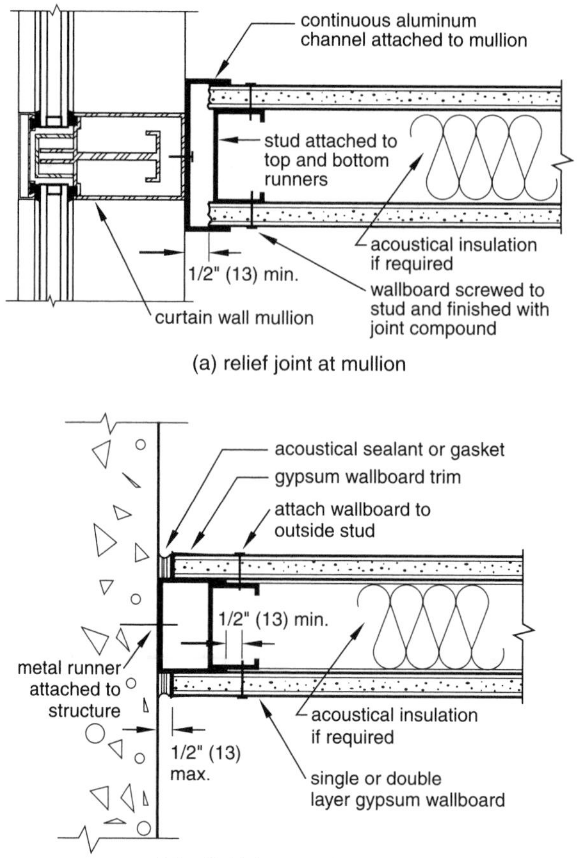

(a) relief joint at mullion

continuous aluminum channel attached to mullion

stud attached to top and bottom runners

acoustical insulation if required

wallboard screwed to stud and finished with joint compound

1/2" (13) min.

curtain wall mullion

(b) relief joint at wall or column

acoustical sealant or gasket

gypsum wallboard trim

attach wallboard to outside stud

1/2" (13) min.

metal runner attached to structure

1/2" (13) max.

acoustical insulation if required

single or double layer gypsum wallboard

generic materials or a proprietary product can be used. The amount of deflection expected should be verified by a structural engineer.

Use Building Expansion Joints

When very large movement is expected a different type of joint must be used. Such movement is caused by entire sections of a building moving at different rates or by earthquakes. Joints for these kinds of movement are called building separation joints and seismic separation joints. They are typically located and designed by the architect and structural engineer as part of the design of the building. Proprietary products are available to accommodate different magnitudes of movement in floors, walls, and ceilings and the interior designer may encounter these types of joints in large buildings. Two such joints are shown in Fig. 4-12. Generally, manufacturers provide a method to incorporate the adjacent finish material on the joint.

Provide Clear Space

The simplest way to accommodate small or large building movement is to separate interior construction assemblies and components from the building structure. This is diagrammed in Fig. 4-13. This allows the building to move without transferring any damaging forces to interior materials or components, and it allows interior construction to move separately from the building structure. Of course, this is only possible if the connection can be open from a

Figure 4-12 Building separation joints

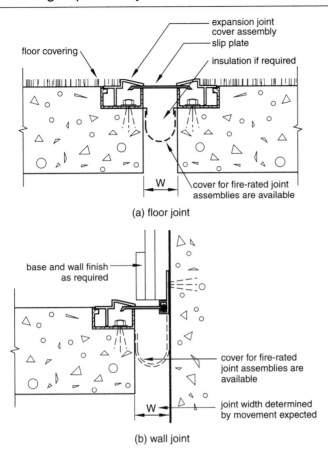

(a) floor joint

(b) wall joint

functional standpoint, For example, a partition held away from the ceiling and exterior walls could not provide complete visual or audio separation.

4-5 TOLERANCES

Tolerance is the acceptable deviation in size, position, shape, or location from a theoretically exact value. Tolerances in building construction recognize that nothing can be built perfectly. The amount of tolerance of a building material or the installation of a product depends on the material itself, manufacturing tolerances, fabrication tolerances, and installation tolerances. Some tolerances in construction are very small while some are quite large. For example,

Figure 4-13 Provide clear space

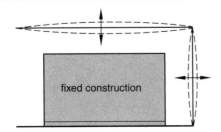

Table 4-1 Common Industry-Standard Construction Tolerances

Building Element	Tolerance	Source
Concrete slab on grade, level from stated elevation	±3/4″ (±19)	ACI
Concrete slab on grade, flatness under 10′ (3 m) straightedge	±3/8″ (±10)	ACI
Concrete suspended slab, level from stated elevation	±3/4″ (±19)	ACI
Concrete suspended slab, flatness under 10′ (3 m) straightedge	±1/2″ (±13)	ACI
Position of concrete beams and walls	±1″ (±25)	ACI
Concrete opening size, vertical openings, like windows and doors	+1″, −1/2″ (+25, −13)	ACI
Size of concrete columns over 12″ (305 mm)	+1/2 ″, −3/8″ (+13, −10)	ACI
Concrete block, position in plan	±1/2″ in 20′ (±12.7 in 6.1 m)	ACI
Concrete block, plumb	±1/4″ in 10′ (±6.4 in 3.05 m)	ACI
Interior stone wall cladding size	±1/8″ (3)	MIA
Stone tile size	±1/32″ (0.8)	MIA
Rough lumber framing, position	±1/4″ (6)	RCPS
Rough lumber framing, plumb	±1/4″ in 10′ (6 in 3050)	RCPS
Rough floor framing with subflooring in 10′	±1/4″ in 10′ (6 in 3050)	RCPS
Rough floor framing with subflooring overall	±1/2″ in 20′ (13 in 6100)	RCPS
Woodwork field joint installation of wood to wood items:		
Flushness and gap width, premium grade	±0.012″ (±0.3)	AWI
Flushness and gap width, custom grade	±0.025″ (±0.65)	AWI
Woodwork field joint installation of wood to nonwood items:		
Flushness and gap width, premium grade	±0.025″ (±0.65)	AWI
Flushness and gap width, custom grade	±0.050″ (±1.3)	AWI
Curtain wall and storefront installation, plumb	±1/8″ in 12′ (±3 in 3600)	GANA
Gypsum wallboard partitions in horizontal position	±1/4″ (6)	Various
Gypsum wallboard partitions, plumb and ceiling level	±1/4 ″ in 10′ (±6 in 3050)	Various
Maximum bow of 1/4″ tempered glass from 71″ to 83″ long	0.47″ (12 mm)	ASTM

Original source of industry standard:

ACI	American Concrete Institute
MIA	Marble Institute of America
RCPS	*Residential Construction Performance Guidelines 3rd ed.*, Association of Home Builders Remodelors™
AWI	*Architectural Woodwork Quality Standards, 8th ed.*
GANA	Glass Association of North America, *Glazing Manual*
ASTM	American Society for Testing and Materials, C1048

For a complete listing of construction tolerances see *Handbook of Construction Tolerances 2nd ed.*, David Kent Ballast. John Wiley & Sons.

architectural woodwork built in the shop may have tolerances in the range of hundredths of an inch, while site-cast concrete may have tolerances of several inches.

The interior designer must understand both the manufacturing and installation tolerances for construction components and detail accordingly. Table 4-1 gives some common industry-standard tolerances for various construction components, including both basic architectural tolerances on which interior construction is based, as well as interior components themselves. Of course, for architectural tolerances, such as a concrete floor slab, the interior designer must accommodate whatever tolerances and existing conditions are present with the interior construction. For interior components, the designer can choose to design for industry-standard tolerances or specify more restrictive tolerances, recognizing that requiring smaller tolerance values may increase the cost and installation time of a construction element.

The following guidelines are some of the methods that can be used to accommodate tolerances when developing a detail. These are diagrammed in Fig. 4-14.

Provide Shim Space

A shim space allows one construction component that must be installed with close tolerance to be placed within or adjacent to another construction component that may be built with greater tolerances. For example, a door frame must be placed perfectly plumb and level in

Figure 4-14 Methods of accommodating tolerances

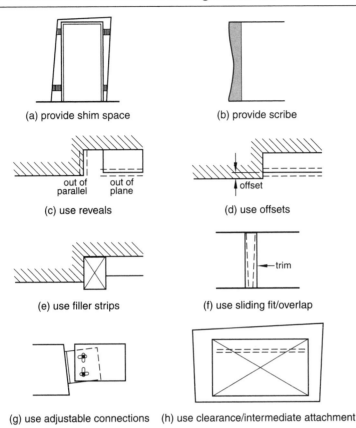

(a) provide shim space (b) provide scribe

(c) use reveals (d) use offsets

(e) use filler strips (f) use sliding fit/overlap

(g) use adjustable connections (h) use clearance/intermediate attachment

order for the door to operate properly but is placed within, and attached to, a rough opening whose edges are usually not plumb or level. See Fig. 4–14(a). Shims are used to provide for the variable space between the two components. Shims are thin pieces of wood (usually tapered), metal, or plastic, which are used to fill the space. Shimming is typically used for the installation of doors, glazed openings, cabinets, wall panels, and any construction element that must be installed plumb and level. In most cases, the resulting irregular shim space and shims must be covered with trim or otherwise concealed by the detail.

Provide Scribe

A scribe, or scribe piece, is a slightly oversized piece of material that is custom trimmed on site to follow the irregularities of another edge. As diagrammed in Fig. 4–14(b) a scribe may be used to set a perfectly straight and plumb cabinet edge against a wall that is bowed or slightly out of plumb. When the gaps are filled by the scribe the variation is generally not noticeable to the eye.

Use Reveals

Reveals visually separate one construction element with another by using a small space, generally in the range of 3/8 in. to 1 in. (10 mm to 25 mm). See Fig. 4–14(c). Reveals may be as deep as allowed by the materials or at the designer's discretion. If the edges and surfaces of the two elements are not parallel or flush, the reveal separates them enough to be unnoticeable. Reveals are an effective device for use in a wide range of construction details. In addition to accommodating tolerances, reveals provide a way to separate and finish different materials and to establish interesting shadow lines. A scribe piece may be recessed to create a reveal if the gap must be physically closed off. Reveals may be finished with the same color and material as one or both of the adjacent materials to help minimize its presence, painted black, or finished with a contrasting color.

Use Offsets

An offset, diagrammed in Fig. 4-14(d) is similar to a reveal in that it visually conceals slight differences in plane between two elements. Offsets are often referred to as reveals. Offsets are most often used to conceal the situation of two adjacent surfaces being slight out of plane with each other. They are commonly used when two pieces of wood trim are joined. Instead of setting the two wood pieces perfectly aligned along their edges, one is set back from the other by a fraction of an inch; for example, the casing trim of a door opening is usually set back from the face of the door frame itself by about 1/4 in. (6 mm).

Use Filler Strips

Filler strips are separate construction elements that extend beyond two edges or planes to visually separate and disguise any discrepancies in flushness or alignment. See Fig. 4-14(e). They conceal minor irregularities in the same way a reveal does, but a filler strip becomes a prominent design element in its own right by extending beyond the primary materials. A filler strip can also be recessed from the two adjacent surfaces to create a reveal but with a separate finish to highlight the strip instead of trying to conceal it. Filler strips can also act as scribe pieces.

Use Sliding or Overlapping Fit

A sliding or overlapping fit is a common way of detailing to conceal imperfect fits between construction elements. As diagrammed in Fig. 4-14(f), a finished piece of wood molding applied over the joint between two adjacent pieces of paneling easily conceals any imperfection in plumb or flush alignment, as well as poorly finished edges of the paneling. Most molding or trim pieces in construction are used for this purpose. A rubber base, for example, conceals the imperfect gap between the floor and the wall surface. Door casing trim covers not only the shim space but also the out-of-plumb tolerance of the rough opening.

Use Adjustable Connections

When two components of a detail must be joined, provide for a connection that can be adjusted slightly. Slotted bolt holes are one way to provide for easy adjustment when detailing attachment of one rigid piece to another, as diagrammed in Fig. 4-14(g). Floor levelers on desks and other cabinets are another way to build in adjustment in a detail and are an example of using a screw fitting to provide a fine level of adjustment that can be used in many types of details. Depending on the detail, adjustment capability may need to be provided for in one-, two-, or three-dimensions.

Give Adequate Clearance and Incorporate Intermediate Attachments

In many, cases the best way to deal with construction tolerances is to provide space for an intermediate material that be used to connect the finish object with an imperfect construction element. For example, as diagrammed in Fig. 4-14(h), if a panel must be installed perfectly plumb, level, and flat over a rough concrete wall one or more hanging strips can be installed on the concrete using any required shimming and structural fasteners independent of the finished panel itself. The panel is then suspended from the hanging strips as required by its construction. This approach requires that sufficient space be detailed between the concrete surface and the back of the panel for the hanging strip, shims, and any mechanical fasteners.

4-6 CLEARANCES

Clearance is the space between construction elements required for installation, making connections, allowing for tolerances, and providing space for other construction items. The requirement for clearance is often forgotten by detailers because the detail is viewed and conceived on paper as a completed assembly and often in isolation, without regard for the construction and required maneuvering space around it. The best way to avoid clearance problems when detailing is to imagine how the fabricators and installation workers would actually perform the work to build the detail.

Allow Space for Working and Assembly

A detail must provide sufficient space for a worker to use tools and manipulate hands and arms for assembly. Most hand tools do not require a large space, but some power tools may require 12 in. (300 mm) or more of space in addition to space for the worker's hand and arm. For example, a small gap shown on a detail to be enclosed with gypsum wallboard finish must provide space for attaching the wallboard, taping the joints, and applying joint compound.

Sometimes, just a 90-degree change in orientation of a screw or bolt connection may be enough to solve a problem with a fastener installation.

Provide Space for Installation of Pieces

Individual pieces of a detail must be placed into position. This often requires a component to be lifted over something else, tilted into place, rotated, or otherwise manipulated in a space larger than required for its final position. For example, sufficient plenum space must be provided below ducts and piping to tilt and install acoustical ceiling tile, even though the tile and suspension grid themselves only require a narrow envelope of space when they are in their final position.

Allow for Tolerances

As mentioned in the previous section, clearance should be provided to allow the various construction elements to be installed slightly off their theoretical position and for materials to vary in size according to their manufacturing tolerances. When allowing clearances for tolerances the detailer must also consider the accumulation of tolerances, which may be more than the individual tolerances of the various components.

4-7 DURABILITY

Durability is the requirement of a material or detail to withstand the rigors of use. For example, the corner of a partition in a heavily traveled corridor should be durable enough to resist denting, scratching, and chipping as people or goods impact it.

Durability is also an important aspect of sustainability. If a material or detail component must be replaced or repaired frequently, more energy and resources must be used to maintain the detail. Refer to Chapter 3 for more information on detailing for sustainability.

The following suggestions list some of the ways to build durability into a detail.

Self-Durable

Details can be made durable by themselves without any applied protection.

USE HARD, HEAVY, DURABLE MATERIALS

The materials used in a detail, especially the portions exposed to abuse, can be specified as hard, heavy, or otherwise durable. Materials such as concrete, brick, stone, some metals are generally very durable for interior use. Other materials, such as wood, vary in hardness depending on the specific type used. Oak, for example, is harder than pine or poplar. Plaster is a harder finish than gypsum wallboard, although abuse-resistant wallboard is available. Many manufacturers supply variations of their products that are durable. For example, acoustical ceiling tiles are available that are intended for use in schools and other occupancies where intentional or accidental damage are concerns. Very durable materials may cost more initially but have a lower life-cycle cost when replacement and maintenance costs are considered.

The designer can also specify and detail materials that may show wear over time but which age well and can be refinished easily. For example, hardwoods such as oak hold up to impact, rubbing, and similar wear but take on a unique patina with age that many people find attractive. When the finish wears excessively, the wood can be sanded and refinished.

LOCATE FRAGILE SURFACES AWAY FROM ABUSE

If a detail does have a finish, surface, or edge that is susceptible to damage, the designer may be able to position that portion away from damage. For example, instead of using a 90-degree corner on gypsum wallboard, a rounded trim piece can be used. A decorative soft metal strip can be recessed below a wall surface instead of being flush or extending beyond the surface. Decorative wood molding can be located above shoulder level instead of being in a lower position.

Applied Protection

If materials that are susceptible to damage must be used for reasons of cost, availability, design intent, function, or other constructability issues, there are various strategies than can be built into the detail.

COVER FINISH WITH SHIELD

The most obvious method to protect something is to cover it. A kick plate or armor plate on a wood door are simple examples of this strategy. Clear plastic panels can be installed over more fragile wall surfaces or glass can be placed on horizontal wood surfaces. However, the designer must decide whether covering one part of a detail or surface with a protective material compromises the design intent or creates more problems than it may solve. In many cases, if a material must be covered with a shield, it may be best to replace it with a more durable material or one that can be easily repaired or replaced, as discussed in the next section on maintainability. Alternate, similar materials can also be considered. For example, instead of using a real wood surface for a countertop, a plastic laminate finish with a wood-grain pattern can be substituted.

INSTALL GUARDS AT CRITICAL EDGES AND SURFACES

Instead of covering a finish or portion of a surface, just critical parts of it may need protection. A corner guard on the exterior corner of a partition is an examples of this. If protective guards are needed, the designer may consider making them a design feature instead of trying to hide them. For example, instead of using clear plastic corner guards on a partition, a large, stainless steel pole could be placed at the outside edge of the corner.

SEPARATE FINISH WITH RAILINGS/POSTS

A surface, edge, or other portion of a detail can be physically separated to protect it from damage by maintaining a distance from the material and whatever the damage may come from. For example, a railing or series of simple metal bars can be used in front of a wall surface to prevent carts, people, and goods from damaging the lower portion of a partition.

4-8 MAINTAINABILITY

Maintainability is the quality of a detail that allows it to be kept in its original state or level of use during the life cycle of the interior space. This may involve the ability to clean easily and to make adjustments and repairs to, and replacements of, the detail or its components.

Cleanability

MAKE CLEANING AND OTHER MAINTENANCE EASY

The easier it is to maintain something, the more likely it is to be maintained. This includes details and finishes that are maintained by the users or occupants, such as residences, or by separate maintenance personnel. Making a detail easy to clean is especially important for occupancies that must be maintained in a sanitary condition on a daily basis such as restaurants, hospitals, restrooms, kitchens, hotel rooms, and the like. Interior components that must be cleaned frequently should have the fewest number of materials and connections possible. Different materials may require different cleaning products, but in practice, cleaning personnel often use only a limited number. Many connections, edges, corners, and joints also make a detail difficult and time-consuming to clean.

Use Smooth, Nonabsorbent Surfaces

In most cases, the smoother and more nonabsorbent a material is, the easier it is to clean. However, some materials, such as brass or flat-painted gypsum wallboard, may scratch or streak easily if not cleaned properly. As with all aspects of cleanability, the designer must understand who will be maintaining the space and what procedures will be used. Professional cleaning personnel may be more likely to correctly clean materials and surfaces than user/occupants.

Avoid Sharp inside Corners and Small Areas

Sharp, inside corners and small gaps and recesses are especially difficult to clean. Cove bases and other types of rounded corners allow mops and cleaning rags to be wiped over surfaces quickly and easily. In addition, any type of connector, edge, or joint that has a small dimension should also be avoided when sanitation or ease of cleaning is an issue. Something as simple as a screw head can collect dirt and grease and be nearly impossible to clean. If possible, individual components that create small joints or corners can be made removable to make cleaning easier.

Minimize Number of Connections to Cleanable Surface

The simplest surface to clean is one that is smooth, flat, and without interruptions. Floors are relatively easy to clean, except for all the cabinets, table and chair legs, and other furnishings and construction elements that intersect the floor. The detailer must consider how frequently and by what method something will be cleaned. For example, a clear glass panel used for a sign suspended from a partition with standoffs may be an interesting design feature, but any dust or dirt accumulation behind the glass may be difficult to remove because of the various connectors and the small gap between the glass and partition. An alternative detail could mount the sign on a four-sided frame set directly against the partition providing just one large element to clean around. Benches or cabinets can be cantilevered or suspended from partitions instead of resting on the floor to make mopping easier.

Select Products That Do Not Need Toxic Cleaners

Although maintenance of facilities is not the responsibility of the interior designer, materials and finishes can be selected and specified that do not require complex cleaning procedures or toxic cleaners that may compromise indoor air quality. As part of the selection process, the interior designer should review the manufacturer's cleaning instructions to determine if any toxic substances are required for routine maintenance. The material safety data sheets for recommended cleaners can also be reviewed to help determine toxicity.

Adjustability

Many times a construction detail must have some degree of adjustability, to accommodate tolerances when the detail is constructed, to provide for realignment after a period of use, or to allow the detail to function as intended. Some building products, such as door closers, have adjustability built in, while other times the interior designer must design the detail to be adjustable.

PROVIDE LOOSE CONNECTIONS

Loose connections are those that provide some amount of movement while still holding materials in place. Loose connections are generally employed in details that must provide for movement, from either material expansion and contraction or movement of the adjacent construction, as well as to allow for minor adjustability or easy disassembly. Examples of loose connections include the following.

- Wire-suspended elements. Suspended ceilings, for example, allow for fine adjustment to level the ceiling during construction, while allowing for deflection of the floor above without compromising the integrity of the ceiling.
- Clips that provide for one-way sliding. For example, wall-mounted panels set on Z-clips can be shimmed to accommodate wall tolerances, provide for adjustment during construction, and allow the panels to accommodate slight movement during use.
- Clips or other components that provide for friction fit. For example, freestanding wall panels can be connected with clips for easy installation and removal. Glass is held in place with tightly fitting glazing tape or elastomeric material.
- Loose components held in place by gravity. Adjustable shelving can rest directly on supports or slide into dados to make repositioning easy. Connections using metal tabs that fit into slots also utilize gravity to hold materials in place, as with adjustable shelving standards.
- Joints in wood without adhesive or mechanical fasteners. Spline and tongue-and-groove joints, for example, allow the wood to expand and contract and can accommodate minor building movement.
- Sliding joints such as those illustrated in Figs. 4-8 to 4-11.

USE REPOSITIONABLE FASTENERS AND CONNECTIONS

Repositionable fasteners create a tight connection after installation but allow for adjustment during construction as well as repositioning of a building component after use. For example, an adjustable hinge allows a cabinet door to be reset if it sags slightly during use. Because this type of connection must be capable of multiple tightening and loosening, it most often must employ some type of bolt and nut or set screw in a threaded fitting. Figure 4-15 shows three types of repositionable connections.

A leveling bolt, shown in Fig. 4-15(a) allows for adjustment parallel to the length of the bolt. Once the piece is in position both bolts are tightened against it to hold it tight. Used in conjunction with a slotted bolt hole, this type of connection can provide for adjustment in two directions. Although Fig. 4-15(a) shows vertical adjustment, the detail can be oriented

Figure 4-15 Repositionable connections

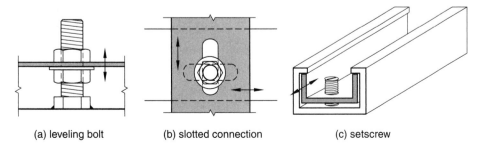

(a) leveling bolt   (b) slotted connection   (c) setscrew in any direction to provide for fine adjustment. Floor levelers used on desks and cabinets are one example of a leveling bolt.

Slotted connections, shown in Fig. 4-15(b) allow for adjustment perpendicular to the length of the bolt. Used in conjunction with a slotted hole in the adjacent piece this connection can provide for two-way adjustment.

Setscrews are small screw-type fasteners that are threaded into mating holes in one of the adjustable pieces. See Fig. 4-15(c). When the two elements are in position the setscrew is tightened and holds the two pieces together by pressing one against the other. This type of connection requires that one of the pieces be configured so that one piece is held in place by the other. Setscrew fasteners generally provide for adjustment in only one direction.

USE FLEXIBLE JOINTS

A flexible joint is a semirigid joint that uses the stiffness of the connector to hold two pieces together while still allowing movement. Springs, metal spring clips, and hard elastomeric sheets are examples of flexible joints. Flexible plumbing connections are often used to connect drain lines to prevent buckling or breaking caused by building movement. Although flexible joints are not used much in interior detailing, they can provide a useful way to join two construction elements.

Repair and Replacement

Nearly all interior finishes wear out eventually or become damaged through normal use or accidents. Interior details should provide methods to easily repair all or a portion of a detail or replace it, especially those vulnerable to damage.

USE PATCHABLE MATERIAL

The simplest way to provide for repair is to use materials and finishes that can be patched and refinished. Gypsum wallboard and plaster are two materials that can be patched and repainted by qualified trade workers to look like the original finish.

If a material cannot be successfully patched in a small area, the designer can detail the finishes in small sections so that only one section needs to be replaced edge to edge instead of an entire surface. For example, a large wall can be built in sections separated by reveals. If a small area is damaged just one section between the reveals needs to be replaced or repaired. Any minor differences between the existing wall and the repaired section is not noticeable.

USE INTERCHANGEABLE PIECES

When a material or finish cannot be successfully patched the detail can be designed to use replaceable parts. Carpet tile and ceiling tile are two common examples of this approach. For other types of interior details, individual pieces can be attached with removable fasteners or otherwise designed so a damaged part can be replaced with a new one. If the pieces are unusual, unique, or are from a particular dye lot, the designer should specify that replacement pieces be provided as attic stock for maintenance by the client.

For example, walls in areas susceptible to abuse can be finished with individual panels mounted on clips so that, if one is damaged, it can easily be removed and replaced with an identical unit. Likewise, a woodwork detail may use a removable strip of molding along an edge that receives the most wear. When the wood is dented, scratched, or chipped, it can be replaced with a newly finished member.

ALLOW FOR EASY MAINTENANCE ACCESS

Details should be configured to make whatever maintenance may be required easy to accomplish. This includes providing sufficient clearance for workers and tools, using connections that can be easily disassembled, and orienting fasteners in accessible locations.

4-9   CONSTRUCTION PROCESS

Construction process is the sequence of steps taken by various trade workers to complete the building of an interior space. Regardless of the design intent of a detail or how it meets functional needs, all details reflect the fact that buildings are composed of both manufactured and field-fabricated elements, require a certain sequence of activities, and are built by trade workers who may belong to different unions and who have various levels of skills.

In addition to simple physical buildability, the construction process is most often closely related to cost and time. A complicated detail using a variety of materials will most likely cost more and take more time to build than a simpler detail. The following suggestions provide some ways to make construction more efficient when designing interior details.

Number of Parts

MINIMIZE TOTAL NUMBER OF PIECES

The detailer should try to minimize the total number of pieces and parts of a detail. This simplifies construction, reduces the chances for errors, speeds construction time, and minimizes cost. As described below, using the maximum amount of prefabricated components also simplifies construction and generally improves quality.

MINIMIZE VARIATION IN SIZE AND TYPE OF COMPONENTS

If possible, the individual components of a detail should be the same size, type, and configuration. Not only is it more difficult to order and stock a variety of materials, but the chances of a worker using the wrong one also increases as the number of different materials increases, especially if they are similar in size, shape, and material. However, minimizing variation in individual components does not necessarily mean a uniform, simplistic appearance in the final design. By coordinating all the detailing on a project, the designer can develop a few well-crafted details and use them in a variety of ways to satisfy the design intent of the problem while resolving the other functional issues. The following are some ideas to consider.

- Limit the number of different partition types. For example, a fire-rated partition may also be used as an acoustical partition in some situations.
- Develop a limited vocabulary of wallboard trim and finishing.
- Minimize the number of different door, frame, and glazing types.
- Develop a few ceiling details and use them in different ways throughout the job.
- Use a limited number of wood trim profiles and sizes. This not only provides more design consistency but also may reduce costs.
- Minimize the number of different types and sizes of ornamental metals.
- When fasteners are needed, they should all be the same size and material.

Sequence

SIMPLIFY SEQUENCE OF CONSTRUCTION

Most details require more than one worker to assemble and a certain number of steps for the complete process. Whenever possible, design details to require the least number of individual steps consistent with the design intent, constraints, and functional issues. Also consider what tools and equipment will be needed. For example, using an aluminum frame will require fewer steps to complete the installation of an interior glass panel than one using wood that may require several steps for the installation of the frame, glazing stop, and casing trim.

SEQUENCE CONSTRUCTION FROM ROUGH TO FINISH

Think through how a contractor will need to construct a detail. Generally, design a detail as though all rough construction will be completed first and progressively move to more refined finishing. Do not develop a detail that requires rough construction, such as metal or wood framing, to be installed *after* some of the finished part of the detail. All dirty and wet work, such as wall framing, mechanical installation, wallboard finishing, plastering, and tile work, should be complete before finish work and installation of architectural woodwork.

EMPLOY REPETITIOUS ASSEMBLY WHEN POSSIBLE

As on an assembly line, there is efficiency and lower cost in repetitive work. Details, and all interior construction in general, should be designed to use as much repetitive assembly as possible. For example, all wall panels should be installed using the same method, doors should fit into frames in a consistent manner, glazing details should be consistent, and tile installation should be uniform. Modular units should be used whenever possible.

Trade Division of Labor

MINIMIZE NUMBER OF TRADES NEEDED FOR ASSEMBLY

Because labor is a significant portion of total construction cost anything that reduces labor saves cost. Generally, a detail that requires the fewest number of different trades will cost less than one that uses more. This approach has the added advantage of reducing the possibility that trade disputes will develop on the job site.

SEQUENCE SO THAT EACH TRADE IS INVOLVED ONLY ONCE

Details should be designed so each required trade is involved only once. For example, framers and wallboard finishers should not build a portion of a detail or wall and then have to return to the job site to complete additional work after carpenters or millwork installers have done their portion of the work. Imagining construction of a detail from a rough-to-finish progression as described in the previous section is one way to think about the sequence of trade workers.

CONSIDER UNION JURISDICTIONS

Depending on the geographical region where a project is being constructed, union jurisdiction may influence how a designer develops a detail. In some areas, unions may have very strict rules about the limits of each unions work and how workers may (or may not) cooperate. Limits on what type of work is done may result in a single trade having to be involved more than once as discussed in the paragraph above. If the designer is working in a new geographical area for the first time, they should talk to other designers or contractors in the area to get an idea of unique problems or concerns related to union requirements.

CONSIDER AVAILABILITY OF LOCAL LABOR

If the interior construction of a project is complex and incorporates nonstandard construction techniques the job may require highly skilled and specialized workers or a large number of workers. It may be difficult to find such workers in some geographical areas. If this is the case, either the quality will suffer, if less qualified workers are used, or workers will have to be brought in from another area, raising the cost of the project. Therefore, the availability of local labor, in terms of both number and quality, may influence how a project is designed and detailed. If certain types of skilled labor are unavailable, the designer may consider simplifying details or using prefabricated components rather than site-built construction.

Off-Shelf versus Custom Parts

Whenever possible, the designer should incorporate standard, off-the-shelf components instead of designing custom parts. This costs less and makes repair and replacement easier. For example, instead of developing a custom profile for a piece of ornamental metal, the designer should investigate the standard shapes and sizes of whatever metal type is being considered. Likewise, instead of detailing a gypsum wallboard edge trim or soffit for a ceiling detail, there may be standard manufactured components that will function as well or better at a lower cost and with a faster construction time.

Shop versus Field Fabricated

Although much of construction includes standard practices regarding what is site built and what is manufactured or shop fabricated, there are still times when the contractor or designer can decide on how a particular part of a job can be completed. For example, many woodwork items can be built on site by a qualified finish carpenter or fabricated in a mill shop and installed by the mill shop workers. On-site construction has the advantage of providing for tolerances and making an exact fit, while shop-fabricated items are generally higher quality and shorten construction time because they can be built while other construction is taking place. Shop-fabricated items may also be necessary if qualified labor is not available for on-site work, as described in the section above. When a decision must be made, it is a matter of balancing quality, time, cost, and availability of labor.

PART 2

ELEMENTS

CHAPTER 5

DIVIDING AND CREATING SPACE WITH PERMANENT BARRIERS

5-1 INTRODUCTION

One of the most fundamental construction elements in interior design and architecture is the permanent vertical barrier. Although commonly called a wall or partition the designer should think of this construction element as a vertical barrier during preliminary design. Thinking of this element as a barrier focuses attention on the important *qualities* that the element must have to meet both the aesthetic and functional requirements of the problem. Then, the designer can apply the techniques and materials necessary to meet the requirements within the given conditions of the problem.

In most cases, exterior walls, columns, and overall ceiling height are beyond the designer's control. However, vertical design elements, such as partitions, are one of the major elements that interior designers can control and use to define space and modulate the appearance of interiors. They are often an underutilized design element. Although exterior walls, window placement, interior bearing walls, columns, and beams may suggest how the division of interior space should be created, nonbearing vertical barriers can be placed anywhere as long as they satisfy the program and meet regulatory requirements.

Vertical barriers may be used to divide one space into two or more smaller spaces, to define space with one or more barriers, to block vision from one area to another, to stop the transmission of sound, to provide a fire barrier, to provide support for a decorative surface, or any combination of these functions.

This chapter discusses the use of barriers that are permanent in that they are firmly attached to the substrates of the building and are intended to remain in position throughout the life of the space. Refer to Chapter 6 for movable or temporary types of vertical barriers that may be repositioned as the needs of the users change.

5-2 ELEMENT CONCEPTS

Vertical barriers can be created in an almost unlimited number of ways. Surfaces can range from simple flat planes with applied finish to complex constructions holding storage elements and electrical services. Barriers can be solid, translucent, clear, or a combination of visual transparencies. They can be straight, curved, angled, full-height, or partial height. Even when limited by constraints such as fire resistance or security, partitions can take on a wide range of configurations.

Figure 5-1 shows some of the many ways permanent vertical barriers may be designed. Although there are several methods of categorizing them and countless possible variations, they are grouped here as planar, panelized, openings, translucent, partial height, and thick. These illustrations show some of the basic ways a barrier can be designed without regard to a specific material or detailing method. They are discussed in more detail in the sections that follow.

5-3 FUNCTION

Permanent partitions generally serve a variety of functions. Most fundamental is dividing one use of space from another and creating a visual and physical barrier. The common response to these needs is usually a standard gypsum wallboard partition. However, by first thinking through all the specific functions that a barrier must serve, the designer can make a better choice of materials and detailing than simply relying on gypsum wallboard to serve all needs.

Permanent partitions generally provide one or more of the following functions:

Defining space

Suggesting limits on travel

Controlling physical passage

Creating security

Controlling vision

Controlling light

Controlling sound

Limiting the spread of fire and smoke

Limiting radiation

Supporting shelving and other fixtures

Providing support for art or decorative work

If, for example, a vertical barrier is intended to suggest limits on travel and define space, the corresponding physical response to these needs could be a standard gypsum wallboard partition or as simple as a fabric suspended from the ceiling or a freestanding screen as long as fire resistive requirements were met. Only when additional functions are defined would the material or physical configuration of the barrier need to be modified.

Figure 5-1 Vertical barrier concepts

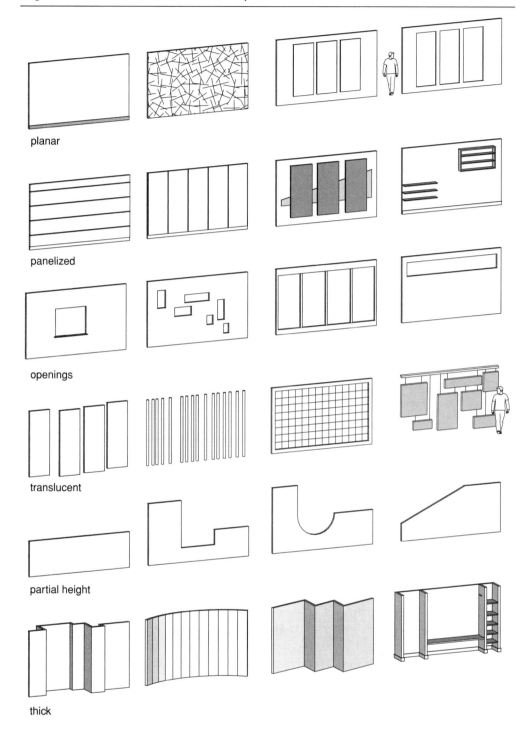

planar

panelized

openings

translucent

partial height

thick

5-4 CONSTRAINTS

For permanent partitions, constraints generally include the existing building floor and ceiling substrates, building code requirements of noncombustibility, fire resistance, and flame spread, budget, and material availability.

Table 5-1 Fire-Resistive Tests Applicable to Permanent Partitions

Test Number	Test Name	Description
ASTM E84	Standard Test Method for Surface Burning Characteristics of Building Materials (also called the Steiner Tunnel Test)	Tests a finish material for flame spread and smoke developed
ASTM E119	Standard Test Methods for Fire Tests of Building Construction and Materials	This is the standard test for fire resistance of building assemblies, such as partitions
ASTM E136	Test Method for Behavior of Materials in a Vertical Tube Furnace at 750°C	This is the test for the noncombustibility of elementary materials
NFPA 258	Recommended Practice for Determining Smoke Generation of Solid Materials	Evaluates the specific optical density of the smoke developed from flaming and nonflaming materials and assemblies
NFPA 265	Method of Fire Tests for Evaluating Room Fire Growth Contribution of Textile Wall Coverings on Full Height Panels and Walls (also called the Room Corner Test for Textile Wall Coverings)	Evaluates the contribution of textile wall finish to fire growth in full-scale mockup
NFPA 286	Standard Methods of Fire Test for Evaluating Contribution of Wall and Ceiling Interior Finish to Room Fire Growth (also called the Room Corner Test)	Evaluates the extent to which wall and ceiling finishes (other than textiles) contributes to fire growth

Floor and ceiling substrates may have implications for how the partition can be fastened and the distance between the floor and ceiling or structure may suggest the type and size of partition materials to span the distance.

For commercial construction, most finish materials meet flame-spread requirements for use in spaces other than exit enclosures, exit passageways, or corridors. However, the use of fabrics and plastics may be problematic. Specific tested flame-spread ratings for individual material must be verified for a given use. Refer to Table 5-1 for a summary of fire-resistive-related tests that may apply to permanent partitions.

Finish materials for commercial construction must be Class A, B, or C, based on the occupancy group, where they are used in a building, and whether the building has a sprinkler system or not. These requirements are given in Table 803.5 of the IBC.

5-5 COORDINATION

Vertical barriers must always be coordinated with ceiling and floor conditions for attachment, base conditions, tolerances, and structural support. In addition, permanent partitions may also contain electrical and communication services, plumbing pipes, and blocking for architectural woodwork, artwork, electronics, or other wall-supported items.

See Chapter 10 for more ideas on ceiling and floor connections.

Tolerance Coordination

Construction tolerances can affect the installation of permanent partitions in several ways. Most notably, the floors of commercial buildings and many residential buildings are not level. Concrete slabs poured on metal decking are especially troublesome, sometimes deflecting as much as 1-1/2 in. (38 mm) in the center of the span. Although studs and gypsum wallboard can be cut to fit the variations, out-of-level floors are problematic when rigid wall materials, such as glass, metal panels, cabinets, or premanufactured finishes, are installed. Out-of-level floors also create problems with the application of some bases.

Table 5-2   Standard Industry Tolerances for Floors

Floor Type	Tolerance	Tolerance Source
Slab-on-grade elevation from theoretical elevation plane	±3/4 in. (19 mm)	ACI 117[a]
Slab-on-grade flatness, conventional, 90% compliance[b]	±1/2 in. (13 mm)	ACI 117
moderately flat, 90% compliance	±3/8 in. (10 mm)	ACI 117
flat, 90% compliance	±1/4 in. (6 mm)	ACI 117
Wood floor framing, perpendicular to joists	±1/2 in. in 20 ft (13 mm in 6100 mm)	*Residential Performance Guidelines*[c]
Wood floor framing, parallel to joists	±1/4 in. in 32 ft (6 mm in 813 mm)	*Residential Performance Guidelines*[c]

[a]ACI 117: Specifications for Tolerances for Concrete Construction and Materials and Commentary, American Concrete Institute
[b]90% compliance means that a number of measurements equal to a minimum 0.01 times the area of the floor measured in ft.^{2} (0.1 times the area in m^2) must taken and 90% must be within the value in the second column.
[c]*Residential Construction Performance Guidelines*, 3rd ed. Association of Home Builders Remodelors™ Council.

Refer to Table 5-2 for some of the industry standard tolerances for floors that should be expected and considered in detailing.

When levelness is critical to the application of interior construction, high spots in concrete floors can be ground down and low spots filled with leveling compound within structural limits for adding extra dead load to the floor. Access flooring can also be used to deal with out-of-level floors, while providing space for mechanical, electrical, and communication services.

5-6   METHODS

Although there are many ways to detail the conceptual ideas shown in Fig. 5-1, the sketches shown in this section provide useful starting points.

Planar

FLAT PARTITION

A flat partition is the simplest method of dividing space. It is easy and inexpensive to build and can accommodate a variety of finishes. The most common construction is gypsum wallboard on metal or wood studs, either built to the structure above or to the underside of a suspended ceiling for commercial construction or to the ceiling plane in residential construction. See Fig. 5-2(a).

APPLIED TEXTURE

Texture can be applied to a flat surface directly, as with paint, plaster, or other coatings, or as a separate finish, glued or screwed to the substrate. Table 5-3 lists some of the many manufacturers that supply such textures. Consult individual manufacturers for the recommended method of application. Applied textures are useful when the base structural partition is needed for acoustic, security, or fire-resistive reasons but a more decorative surface is needed. If they are applied as a separate construction element with easily removable connections, applied textures

Figure 5-2 Types of planar barriers

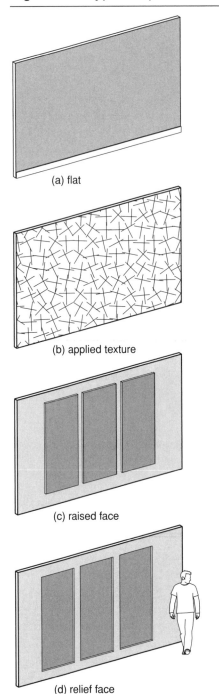

(a) flat

A flat wall with an applied base is the most common type of partition. It is easy to build, inexpensive, and provides a good base for a wide variety of smooth interior finishes. Most commonly, such partitions are gypsum wallboard applied to wood or metal studs. They can also be constructed of veneer plaster, solid plaster on metal lath, or concrete masonry units.

(b) applied texture

Applied texture partitions are a variation of the simple flat partition but with a deep texture applied. The texture may be part of the finish material, such as textured plaster, or be a separate manufactured product that is applied or attached to the base partition. With this type of partition, the functional requirements of security, fire resistance, and sound attenuation can be accomplished with the base partition, while the applied texture is mainly decorative.

(c) raised face

A raised face partition is used to give depth to an otherwise flat wall or to serve a functional reason, such as an applied acoustical panel. The raised face may be constructed of something as simple as an additional layer of gypsum wallboard or be a separate material, such as a fabric, wood, or metal panel. The panels can be the same size applied symmetricaly or be different sizes in an irregular pattern.

(d) relief face

A relief face partition serves similar purposes to a raised face partition, but the emphasized planes are below the plane of the main partition surface. These types of partitions are typically more expensive and difficult to construct because two or more layers of finish material must be constructed to provide the effect. For example, if constructed of gypsum wallboard, one complete layer of wallboard must be attached to the framing with the second layer cut, fit, and trimmed to provide the finish layer.

can be replaced if they become dirty or damaged or if a change is wanted, without affecting the integrity of the supporting partition.

RAISED FACE

A raised face effect, as shown in Fig. 5-2(c), can be created in a number of ways, from the direct application of a thin panel to the construction of a separate element with substantial thickness. Because the construction element used to create the raised face must be attached

Table 5-3 Specialty Wall Finish and Accessory Manufacturers

Manufacturer	Web Site	Comments
Applied textures		
Architectural Systems, Inc.	www.archsystems.com	Carved, woven, and embossed wood panels made with sustainable materials
Brush	www.robin-reigi.com	Clay Solutions custom-formed panels of solid surfacing materials, solid or translucent
Ceilings Plus	www.ceilingsplus.com	Metal wall panel wall systems
Forms + Surfaces	www.forms-surfaces.com	Wide variety of metal panels in various finishes and surface patterns and textures
Fry Reglet	www.fryreglet.com	24 in. × 24 in. standard and custom panels of steel, aluminum, wood, glass, laminate on grid attached to gypsum wallboard
GageCast	www.gagecorp.net	Cast metal surfacing mastic applied or mounted with Z-clips or rail system
Interlam	www.interlam-design.com	Wide variety of textured panels on sustainable core material
Rimex Group	www.rimexmetals.com	Colored and patterned stainless steel
Illuminated panels		
Evonik Industries	www.acrylite-magic.com	Acrylite® brand edge lighted acrylic sheet for signage and wall panels
Green American Lighting, Inc.	www.greenamericalighting.com	Thin wall and floor panels up to 5 ft × 10 ft edge illuminated with LEDs in white and colors
Gypsum wallboard trim		
Fry Reglet	www.fryreglet.com	Aluminum trim pieces
Gordon Grid	www.gordongrid.com	Aluminum trim pieces
Plastic Components, Inc.	www.plasticcomponents.com	PVC trim pieces
Trim-tex	www.trim-tex.com	Vinyl trim pieces
Superior Metal Trim	www.superiormetaltrim.com	Steel, aluminum, zinc trim pieces
Woven wire fabric		
Cascade Coil Drapery	www.cascadecoil.com	Suspended wire mesh or mesh in fixed framing
Gage Woven	www.gagecorp.net	Variety of metal products, including architectural wire mesh
GKD	www.gkdusa.com	Wide variety of products including mesh with integrated LED lighting
Gordon Grid	www.gordongrid.com	Mesh with trim applied to gypsum wallboard with standard or custom painted finishes
Architectural mesh		
Baker "Millennium"	www.bakermetal.com	Wall and ceiling panel system
Cambridge Architectural Mesh	www.architgecturalmesh.com	Wide variety of woven wire and mesh products
GKD Metal Fabrics	www.gkdmetalfabrics.com	Wide variety of woven wire and mesh products
McNichols Co.	www.mcnichols.com	Woven wire mesh, perforated metal
Standoffs		
Doug Mockett & Company	www.mockett.com	Standoffs and other hardware for furniture
Gyford Productions LLC.	www.standoffsystems.com	Wide variety of standoff shapes and sizes for wall and ceiling mounting
Mogg	www.mogg.com	Manufacturers of stainless steel standoffs
Nova Display	www.novadisplay.com	Cable rail systems and standoffs for sign mounting
Wilson Glass	www.wilsonglass.com	Square and round standoffs for glass mounting
Flex-ability Concepts	www.flex.com	Runner track that can be curved for vertical or horizontal curved partitions

to a substrate strong enough to support it, gypsum wallboard partitions are typically used. Figure 5-3 shows some of the methods of creating a raised face, assuming a base partition of studs and gypsum wallboard. Some of the products used as applied textures can also be limited to discrete areas to give the impression of a raised face. As with applied textures, if a suitable connection detail is used, such as Z-clips, the finish face can be easily replaced when necessary.

Figure 5-3 Methods of creating raised faces

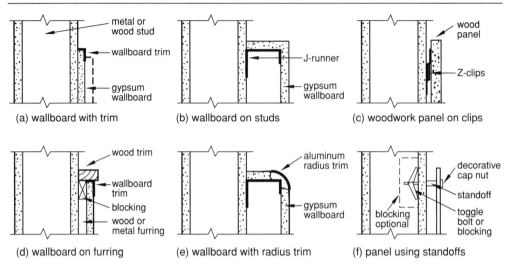

(a) wallboard with trim

(b) wallboard on studs

(c) woodwork panel on clips

(d) wallboard on furring

(e) wallboard with radius trim

(f) panel using standoffs

When the raised face is a simple application of one or two layers of wallboard, various trims can be used to finish the edges, as shown in Fig. 5-4. However, this type of installation results in more damage if the finish needs to be replaced. Refer to Table 5-3 for a listing of some manufacturers of wallboard trim.

RELIEF FACE

Relief faces, those indented from the main surface of the partition, can be created by using some of the same techniques as raised faces, only in the opposite direction. Shallow reliefs can

Figure 5-4 Gypsum wallboard trims

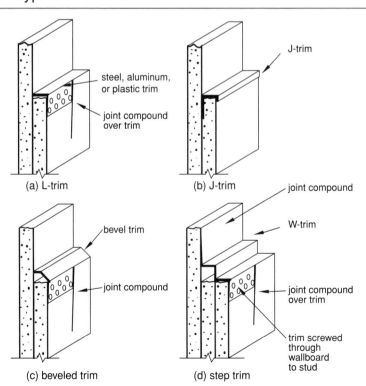

(a) L-trim

(b) J-trim

(c) beveled trim

(d) step trim

Figure 5-5 Methods of creating relief faces

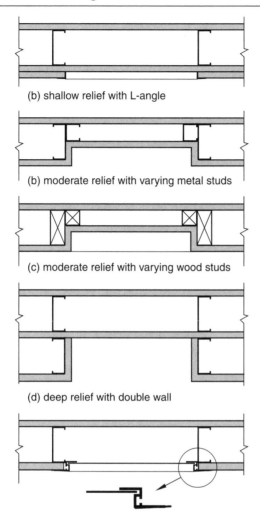

(b) shallow relief with L-angle

(b) moderate relief with varying metal studs

(c) moderate relief with varying wood studs

(d) deep relief with double wall

(e) shallow relief with aluminum infill

be formed with gypsum wallboard trim, as shown in Fig. 5-5(a), (b), and (c). Deeper reliefs may need a double-wall construction similar to Fig. 5-5(d). Reliefs may be framed on four sides for a picture-frame effect or may run full height, from floor to ceiling as a type of reverse panel. Reliefs are useful for highlighting or emphasizing a wall-hung element or as a way of creating a large-scale textured effect on a large expanse of partition.

When shallow reliefs are created, it usually requires a double or triple layer of wallboard, which is costly for the effect achieved. For smaller reliefs, one manufacturer makes a trim piece that accepts an aluminum panel infill so a double layer of wallboard is not necessary. See Fig. 5-5(e). This is sufficient if the partition does not have to have a fire rating or a high acoustical attenuation rating. When using different depths of studs as shown in Fig. 5-5(b) and (c) verify that any required fire rating is not compromised by reducing the overall thickness of the partition.

Panelized

Panelized partitions are those that are comprised of several visually distinct areas.

HORIZONTAL REVEAL

Horizontal reveals, as shown in Fig. 5-6(a), are used for a variety of reasons. In addition to aesthetic reasons, reveals are a good method to accommodate imperfections in construction when placing one material next to another because the reveal space conceals slight imperfections in alignment or abutment.

Reveals may be detailed as with a raised face shown in Fig. 5-4 or more simply with preformed reveal profiles as shown in Fig. 5-7(a). When preformed reveals for standard L-angle

Figure 5-6 Types of panelized barriers

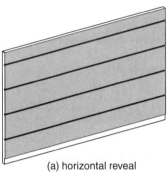

(a) horizontal reveal

Panalized partitions are used to reduce the scale of large expanses of partitions, to emphasize horizontal line, to make construction easier, to enable different sections of the same wall to be finished with different materials, and to make it easier to install and replace sections of the same partition, among others. A panelized partition can literally be made up of separate panels hung on the substrate with clips or other fasteners or the illusion of separate panels can be created with reveals or other materials that separate the individual portions of the finished surface.

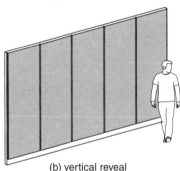

(b) vertical reveal

Vertical panels are often used when the panels are separate pieces of construction, like wood paneling, and are attached to the partition. Although some paneling can be butted together, a reveal conceals any small imperfections in alignment and adds a shadow line to emphasize the paneling effect. The surface of the panels may be in the same plane as the base or be in front of or behind the base.

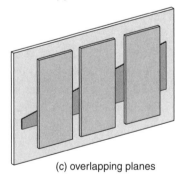

(c) overlapping planes

Overlapping planes add depth and texture to a normally planar partition, depending on the thickness of the panels and how much they are held away from the main portion of the partition. Any number of panels and overlaps may be developed, depending on the effect desired and the budget.

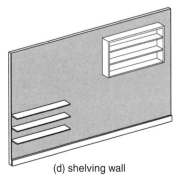

(d) shelving wall

A shelving wall can be thought of as a collection of one or more three-dimensional panels. Shelving can be open on the sides and top but an enclosed grouping, as shown on the right of the diagram, emphasizes the panelized nature more effectively.

Figure 5-7 Methods of creating reveals

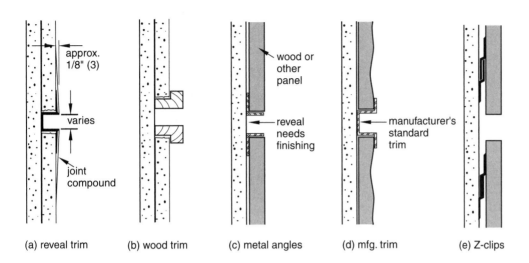

(a) reveal trim   (b) wood trim   (c) metal angles   (d) mfg. trim   (e) Z-clips

trim are used the edge extends about 1/8 in. (3 mm) beyond the thickness of the gypsum wallboard. This usually is not a concern with reveals but may be important when trying to detail a trimmed piece of wallboard to be flush with another material, such as woodwork, stone, or a doorframe. Most of the premanufactured reveals are designed for use with gypsum wallboard, but metal angles or wood trim can be also be used for other materials. See Figs. 5-7(b). (c), and (d). Wood trim must be sized to allow for attachment with screws or brads to avoid splitting the wood. Lightweight materials adhesively applied to a substrate may only require a manufacturer's supplied trim or a metal angle, as shown in Fig. 5-7(d). Separate panels hung on Z-clips can create their own reveals, as shown in Fig. 5-7(e).

VERTICAL REVEAL

Vertical reveals, as shown in Fig. 5-6(b), are used for many of the same reasons as horizontal reveals but mainly to emphasize joints between panels hung on a partition. As with horizontal reveals, the gap between panels allows some imperfection in alignment that is not possible with tightly fit butt joints. Individual panels are also useful in situations where abuse is likely—one panel can be refinished or replaced without the need to replace or refinish an entire wall.

OVERLAPPING PLANES

Overlapping planes, shown in Fig. 5-6(c) are generally created for strictly aesthetic reasons to add depth and interest to a vertical plane. However, the outermost plane may have a functional purpose such as signage or informational displays. Any number and shape of planes may be placed over the basic substrate partition to create a variety of effects. The overlapping planes may be opaque, translucent, or transparent. Translucent or transparent planes may have lighting effects behind.

Two methods of detailing overlapping planes are shown in Figs. 5-8 and 5-9. In Fig. 5-8 the standoff panel is supported with a standard jamb strut used in wallboard framing. This is a useful method when the panel is heavy. With lighter panels, square or round metal standoffs may be used screwed into wood blocking or attached with molly anchors. Refer to Table 5-3 for some standoff manufacturers. Figure 5-9 illustrates one method of suspending overlapping

Figure 5-8 Wall-supported overlapping planes

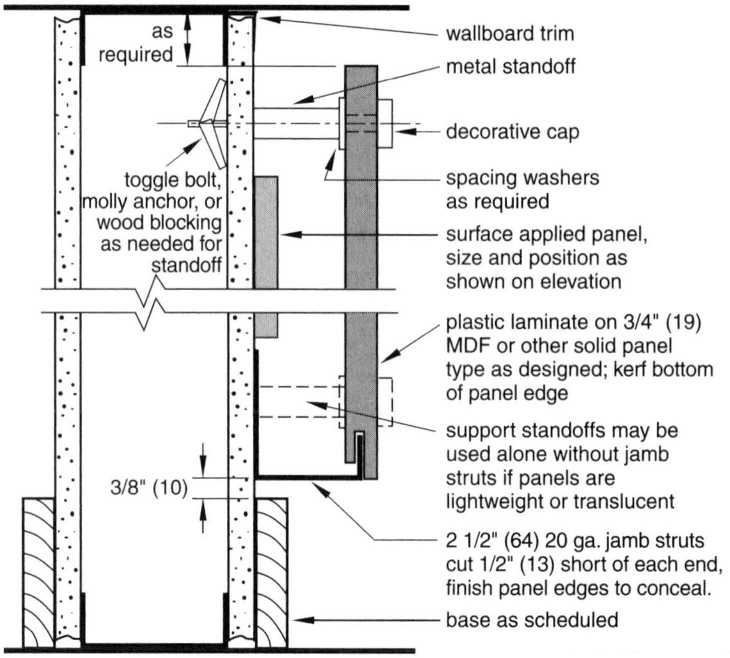

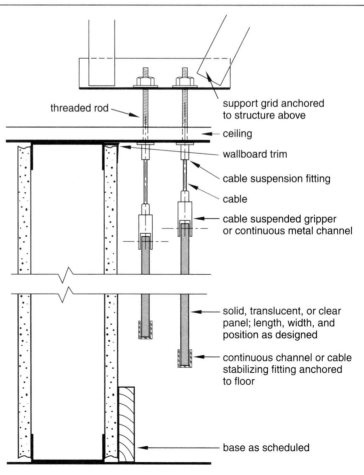

as required

wallboard trim

metal standoff

decorative cap

toggle bolt, molly anchor, or wood blocking as needed for standoff

spacing washers as required

surface applied panel, size and position as shown on elevation

plastic laminate on 3/4" (19) MDF or other solid panel type as designed; kerf bottom of panel edge

support standoffs may be used alone without jamb struts if panels are lightweight or translucent

3/8" (10)

2 1/2" (64) 20 ga. jamb struts cut 1/2" (13) short of each end, finish panel edges to conceal.

base as scheduled

Figure 5-9 Ceiling-suspended overlapping planes

threaded rod

support grid anchored to structure above

ceiling

wallboard trim

cable suspension fitting

cable

cable suspended gripper or continuous metal channel

solid, translucent, or clear panel; length, width, and position as designed

continuous channel or cable stabilizing fitting anchored to floor

base as scheduled

panels. In this case, the panels may be any type of thin panel such as glass, plastic (if allowed by the local building code), particle board, or acoustic panels.

SHELVING WALL

When used in mass or as a tight grouping, shelving can take on the appearance of a thick, three-dimensional, textured panel. See Fig. 5-6(d). Shelving can be grouped horizontally, vertically, or as a separate patch to create different effects. Unlike thin panels, shelving adds the extra constraint of weight so that both the substrate partition and the shelving and its attachments must accommodate this.

Shelving can be attached to standards securely anchored to the partition, set on brackets also anchored to the wall, or constructed as separate units and hung on the partition with Z-clips or other types of anchors.

Table 5-4 gives the approximate load-carrying capacities of some common fasteners. However, every manufacturer's product has a unique load capability, so they should be verified

Table 5-4 Approximate Load Capacity of Common Fasteners for Interior Use								
	Approximate Range of Working Load Values in Shear and Tension, lbs. (N)[a]							
	Application							
	1/2″ GWB only		5/8″ GWB only		GWB w/ 25 ga. studs		GWB w/ 20 ga. studs	
fastener type and size	Shear	Tension	Shear	Tension	Shear	Tension	Shear	Tension
wood screws in wood studs or backing, 1 in. (25 mm) penetration	110 (490)		110 (490)					
metal screws through GWB into metal studs[b]					25-100 (111-445)	15-60 (67-267)	34-135 (151-600)	20-85 (89-378)
anchor screws[c]	60 (300)	20(100)	90 (400)	35 (200)				
nylon wall drillers	18-38 (80-170)	10-15 (45-67)	25-50 (111-222)	12-23 (53-102)				
hollow wall anchors	40-45 (178-200)	20-36 (89-160)						
molly bolts								
1/8 in. (3.2)	43 (191)	38 (169)	50 (222)	40 (178)	100 (445)	70 (311)		
3/16 in. (4.8)	45 (200)	45 (200)	53 (236)	48 (213)	125 (556)	80 (356)		
1/4 in. (6.4)	50 (222)	50 (222)	55 (245)	55 (245)	175 (778)	155 (689)		
toggle bolts								
1/8 in. (3.2)	40-50 (178-222)	20-50 (89-222)	66 (294)	63 (280)				
3/16 in. (4.8)	50-70 (222-311)	30-60 (150-300)	88 (391)	79 (351)				
1/4 in. (6.4)	60-90 (267-400)	40-75 (178-334)	96 (427)	88 (391)				
Toggler® system								
1/4 in. (6.4) (BB)	60 (300)	66 (294)	81 (360)	90 (400)	81 (360)	116 (516)		
3/8 in. (9.5) (BC)	73 (325)	–	100 (445)	144 (640)	100 (445)	122 (543)		

[a]Values given are from various manufacturer's sources and are approximate only. Exact values should be verified with the manufacturer for proprietary fasteners. These are working values and are four times less than the ultimate values often shown in tests and manufacturer's literature.
[b]Values for metal screws depend on the screw size, thread type.
[c]An anchor screw is a proprietary screw with high-profile threads designed for wallboard and other masonry materials.

when specifying a particular type of fastener. When loading is especially critical, consult a structural engineer for specific recommendations.

The values shown in Table 5-4 are working values; that is, load-carrying capacities after a factor of safety has been applied. When manufacturers publish load capacities, they often give the *ultimate* load-carrying value. If this is the case, a safety factor of four should be applied; that is, divide the rated ultimate load-carrying capacity by 4 to get the actual working load that should be used. For extremely heavy loads a separate structural steel tube, angle, or other shape may need to be bolted to the floor.

Barriers with Openings

Although there is overlap between a glazed partition and interior glazing, the difference in this book is that a glazed partition is primarily a solid partition with some glazing, while interior glazing is primarily glazing material with framing as required to support it. Refer to Chapter 9 for a discussion of other types of glazed openings.

Barriers in this category generally include variations of the following types.

SINGLE WINDOW

A single opening, as shown in Fig. 5-10(a), is the classic window-in-a-wall, where there is a much higher percentage of solid partition than glazed opening. The size of the opening may be limited by function, fire rating requirements, or cost. Generally, this type of opening is not used to transmit daylight to interior spaces but to provide functional visual communication. Glazing is held in place with traditional metal or wood framing or some variation of frameless glazing may be used to minimize the appearance of a frame. Refer to Chapter 9 for framing options.

In most cases glass is used, but the glazing may also be ceramic for fire-resistive partitions, glass unit masonry, or plastic if fire rating requirements permit. The thickness of the glass depends on the size of the glazed area, the allowable deflection, and acoustic requirements. Except for very small glazed openings, 1/4-in. (6 mm) glass is typically used. Full-height glass panels framed on four sides, as shown in Fig. 5-10(b), are typically 1/4 in. (6 mm) to 3/8 in. (10 mm) thick. Refer to Chapter 9 for recommendations for butt-glazed glass panels supported only at the top and bottom.

WINDOW WALL

A window wall gives the sense of a partition but with large openings for vision and light transmission. It is useful for bringing daylight deeper into the interior of a space and gives a visual expansion of otherwise small rooms. See Fig. 5-10(b). Safety glazing is required for glass panels next to a door or with the sill lower than 18 in. (457 mm) above the floor. In lieu of safety glazing, a crash bar may be used. Refer to Chapter 9 for more information on safety glazing.

If the partition must have a fire rating, then *fire-resistance-rated glazing* can be used. This is glass or other glazing material that has been tested according to ASTM E119, including the hose stream test. Fire ratings up to two hours are possible with no limitation on area except that limited by the manufacturer's requirements based on fire testing. Refer to Chapter 9 for more information on this type of glazing.

HIGH WINDOW

As shown in Fig. 5-10(c), high windows are useful for giving a sense of openness and transmitting some daylight, while still providing privacy. If the sill is more than 60 in. (1525 mm)

Figure 5-10 Barriers with openings

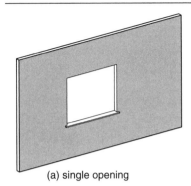

(a) single opening

A single opening in a barrier is generally used for strictly functional reasons, such as a pass-through, specific visual communication between the spaces, or as a way to allow people to see the activity in the next room. The opening may be left open or be glazed if acoustical separation is needed or if the partition must have a fire-resistance rating. The size of the opening defines the degree of separation that the partition has.

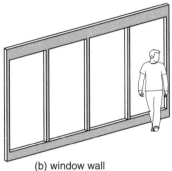

(b) window wall

Window wall openings maximize the amount of open area in a partition while still dividing a space and directing movement. In most cases, the openings are filled with glazing to reduce sound transmission or prevent entry, but may be left open. The edges of the openings may be covered with the same material as the partition or wood or other type of trim may be used. Refer to Chapter 9 on glazing for other options.

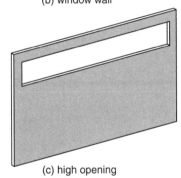

(c) high opening

High openings provide visual privacy while allowing light to pass from one space to the next and to make a space appear more open. A variation of the concept shown here is to eliminate the framing at the top of the opening to let the ceiling pass uninterrupted from one space to the next. A thin metal channel can be used to frame the glazing, if used.

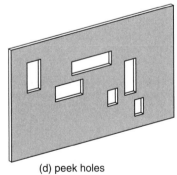

(d) peek holes

Instead of one or more large openings, many smaller openings can be placed in a wall to break up the view and add a sense of playfullness to the partition. Openings can be located randomly, as shown here, or symmetrically. They can be the same size or a variety of sizes and filled with clear glazing material or translucent material to increase visual privacy. The openings can be made frameless or framed with wood or other materials.

above the floor, standard glass, instead of safety glazing, may be used. Standard wood or metal framing may be used or frameless glazing may be incorporated.

PEEK HOLES

Multiple, smaller glazed openings, as shown in Fig. 5-10(d), may be used for a variety of reasons. They can reduce the scale of an otherwise large expanse of partition, give a sense of playfulness, transmit light, focus views, eliminate the need for safety glazing if small enough (less than 9 ft² [0.84 m²]), and create patterns to reinforce the design of the space. If the openings are not glazed, the partition can limit and control movement while giving a sense of openness and allowing sound to penetrate spaces.

Translucent

Translucent barriers are those that define space and limit travel but allow varying amounts of visibility. In addition to glazing, some of the various approaches to creating translucent barriers are shown in Fig. 5-11. The only limit on the types of translucent barriers is the

Figure 5-11 Types of translucent barriers

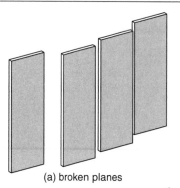

(a) broken planes

Translucent barriers are those that are perceived mainly as a defined plane but that allow vision and/or sound transmission. They clearly define space and direct movement but give a sense of connection between the spaces they separate. Broken planes are simple to build and, by varying the space between the edges and surfaces of the planes, the amount of separation can be varied as required. Broken planes can be rigid, solid material, such as gypsum wallboard or as simple as wood panels or suspended fabric.

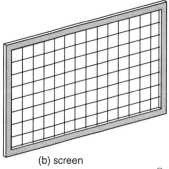

(b) screen

A screen wall can be any uniform, nonsolid material such as a wood lattice, metal rods, or perforated metal. By varying the density of the material used, the amount of separation can be varied. If the spaces are filled with glazing for acoustical control the screen can be a variation of the window wall barrier type. Screens can be the full height of the ceiling or can be constructed short of the ceiling to make construction easier and allow the ceiling plane to continue over the screen. Screens can also be suspended from the ceiling to simplify construction and allow the flooring material to continue uninterrupted.

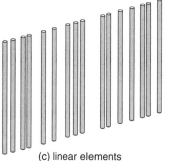

(c) linear elements

Individual linear elements can be used to create a screen effect when the design of the space suggests that type of design element. They can be oriented vertically, horizontally, or at an angle for a more dynamic appearance. The scale can be reduced by developing a basketweave or herringbone pattern. In most cases, smaller individual elements must be anchored to an intermediate piece of construction before being attached to the floor, wall, or ceiling.

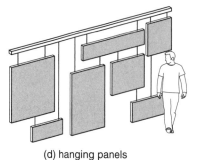

(d) hanging panels

Hanging panels simplify construction of a translucent barrier and allow the flooring material to continue from one space to another, giving a stronger sense of connection between the spaces. The panels may be suspended directly from the ceiling, if appropriate, or can be suspended from an intermediate support, which is, in turn, attached to the ceiling. Panels may be any type of material, including wood, metal, fabric, plastic, or fabric-wrapped panels for acoustical control.

Table 5-5 Specialty Glazing Materials for Translucent Barriers

Manufacturer	Web site	Comments
Avanti Systems USA	www.avantisystemsusa.com	Straight and curved glass wall system
Berman Glass	www.bermanglasseditions.com	Cast, textured
Evonik Industries	www.acrylite-magic.com	Wide variety of acrylic sheet products
Forms + Surfaces	www.forms-surfaces.com	Patterned glass for doors, railings, and panels
Meltdown Glass	www.meltdownglass.com	Wide variety of custom kiln-cast glass
McGrory Glass, Inc.	www.mcgrory-glass.com	Laminated, acid-etched, and sandblasted glass
Meltdown Glass	www.meltdownglass.com	Wide variety of custom, kiln-cast glass
Nathan Allan Glass Studios, Inc.	www.nathanallan.com	Textured, colored, cast, and dichroic glass
Oldcastle Glass	www.oldcastleglass.com	Patterned, silk-screened, colored, and rice paper textured glass in their Montage series
Polytronix	www.polytronix.com	Electrochromic glass using polymer dispersed liquid crystal technology
Priva-Lite by Saint-Gobain	www.sggprivalite.com	Electrochromic glass
Pulp Studios	www.pulpstudio.com	Wide variety of specialty glass products, including colored, textured, electrochromic, and laminated glass with wide selection of textures and decorative patterns
Glow	www.robin-reigi.com	"Glow" custom translucent solid surfacing available with LED backlighting
Palace of Glass	www.palaceofglass.com	Stock and custom art glass
Saint-Gobain Glass	www.saint-gobain-glass.com	Embossed, patterned, and colored glass
Schneller, Inc	www.veritasideas.com	Veritas architectural resin panels custom detailed or with manufacturer's aluminum pole system for mounting
SmartWall	www.insightlighting.com	Transparent, translucent, or opaque panels up to 32 ft^2 (3.0 m^2) edge lit with LEDs, which can change colors
Studio Production	www.studio-productions.com	Scrim fabric for theatrical scrim effects
Switch Lite Privacy Glass	www.switchlite.com	Electrochromic glass
Visual Impact Technologies	www.vitglass.com	Holographic laminated and patterned glass

designer's imagination. Common materials can be used in common or uncommon ways or custom, proprietary materials can be used with a variety of installation methods.

With translucent glazing, visibility and light transmission can be allowed while sound transmission is limited. Some of the many possible custom glazing materials are listed in Table 5-5. With some types of translucent barriers, such as wire mesh, lighting can be used to highlight the barrier while making the space beyond visible or not. This is much the same effect as a theater scrim, where what is beyond the scrim can be made invisible by increasing the light on the scrim and decreasing the light behind the scrim.

BROKEN PLANES

Broken planes establish several separate surfaces either in line or in a staggered pattern, as shown in Fig. 5-11(a). Depending on how the planes are arranged, this focuses the view either perpendicular to the plane of the partition or at an angles to the partition. The planes can be closely spaced or with large gaps between to modulate the amount of vision, light, and sound that is transmitted. Some methods of detailing and anchoring broken planes are shown in Fig. 5-12. Broken planes may be constructed of standard partition materials as shown in Fig. 5-12(a) and (b) or with sheets of glazing or other panel products mounted in metal channels at the floor and ceiling.

SCREENS

A screen effect can be created with any material that allows some degree of light or sound transmission while modulating vision. A shoji screen, for example, allows sound and light to

Figure 5-12 Detailing broken planes

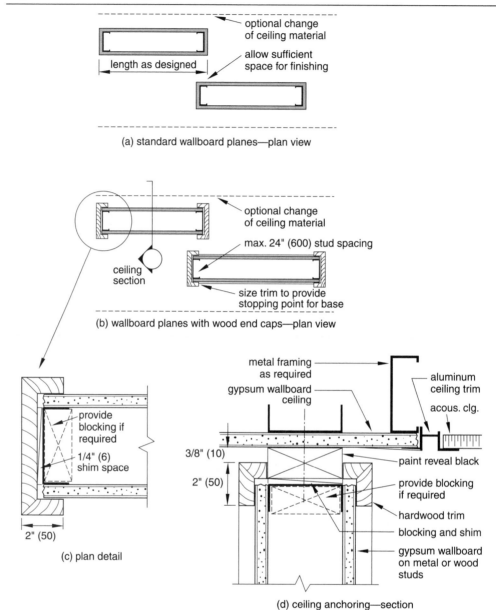

(a) standard wallboard planes—plan view

(b) wallboard planes with wood end caps—plan view

(c) plan detail

(d) ceiling anchoring—section

pass through while limiting vision. Perforated metal, on the other hand, allows some visibility through the screen but limits light transmission, depending on the percentage of open area. Screens can be attached to both the floor and ceiling structure or can be held short of the ceiling or floor to simplify construction and allow for variations in the ceiling or floor plane.

Some of the materials that can be used for screens include curtains, woven wire mesh, perforated metal, lattice work, translucent glass or plastic, stretched fabric, or shoji screens. Generally, these materials tend to be thin and are not self-supporting, so some type of mounting to the structure is necessary. There are typically five different ways to do this, as shown in Fig. 5-13.

All of the methods shown rely on the screen-supporting system to be permanently attached to the building structure. Some of the methods, such as post supports, can be modified to be freestanding. The simplest method, shown in Figs. 5-13(a) and (b) uses a

Figure 5-13 Methods of mounting screen material

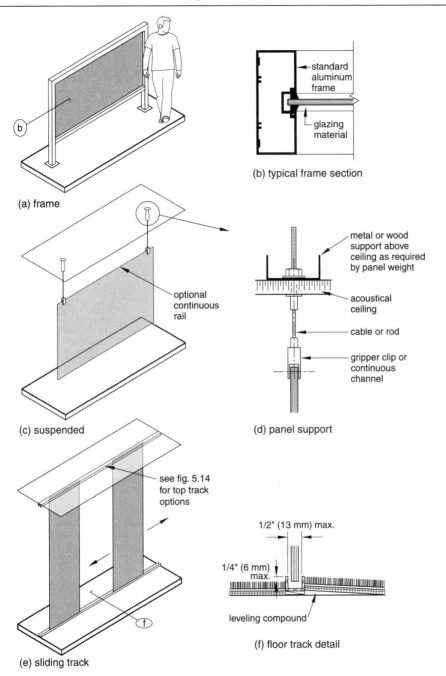

(b) typical frame section

standard aluminum frame

glazing material

(a) frame

optional continuous rail

(c) suspended

metal or wood support above ceiling as required by panel weight

acoustical ceiling

cable or rod

gripper clip or continuous channel

(d) panel support

see fig. 5.14 for top track options

(e) sliding track

1/2" (13 mm) max.

1/4" (6 mm) max.

leveling compound

(f) floor track detail

frame, much like a window frame, to support the material. This can be accomplished with a partial-height frame as shown or within a full-height partition. A suspended system uses either point supports or a continuous rail, as shown in Figs. 5-13(c) and (d).

When the screen must be adjustable, a track system can be used. Sliding track supports may use a top and bottom track, as shown in Figs. 5-13(e) and (f) or just a top track. For rigid materials, such as glass or plastic, a bottom track or floor-mounted guides are typically required to hold the screen in place. However, continuous bottom tracks can be problematic because they must be shimmed to be level, interrupt the flooring material, pose tripping hazards unless they are completely recessed, and can create accessibility problems if the track is too high.

Figure 5-13 Methods of mounting screen material (*continued*)

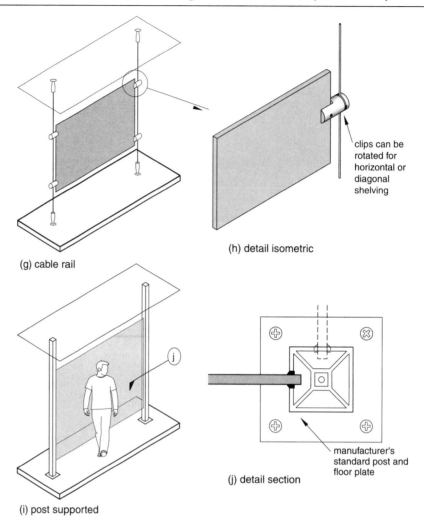

(g) cable rail

(h) detail isometric

clips can be rotated for horizontal or diagonal shelving

(i) post supported

(j) detail section

manufacturer's standard post and floor plate

Using leveling compound to minimize any vertical projections, as shown on the right side of Fig. 5-13(f), is the preferred method. Most materials can be completely suspended from the ceiling, avoiding these issues, using short floor guides placed out of the way of the traffic pattern. Top tracks can be mounted in several different ways, as shown in Fig. 5-14. Consult individual manufactures for exact dimensions and attachment methods.

Cable rail systems, as diagrammed in Fig. 5-13(g) and (h), provide an airy support system for vertical panels as well as horizontal and diagonal shelving. Some of the manufacturers of cable rail systems for this application are listed in Table 5-6.

Point supports required for cable rail systems can be problematic for acoustical suspended ceilings because the cable must be stretched tightly, but most manufacturers have methods of attaching the top of the cable directly through ceiling tiles to the structure above.

The methods of mounting screen material with posts are relatively straightforward. As shown in Fig. 5-13(i) and (j), the post is commonly attached to a bottom plate, which is screwed or bolted to the floor. Similar attachments are used at the ceiling, either to a suspended ceiling or continuing through the ceiling to the structure above if the screen material is heavy. Unless the installation is custom, most screen material manufacturers also provide standard post-mounting hardware as part of their system.

Figure 5-14 Overhead track mounting

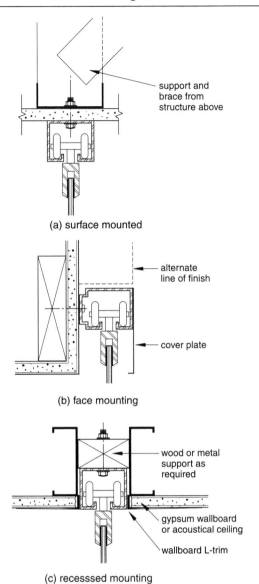

support and
brace from
structure above

(a) surface mounted

alternate
line of finish

cover plate

(b) face mounting

wood or metal
support as
required

gypsum wallboard
or acoustical ceiling

wallboard L-trim

(c) recesssed mounting

Linear Elements

Multiple pieces of long, relatively thin elements can be used as a type of translucent barrier. By varying the thickness and spacing of the individual elements varying degrees of separation are created. Elements can be installed vertically, as shown in Figure 5-11(c), horizontally, diagonally, or in any combination. Unless the linear elements are part of a premanufactured system, the cost of materials and installation can be significant because each has to be installed separately. Cable railing systems, normally used for stair and balcony railings can be used for this application if very thin linear elements are desired. Some of the cable railing manufacturers are listed in Table 5-6.

Hanging Panels

Hanging panels or other construction elements can provide a sense of separation while allowing a wide range of visibility. Practically, hanging materials avoids any irregularities of the floor

Table 5-6 Cable Rail and Support Manufacturers

Manufacturer	Web site	Comments
Panel and shelving support systems		
Arakawa Hanging Systems	www.arakawagrip.com	Wide variety of ceiling and floor anchors and shelving grippers as well as railing systems and picture hanging rails
Gyford Productions LLC.	www.standoffsystems.com	Cables systems for shelving, panels, signage as well as integrated with line of freestanding extrusions for panel systems
Jakob	www.jakobstainlesssteel.com	Inox line of shelving supports on cable system
Nova Display	www.novadisplay.com	Cable, rod, and floor stand display systems with variety of clamping options
PosiLock	www.s3i.co.uk	Sign, picture, and shelf handing systems
Secosouth Architectural Systems	www.secosouth.com	Stainless steel systems for shelving, signage, grills, and architectural rigging
Veritas Hardware Systems	www.veritas.com	Stainless steel cable and rod systems for suspending Veritas panels as well as other shelving and hanging panels
Cable railings		
Atlantis Rail Systems	www.atlantisrail.com	Stainless steel cable railing and accessories
Feeney Wire	www.cablerail.com	Cable rail system for interior stairs and guards
Hansen Architectural Systems	www.aluminumrailing.com	Cable rail systems and other railing products
Johnson Architectural Hardware	www.csjohnson.com	Stainless steel cables, rods, and accessories for interior or exterior use
PosiLock	www.s3i.co.uk	Wire rope assemblies and fittings
Ronstan	www.ronstanusa.com	Mainly heavy duty architectural rigging systems for exterior use but also has railing system for interior use
Secosouth Architectural Systems	www.secosouth.com	Stainless steel handrail and guard systems
TriPyramid Structures, Inc.	www.tripyramid.com	Architectural support systems, including railing system for interior use
Ultra-tec	www.ultra-tec.com	Stainless steel railing for handrails

and prevents damaging the flooring material with attachment hardware. Depending on the attachment method, hanging panels can be relocated easily as the user's needs change. Many of the suspension methods illustrated in Fig. 5-13(c) and (d) can also be used for hanging panels.

In commercial construction, products can be suspended from a suspended acoustical ceiling or from the structural floor above. Lightweight materials can be hung from acoustical ceiling grids with clips that attach to the grid, with screws directly through the grid, or with toggle bolts through the tile. Heavier materials can be suspended with heavy-gauge wire or metal framing attached to the structural floor above or from a steel framework directly above the suspended ceiling. See Figs. 5-9 and 5-13(d).

Partial Height

Partial height partitions are commonly used to define space, direct movement, and/or provide a backing for furniture, equipment, and electrical services while keeping the space open and allowing views, light, and sound between spaces. While freestanding panels and systems furniture can also meet these functions, permanent partitions look more like an architectural element in a space rather than a furnishings element. Several variations are shown in Fig. 5-15.

When the design intent is to have the partial height walls look like an architectural element, they are typically constructed with gypsum wallboard on studs.

Straight, partial height partitions, as diagrammed in Fig. 5-15(a) are typically not strong enough to support lateral loads (like someone leaning on them) if they are just attached to the floor with fasteners commonly used for full-height partitions. One way to solve this problem is to use a curved or angled shape, as shown in Fig. 5-18(b) and (c). The shape of the low partition itself provides the necessary strength, acting as a shaped beam oriented vertically.

Figure 5-15 Types of partial-height barriers

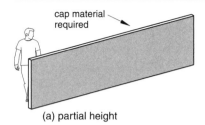

cap material required

(a) partial height

Partial height partitions are typically used to define space and direct movement when audio separation is not required while allowing vision and light transmittance in. They are also used as a backdrop or shield for furniture, equipment, and anything that needs to be hidden from view. When low enough for people to lean on or place object on, the top edge usually needs to have some type of durable cap.

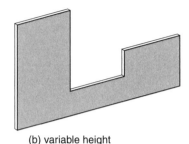

(b) variable height

Variable-height partitions are used for the same reason as single-height partitions except the different heights may provide more privacy where it is desired, act as a support for wall-mounted items, to direct views, or simply add interest to the partition. The height of the partition affects the sense of separation.

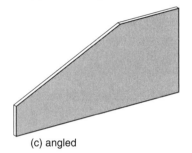

(c) angled

Angled partitions vary the amount of separation within a single plane and provide a more dynamic line and shape to the space it defines. Variations include using two or more angles to give the partition even more interest or to modulate the wall to meet the needs of the spaces in which it is used.

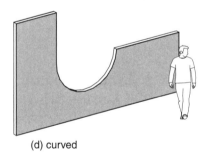

(d) curved

Curved partial-height partitions serve some of the same functions as angled and variable height walls but with a different shape. Curves may be convex or concave. Curves such as the one shown in this diagram are an elegant way to make the transistion from one height to another. The radius of the curve can be varied to suit the functions of the partitions. One disadvantage to this shape is that the top of the curve is more difficult to cap with some type of durable material.

Another way to provide support for a straight, low partition is to provide a steel plate bolted to the floor with a steel post welded to the plate, as shown in Fig. 5-16.

UNIFORM PARTIAL HEIGHT

Partial-height dividers of uniform height are typically used to create individual workstations or as a backup for storage, bars, and work surfaces or to conceal unsightly equipment and cords. The dividers may be high to block views if privacy is needed or low to allow the maximum amount of light transmission and vision. For short runs of partition designed to support work surfaces or storage units, a U-shaped or L-shaped partition should be constructed to provide lateral support without the need for structural steel supports.

When the height of the partition is low enough for people to lean on or place objects on some type of durable material should be used to cap the partition. Some of the possible ways of

Figure 5-16 Low-partition bracing

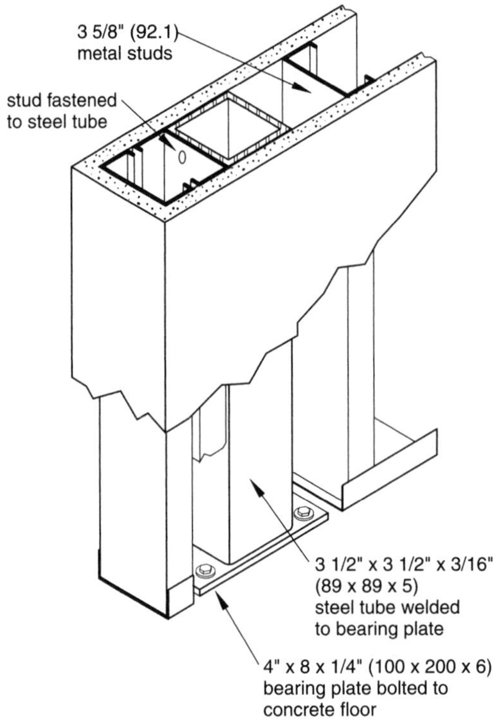

3 5/8" (92.1)
metal studs

stud fastened
to steel tube

3 1/2" x 3 1/2" x 3/16"
(89 x 89 x 5)
steel tube welded
to bearing plate

4" x 8 x 1/4" (100 x 200 x 6)
bearing plate bolted to
concrete floor

note: lower portion of wallboard and one
stud not shown for clarity; 2 1/2" 63.5)
studs may also be used

doing this are shown in Fig. 5-17. To discourage placement of objects on the wall rounded or angled tops can be used. All of these terminations can also be used for vertical or sloped edges.

VARIABLE HEIGHT

Variable-height partitions, as diagrammed in Fig. 5-15(b), are useful for all of the reasons as a uniform-height partition, while limiting views in some areas or providing walls where full-height construction is necessary.

ANGLED

Angled partitions, as shown in Fig. 5-15(c), are a variation of the variable height partition but provide a more dynamic line from a strictly design standpoint. When multiple angled partitions are used at different angles or in opposing directions, they can create a dynamic rhythm in a space. The straight lines also make it easy to cap the edge of the partition with wood, metal, wallboard trim, or other materials, as shown in Fig. 5-17, to protect the corners and thin edge.

CURVED

Partial-height partitions curved in the vertical direction create dynamic forms and which can be used with curved lines elsewhere in a space as a basic design element. Curves may also be combined with straight and angled shapes, as shown in Fig. 5-15(d). Curves can be difficult to form with standard wallboard framing techniques, but one manufacturer makes metal stud track that can be curved vertically to make forming inside or outside curves fairly easy. While

Figure 5-17 Gypsum wallboard caps

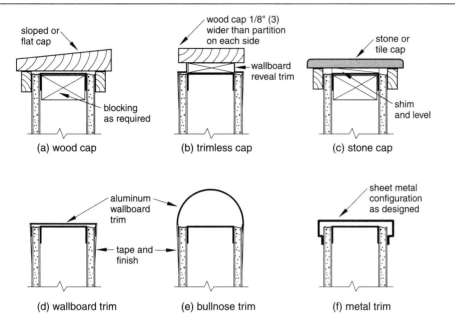

(a) wood cap   (b) trimless cap   (c) stone cap

(d) wallboard trim   (e) bullnose trim   (f) metal trim

curved edges can be easily formed with flexible vinyl corner bead or L-trim, one of the main difficulties with this type of partition is providing a durable cap (other than gypsum wallboard) to finish the curved edge. Curved shapes may also be curved in two directions, although these are more difficult and costly to construct, usually requiring a plaster finish instead of standard gypsum wallboard.

Thick

Thick partitions refer to those that occupy a significant amount of floor space beyond just the depth of the partition itself. Some types of thick partitions are shown in Fig. 5-18.

Modulated Thickness

Modulated partitions create an in-and-out shape based on planning requirements for the spaces on both sides of the partition, for the accommodation of equipment or storage, or simply as a way to create interest or break up a long run of an otherwise plain wall. Modulated partitions can also result from concealment of structural columns or pipe chases.

Curved Full Height

Curved walls and complete circles are strong geometric forms. They focus attention on the concave side and can be useful for meeting rooms, gathering spaces, or any place where the designer wants to establish a special interior space. Broad curves can also be used along a circulation space to create a sense of dynamic movement through a rectangular building. A complete circle emphasizes a space, especially when placed in a rectangular grid. However, depending on the radius, the convex opposite sides of curved partitions can be problematic for space planning, furniture arrangement, or equipment placement.

Figure 5-18 Types of thick barriers

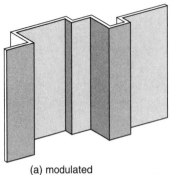

(a) modulated

Modulated partitions can be used to define space for activities, create niches for furniture, or simply add interest and reduce the scale of an otherwise large partition. As with any thick partition, the size and shape on one side has implication for the other side, so the placement and design must be carefully though out and resolved in the space-planning process.

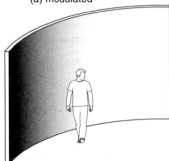

(b) curved full height

Curved partitions create dynamic spaces. The concave portion emphasizes and tightens a space, while the opposite convex side expands the sense of space. While providing exciting spaces, curved partitions are slightly more expensive to build and make it difficult to hang artwork and support rectilinear furniture and fixtures. Generally, curved partitions stand on their own as a strong definition of space.

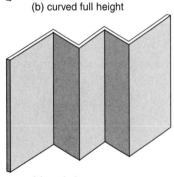

(c) angled

Like modulated partitions, angled partitions reduce the scale of a long wall and create a more dynamic spatial edge. The size and number of angles can be varied to suit the purposes of the partition. Small divisions can reduce the scale while large divisions can serve practical purposes such as providing spaces for furniture or emphasizing artwork. In a corridor, the negative spaces can provide a space to step aside to view wall hangings or as a space for doors to swing out without encroaching on the corridor space.

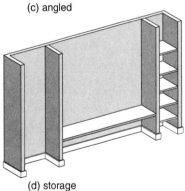

(d) storage

Storage walls let a partition do double duty as space dividers as well as storage spaces. One side can be a flat wall, as shown here, or one half of the partition can face one room while the other half faces the opposite room. Storage walls make good acoustical separations, keeping noise and activities away from the partition itself, preventing bumping the wall with furniture or accidental human contact. With closet doors, the inside space makes an acoustical barrier.

ANGLED

Angled or folded wall surfaces are similar to modulated walls but create a more dynamic statement of surface and rhythm. Angled surfaces can have a strictly functional purpose, such as providing individual spaces for art or other displays or can simply be a way to reduce the scale of a long partition. As with curved walls, a shape that may work on one side may not work on the other side, so careful space planning is required to minimize wasted floor space.

STORAGE

Storage walls divide space, serve a functional purpose, and can create an interesting surface texture. When used with closet doors and other drawer fronts, storage walls also serve as a double wall, providing additional acoustical separation between two spaces. With one flat wall on the opposite side, there is no space-planning problem with the side opposite as there is with curved or angled walls. For two identical spaces planned back to back, half of the wall can face toward one space with its mirror image facing the other space; for example, with two closets for two adjacent bedrooms.

CHAPTER 6

DIVIDING AND CREATING SPACE WITH TEMPORARY BARRIERS

6-1 INTRODUCTION

Like permanent vertical barriers, temporary barriers provide the interior designer with the means to shape space and solve specific functional problems. Temporary barriers also help the designer meet the challenges of accommodating the changing needs of clients and reducing the time required for initial construction and relocation.

There are two basic categories of temporary barriers: those that are designed to replace permanent, full-height partitions for complete enclosure of a space and those that do not extend to the ceiling or are not intended to provide a complete separation between two spaces. Barriers that do not offer complete separation may be panel systems or be part of a furniture system. Both types of barriers can accommodate the rapid change typically encountered in commercial interiors.

Movable partitions intended to replace standard gypsum wallboard partitions are most frequently used for commercial office application and offer a number of advantages in this application:

- Ease of reconfiguration to meet changing office needs
- In most cases, lower life-cycle costs if partition locations must be changed frequently
- Clean installation without the wet work of joint compound application
- In many cases, single-source responsibility by one trade for partitions, doors, glazing, and electrical and data cabling
- In some cases, tax advantages as movable equipment rather than a fixed asset
- Shorter construction time with finishes already applied
- In most cases, the product uses recycled materials and is easy to disassemble and recycle.
- Readily accommodates out-of-level floors and ceiling tolerances

However, movable partitions cannot provide a fire-resistant rating, have limited security capabilities, cannot conceal plumbing, cannot accept some types of finish materials, and some are limited in the ability to provide support for cabinets and other architectural woodwork.

This chapter discusses the use of temporary barriers that can be easily moved, relocated, reconfigured, or dismantled and removed without affecting the surrounding construction. It does not include *operable walls*, which are fixed construction elements used to divide larger spaces into smaller spaces such as hotel ballrooms, classrooms, and meeting rooms along a fixed track support. This chapter also does not include *furniture systems* that may also include movable panels as part of the system, although some movable panel products described in this chapter do include provisions for hanging work surfaces and storage units or may be designed to work with a particular manufacturer's other products.

6-2 ELEMENT CONCEPTS

Temporary barriers as described in this chapter can take on a variety of forms. As described above, they can substitute for fixed partitions or be partial-height dividers. The barriers can be solid, glass, or some combination of both. They may be attached to the base building structure or be freestanding. Figure 6-1 shows some of the basic types of temporary barriers.

Figure 6-1 Temporary barrier concepts

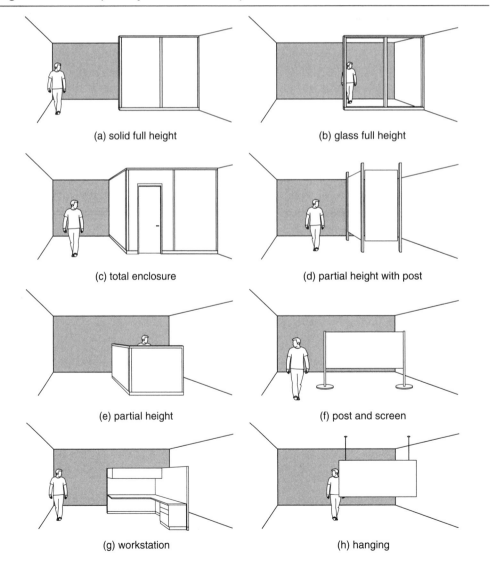

(a) solid full height

(b) glass full height

(c) total enclosure

(d) partial height with post

(e) partial height

(f) post and screen

(g) workstation

(h) hanging

In most cases, temporary barriers are part of a manufacturer's proprietary product and come as a complete system of parts. However, custom barriers can be designed, either from basic building materials or with proprietary materials specifically intended for custom panel systems.

When temporary barriers are intended to replace standard partitions, they are called *demountable partitions*, which consist of a system of individual components that can be quickly assembled, disassembled, and reused with total for near-total salvageability.

There are two basic types of demountable partitions: progressive and nonprogressive. Progressive partitions systems require that the walls be assembled in a particular order and then disassembled in the reverse order. With nonprogressive systems, any individual panel can be removed and replaced without disturbing adjacent panels. Most systems today use designs in a nonprogressive system.

The configuration and design of individual components varies with each manufacturer but generally consists of several components: floor runners, ceiling runners, vertical sections or posts with connectors to hold the panels, and prefinished panels of solid material or glazing. All manufacturers provide accessories to make corners, connect to existing construction, and accommodate doors. Most manufacturers also provide for electrical and data cabling.

Partial height barriers can be supported by posts anchored to the floor and ceiling, supported by posts mounted on large feet, cable supported, or self-supporting with two or more connected sections at an angle to each other.

6-3 FUNCTION

As with permanent vertical barriers, discussed in Chapter 5, temporary barriers serve a variety of functions. Full-height partitions can be used to divide space to provide visual, acoustical, and physical separation or they can serve to simply block vision, define space, or function as a background for other design elements. Partial height panels can also define space or partially block vision, and when used in conjunction with work surfaces and storage units, they become individual workstations as an alternate to private offices constructed with gypsum wallboard. One of the primary functions of temporary barriers is to accommodate change.

Most full-height partition systems are installed by lifting a panel against a ceiling track or a proprietary device clipped to the ceiling. The panel is set plumb and placed against the floor where leveling feet can be used to raise or lower the panel to precisely fit the panel to the space and to level it. A base is then clipped on over the leveling devices.

Some partition systems come with the finish already applied to individual panels. Other systems require that separate panels be applied to the framework, which allows electrical and data cabling to be installed where needed. Finishes include painted steel, gypsum wallboard, wood, high-pressure laminate, fabric or vinyl covered panels, and glass. See Table 6-1 for some of the manufacturers of demountable partitions systems and movable panels.

Although there are some similarities among partition systems produced by various manufacturers, every system is unique and the designer must review each and decide which one meets the requirements of the project. Some of the factors to consider when selecting a partition system include the following:

- The method of assembly and disassembly
- How the system is connected to the existing structure
- Availability of glass units and types and sizes of doors available
- Sizes available and compatibility with the building module (if any)

Table 6-1 Movable Panel and Wall Manufacturers

Manufacturer	Web site	Comments
Avanti Systems USA	www.avantisystemsusa.com	Straight and curved glass wall systems with ability to relocate
Dirtt Environmental Solutions	www.dirtt.net	Several products, including movable walls with solid and glass infill, interior curtain walls for covering existing building walls, curved units, and stick-built walls with solid or glass infill
Haworth	www.haworth.com	Movable wall system in full height or partial height with a variety of options for panels, finishes, doors, and glass units
Infinium Architectural Wall Systems	www.infiniumwalls.com	Full-height, aluminum-framed walls, including doors and glass infill
KI	www.ki.com	Full-height movable wall systems, including doors with solid and glass infill and panels that can accommodate hang-on furniture
Livers Bronze Co.	www.liversbronze.com	Decorative modular wall system of glass panels attached to stainless steel posts for visual separation
LOFTwall	www.loftwall.com	Freestanding aluminum frame system available in two sizes with customizable infill panels for use in residential as well as commercial applications
Modernfold	www.modernfold.com	Provides operable and movable partitions, including ceiling suspended Moveo system with glass panels
Panel Systems Mfg., Inc.	www.roomdividers.org	Provides modular and demountable wall systems
Panelfold Doors & Partitions	www.panelfold.com	Operable and relocatable walls
Steelcase, Inc.	www.steelcase.com	Privacy wall system includes movable wall system of solid or glass panels at various heights with framing and doors and coordinated to work with other Steelcase products
Teknion	www.teknion.com	Provides a variety of products, including Optos and Altos, consisting of modular, relocatable solid and glazed full-height panels with a variety of finish and door options, including wiring and accessories and coordination with wall-mounted storage and work surfaces
Transwall	www.transwall.com	Offers several lines of demountable and movable wall systems, including system integrated with system's furniture

- Availability of connectors to allowed angled installation
- Panel finishes available
- Ability to use customers own material (COM)
- Acoustical rating, if applicable
- Flame spread rating
- Availability of integrated power and data cabling, if needed
- Ability to replace individual finish panels
- Method of resting on existing carpet or other flooring type
- Ability to accommodate work surfaces or storage units, if needed
- Amount of recycled material and recyclability
- Effects on indoor air quality
- Type of base and top track and finishes available
- Overall aesthetics

6-4 CONSTRAINTS

For temporary partitions and other vertical barriers, the primary constraints include the inability for such partitions to have a fire rating, a limited amount of acoustical control, and cost. Partition systems are not designed to be carried above the suspended ceiling.

The lack of a fire rating is generally not an issue because full-height partitions are usually only considered where fire separation is not required. Most systems have a Class A flame spread rating, so they can be used anywhere that type of finish is needed.

Although some manufacturers' systems have a relatively good acoustical control with STC values up to 50 and are suitable for most office uses, actual installed values may be lower, and higher values can only be achieved with other gypsum wallboard constructions.

Partition systems have a higher initial cost per foot than standard gypsum wallboard construction, but costs for large installations must be evaluated on a tax and life-cycle basis, considering how much change in layout is anticipated. Costs for furniture systems with partial-height panels must be based on several considerations, including life-cycle costs, tax issues, flexibility, appearance, single-source responsibility, speed of installation, and function.

Additionally, partition systems cannot be used for very high spaces, provide high security, or allow for plumbing pipes or other recessed items to be placed in them.

6-5   COORDINATION

The type of coordination required for temporary vertical barriers depends on whether the barriers are partial height or full height used in place of standard partitions. Partial-height barriers are usually installed independently of the building structure and other partitions. For barriers that rest on the existing floor, there should be some type of leveling system built into the panels or poles. For suspended barriers, the ceiling structure must be strong enough to support the weight and allow for easy installation and relocation. Figure 5-13 shows some of the methods of installing permanent barriers, some of which are also applicable to temporary barriers.

When partial-height barriers or furniture systems with panels are used for office applications, coordinating acoustical solutions is critical. Ceiling tile must be selected with a high sound absorption average, SAA (formerly called the NRC, or noise reduction coefficient). White sound should also be installed to increase speech privacy. Workstations should also be planned to avoid direct sound paths and placed away from highly reflective materials, such as glass.

Demountable partition systems for large installations are only cost-effective if they are coordinated with other building components and systems, including lighting, HVAC, window mullions, and a suspended ceiling system. Space plans intended for frequent relocation should be laid out on the building grid, which should also coincide with the ceiling. In this way, the relocation of lights, HVAC diffusers and grilles, and sprinkler heads is minimized when partitions change. Figure 7-5 illustrates this type of coordination. Partition systems and other temporary barriers that touch existing construction must have details that allow attachment and acoustical sealing to walls, window mullions, convector covers, and other construction as well as a way to accommodate out-of-plumb construction and other building tolerances.

6-6   METHODS

Although temporary and movable vertical barriers, both full height and partial height, can be custom designed and constructed, they are usually standard manufactured items. In most cases, it is not cost-effective, and many times not structurally sound, to develop new details.

However, some of the ideas shown in Chapter 5 can be modified to develop movable walls. In addition, companies that develop trade show displays can be sources of products that may be adapted to custom-designed partial-height barriers.

Full Height

Full-height movable barriers and partitions are available in a variety of styles. Each manufacturer has its own design and method of assembling and disassembling their system. However, most offer panel and door options, as diagrammed in Fig. 6-2. Some offer clean, contemporary styles, while some are more utilitarian.

Most systems are designed to have the top track clipped to an exposed T-runner ceiling grid, which allows removal from the grid without damaging its appearance. Slotted suspended ceiling grids can also be used, which allows the top track to be screwed into the grid without damage if the system provides for a screw attachment. See Fig. 6-3. Top tracks can also be attached to gypsum wallboard ceilings with a suitable backing of wood or metal channels above the wallboard.

Because of the basic method of installing full-height moveable partitions they all have a visible continuous runner along the ceiling and proprietary clip-on base or a recessed base assembly. As previously mentioned, some systems use a steel framework to which finish is applied. This allows for installation of wiring and an interchangeable variety of finishes.

Partial Height

The type of partial height vertical barrier required for any given application depends on the particular needs of the project. In some cases, only a decorative backdrop is required to define two or more spaces. For other projects, a complete system of flexible, movable workstations with sound attenuation panels is required for a large corporate office.

Figure 6-2 Types of full-height partitions

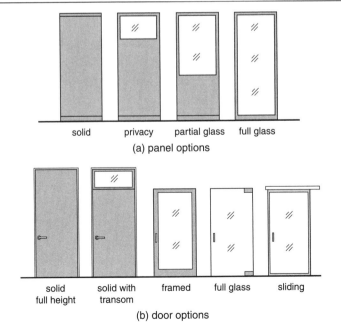

Figure 6-3 Movable panel details

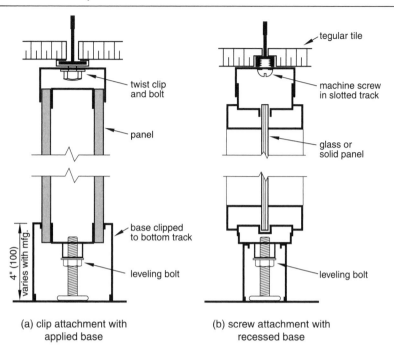

(a) clip attachment with
applied base

(b) screw attachment with
recessed base

Some types of partial height barriers, while being movable and easily disassembled, do require some attachment to the building structure. Post-mounted systems and hanging panels, as diagrammed in Fig. 6-1(d) and (h), are examples of these methods. Refer to Fig. 5-13 for methods of detailing these types of panels. On the other hand, post-and-screen systems and self-supporting panel systems, shown in Fig. 6-1(f) and (e), are completely independent of the existing building structure. Panels incorporated as part of a furniture system are also self-supporting. The difference between these two approaches may have tax consequences, as one type is attached to the structure as a fixed asset, while the other is not.

CHAPTER 7

OVERHEAD LIMITS—CEILINGS

7-1 INTRODUCTION

The overhead limit, or ceiling plane, in any interior space represents one of the most significant elements of interior design. Not only does the ceiling occupy a large proportion of the total visible surface area, but it must also perform a wide variety of functions, such as providing sound control and supporting or containing lighting, HVAC equipment, sprinklers, smoke detectors, and other equipment. For example, consider a room with dimensions of 20 ft by 30 ft with a 9-ft ceiling height (6.1 m by 9.1 m by 2.7 m). Of the total 2,100 ft² (195 m²) of surface area on the floor, walls, and ceilings, the ceiling represents 600 ft² (55.7 m²), or nearly 30% of the area and, unlike the walls and floor, the ceiling is entirely visible. Thinking of this construction element as an overhead limit helps the designer understand what is important in terms of both function *and* aesthetics.

Like vertical barriers, the ceiling plane is one of the major space–defining elements that interior designers can control. To the extent possible, given the fixed structure of the building and mechanical services, the ceiling plane can be created by the interior designer to define and give character to a space as well as provide all the functional requirements. Ceilings can be used to simply cover the structure and mechanical services of a building, to give scale to a space, to create a variety of spaces, and to help establish the design concept.

7-2 ELEMENT CONCEPTS

As with partitions, the ceiling plane can be designed in thousands of different ways. It can be as simple as a flat gypsum wallboard ceiling in a house or suspended acoustical ceiling in a commercial structure to a combination of materials positioned at different heights and orientations with a mixture of lighting types. Ceilings can be a simple plane, curved, angled, a modulated series of heights, a mixture of open and closed areas, richly textured, single color, or a multiple of colors and finishes.

Because the basic architecture, structure, electrical, and mechanical services of a building are predetermined by the architect and engineers, the interior designer has four basic choices

Figure 7-1 Ceiling concepts

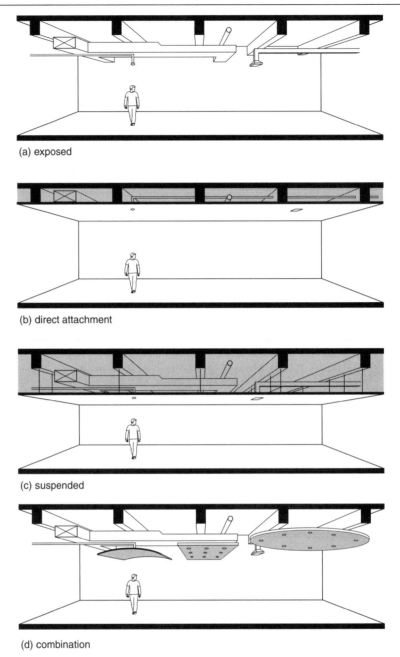

(a) exposed

(b) direct attachment

(c) suspended

(d) combination

when designing the overhead limits of a space as it relates to the base building. These are shown diagrammatically in Fig. 7-1.

Exposing services, as diagrammed in Fig. 7-1(a) is the simplest approach. The underside of the floor or roof structure above is exposed, as are any mechanical and electrical services. Although this approach has the advantages of minimizing cost and improving sustainability by not using any additional materials, sound control may be compromised and there is little opportunity to modulate space and create a finish that will enhance the design intent, unless the intent is a rough, industrial appearance.

Direct attachment, as shown in Fig. 7-1(b), can be as simple as screwing gypsum wallboard onto floor joists in a residence or spray-applied acoustical treatment on a concrete structure.

This method, however, limits any electrical or mechanical services to the space between structural members and generally results in a simple plane surface or all or some of the services being exposed. In most commercial buildings this approach is not even possible because most of the services are installed below the structure.

The most common method of creating a ceiling in commercial construction is by direct suspension of another material, typically acoustical tile in a grid, from the building's structure. See Fig. 7-1(c). These types of ceilings are easy to construct, inexpensive, flexible, work with all building services, and offer a wide variety of finish and design possibilities.

Finally, the designer can use a combination of the previous three methods to tailor the type of ceiling with the functional and aesthetic needs of each space. See Fig. 7-1(d). This is a good way to control costs by placing more expensive ceiling construction in those areas of most importance and choosing less expensive options where it is less important.

Within these four approaches to creating the ceiling plane, there are countless varieties. They can be grouped into closed types and open types. Closed types completely separate the usable area from the plenum. Some of the possible concepts are shown in Fig. 7-2.

The simplest, most common approach shown in Fig. 7-2(a) is a planar, suspended acoustical ceiling, using either an exposed grid or a concealed grid. These are available in a wide variety of grid sizes, tile types, colors, and patterns. A suspended planar ceiling can also be

Figure 7-2 Closed-ceiling concepts

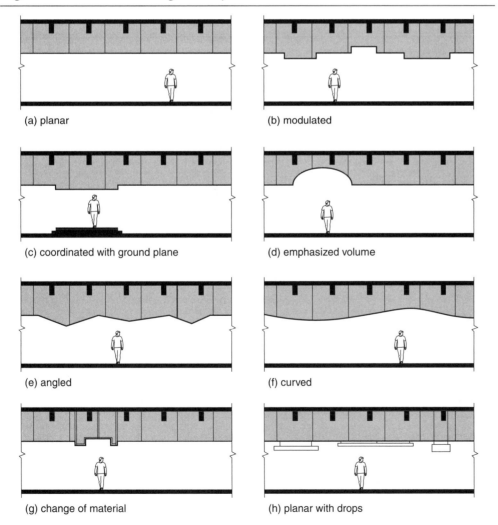

(a) planar

(b) modulated

(c) coordinated with ground plane

(d) emphasized volume

(e) angled

(f) curved

(g) change of material

(h) planar with drops

Figure 7-3 Open-ceiling concepts

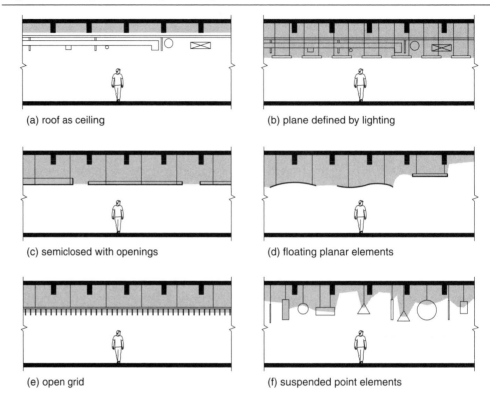

(a) roof as ceiling

(b) plane defined by lighting

(c) semiclosed with openings

(d) floating planar elements

(e) open grid

(f) suspended point elements

constructed of gypsum wallboard. Other varieties of closed ceilings are discussed in more detail later in this chapter.

Open ceilings have all or a portion of the area above the suspended ceiling exposed to view. Some of the possible concepts for this approach are shown in Fig. 7-3.

The most common open concept omits any type of suspended finish ceiling at all, as shown in Fig. 7-3(a). This design concept is used to emphasize the architecture of the space or as a design concept in itself. For residential construction, the underside of the roof is often featured, showcasing, for example, exposed beams, sloping roofs, or some other architectural feature. For commercial construction, exposing the roof or floor above often means exposing all the mechanical and electrical services as well. In both cases, the designer must decide how building services, such as lighting and ventilation, will be provided. Other varieties of open ceilings are discussed later in this chapter.

7-3 FUNCTION

As with partitions, the designer can make the best choice of materials and detailing methods by considering the various functions the ceiling needs to fulfill rather than just relying on standard suspended acoustical ceilings or gypsum wallboard.

Ceilings provide one or more of the following functions:

Covering structure, electrical, and mechanical services

Contributing to the overall design concept of the interior design

Defining space

Controlling sound

Providing light reflectance

Holding luminaires

Holding sprinkler heads

Holding supply air registers and return-air grilles

Holding speakers, smoke detectors, and other electrical equipment

Supporting ceiling-suspended elements, such as signs or curtains

If, for example, a ceiling is to define a lower space within a high volume, that can be accomplished with a standard acoustical grid ceiling. However, it can also be achieved with an open grid of nearly any material, by lighting techniques that only emphasize the lower area of the volume, with a metal mesh, or any number of alternatives as long as the constraints of fire resistance and other requirements are met.

The ceiling can also contribute to the sustainability of a project. Refer to the sidebar for specific ways sustainability can be addressed through the design and detailing of the overhead plane.

Sustainability Issues Related to the Overhead Plane

Sustainability issues related to the overhead plane include the following:

- Specify ceiling tile and other ceiling components with as much recycled content as possible. This includes mineral wool, recycled paper, recycled aluminum and steel, and corn and wheat starch binders instead of traditional binders. Most manufacturers now include recycled content in their product literature.

- Specify ceiling tile that is zero or low-emitting for formaldehyde. The State of California Collaborative for High Performance Schools has a concentration limit of ($33 \ \mu g/m^3$) 27 ppb (parts per billion) when tiles are in place and prior to occupancy with a suggested goal of ($3 \ \mu g/m^3$) 2.5 ppb. For a product to be considered zero-emitting, the formaldehyde concentrations cannot exceed ($2 \ \mu g/m^3$) 1.6 ppb.

- For remodeling projects where existing tile is being replaced, try to recycle old tile. Several manufacturers have recycling programs for certain types and quantities of tile, if certain requirements are met.

- Specify ceiling tile that has antimicrobial protection and conforms to ASTM D3273, Standard Test Method for Resistance to Mold on the Surface of Interior Coatings in an Environmental Chamber.

- If appropriate for the occupancy, select tiles and other components with a high light reflectance to improve daylighting and minimize the need for luminaires.

- When determining ceiling heights and ceiling transitions, consider view planes from the interior of the space to exterior windows to maximize views to the outside and to not obstruct available daylighting.

- Minimize the amount of material used by considering not using suspended ceilings where they may not be necessary. Coordinate with lighting and mechanical requirements because using a continuous suspended ceiling may reduce long-term energy use.

7-4 CONSTRAINTS

For ceilings, constraints most often include the existing slab-to-slab distance, requirements for acoustic control, seismic forces, budget, fire resistance, and flame spread. In commercial construction, most of the functional requirements described above can be satisfied without a separate finished ceiling. Even acoustical control can often be achieved with suspended acoustic panels.

For commercial construction, the common constraints today are acoustic needs, light reflectance, the ability to inexpensively subdivide space with partitions extending to a suspended ceiling, and sustainability. Materials in Type I and Type II buildings must be noncombustible and if the ceiling is part of a floor/ceiling fire-rated assembly in any construction type, the ceiling must be part of a fire-rated assembly. Generally, all the commercial ceiling products on the market meet these requirements. In most cases, lighting, sprinkler systems, HVAC systems, and other services can be installed independently of a finish ceiling, if desired.

7-5   COORDINATION

When a suspended ceiling is used, the most common coordination efforts in overall planning are those required to locate the mechanical and electrical services to work with the design of the grid and to align exposed grid systems or other elements of the ceiling with the architectural elements of the building, such as window mullions, columns, and fixed partitions. The designer may also want to coordinate the location of partitions with the ceiling grid or other main features of the ceiling design such as changes in ceiling material or changes in ceiling height. See Fig. 7-4.

In many cases, compromises must be made because one requirement may take precedence over another. For example, in the short corridor section shown in Fig. 7-4, the layout of the ceiling grid may require the designer to choose between centering the lights and sprinkler head midway between the partitions or in the center of the ceiling tile. Further, if cost is a consideration, sprinkler heads may need to be located at their maximum allowable spacing rather than aligned with other ceiling elements or centered in tiles.

For details, the method of joining the ceiling with vertical elements, such as partitions, columns, and exterior walls, also needs to be considered. This aspect of detailing is discussed in

Figure 7-4 Ceiling coordination items

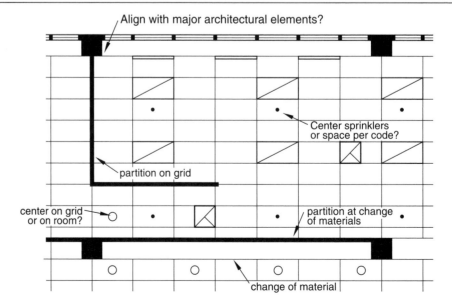

Figure 7-5 20 × 60 ceiling grid

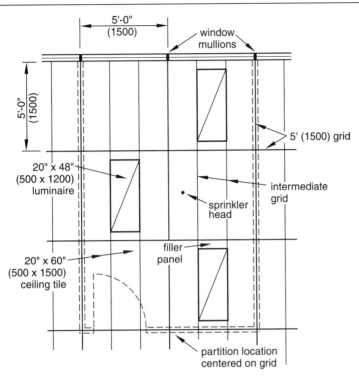

Chapter 10. Additional coordination of details must be made for material transitions, ceiling height transitions, and complex mechanical or electrical installations.

For office planning in which a demountable partition system is used, the size of the ceiling grid must be coordinated with required room sizes and lighting types to allow for the most flexibility in partition relocation. As shown in Fig. 7-5, some demountable partition systems are designed to be located on the ceiling grid lines so that the top runner of the partition can be screwed into a slotted grid (shown in Fig. 7-8(e) and (f)). Lighting, sprinkler heads, and HVAC registers and grilles are designed and specified to be movable within the main planning module, typically 5 ft by 5 ft (1500 mm by 1500 mm) or 4 ft by 4 ft (1200 mm by 1200 mm), allowing partitions to be placed as required.

If a hard ceiling, such as gypsum wallboard, is used, access panels need to be provided to allow access to electrical junction boxes, valves, mechanical equipment, and similar items. If possible, the designer should coordinate with the mechanical and electrical engineers to position the items requiring access in such a way that the panels do not create an unsightly view of the ceiling. In most cases, access panels mounted in a gypsum wallboard ceiling will get dirty with use and the joint compound around the panel will crack over time as the door is open and closed.

Sprinkler Spacing

Sprinklers in commercial construction must be positioned with maximum and minimum dimensions defined by NFPA 13, *Installation of Sprinkler Systems* and NFPA 13R, *Installation of Sprinkler Systems in Residential Occupancies Up to and Including Four Stories in Height*. NFPA 13D, *Installation of Sprinkler Systems in One- and Two-family Dwellings and Manufactured Homes* applies to residential design. The designer should know the basic requirements to make informed design decisions about coordinating sprinklers with the position of luminaires, HVAC air

Figure 7-6 Sprinkler spacing

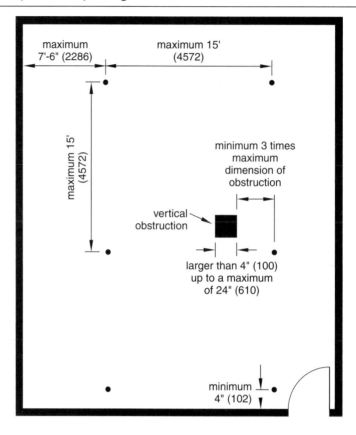

supply, and other ceiling mounted items. With knowledge of the essential spacing limitations, the interior designer can work with the mechanical engineer or fire protection engineer to locate sprinkler heads to work with the overall ceiling plan.

The NFPA 13 standard classifies the relative fire hazard of buildings into three groups: light, ordinary, and extra hazard. Each hazard classification is further divided into groups. The hazard classification determines the required spacing of sprinklers and other regulations. Figure 7-6 shows some of the basic requirements for light hazard occupancies. These include uses such as residential, offices, hospitals, schools, and restaurants. In these occupancies there must be one sprinkler for each 200 ft^2 (18.6 m^2), or 225 ft^2 (20.9 m^2) if the design of the system is designed hydraulically, which most are. Figure 7-6 shows some of the requirement for hydraulically designed systems. There are other requirements for spacing near dropped beams and other obstructions. Refer to Fig. 3-9 for typical clearances above the ceiling required for sprinkler heads and piping. For more detailed design requirements refer to NFPA 13.

HVAC Coordination

In most cases, coordinating the location of air supply registers, return-air grilles, and exhaust fan outlets is straightforward. The mechanical engineer determines the general location and capacity requirements of these items, but the interior designer can work with the engineer to finalize the exact position in the ceiling. The designer may also request that the engineer use a particular type of air control device that is most appropriate for the design of the space. For

Figure 7-7 Types of ceiling-mounted air diffusers

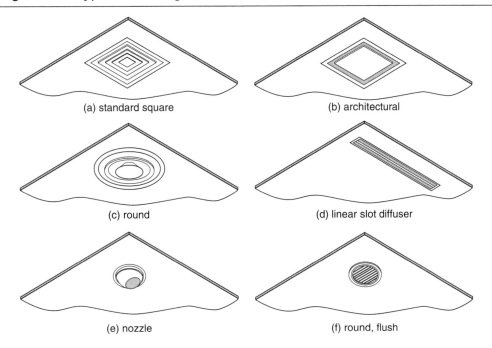

(a) standard square	(b) architectural
(c) round	(d) linear slot diffuser
(e) nozzle	(f) round, flush

example, a linear slot diffuser may be preferable to a standard square air diffuser. Figure 7-7 shows some of the air diffuser types available, and Table 7-1 lists some of the manufacturers of air terminal units.

Tolerance Coordination

Tolerance coordination usually is not an issue because suspended ceilings can be installed very accurately (level, position, and alignment) independent of the building structure. Typical suspended ceilings are installed with laser levels and can generally be constructed level to within ±1/8 in. in 10 ft (3.2 mm in 3050 mm), often to within ±1/8 in. over the entire room area. Of course, if the ceiling does not touch other construction, minor variations in level, position, or size are not noticed. However, if a grid system is to be coordinated with

Table 7-1 Air Diffuser Manufacturers

Manufacturer	Web Site	Description
Acutherm	www.acutherm.com	Provides a variety of diffuser types
AirConcepts, Inc.	www.airconceptsinc.com	Provides a variety of diffuser types
Anemostat	www.anemostat.com	Provides a variety of diffuser types
Carnes Company	wwwlcarnes.com	Provides a variety of diffuser types
Krueger	www.kruegar-hvac.com	Provides round and square diffusers, linear slot diffusers, grilles, and registers
Nailor Industries	www.nailor.com	Linear slot diffusers, square and round ceiling diffusers, and perforated diffusers
Titus	www.titus-hvac.com	Provides a variety of diffuser types
Trox USA	www.troxusa.com	Provides nozzle and swirl diffusers
Tuttle & Bailey	www.tuttleandbailey.com	Provides a variety of diffuser types
Sheiho International	www.seiho.com	Provides nozzle diffusers

the position of recessed downlights or sprinkler heads, additional effort may be needed to coordinate the work of electricians, mechanical contractors, sprinkler contractors, and finish system installers.

7-6 METHODS

Manufacturers have provided hundreds of products for ceiling construction that the designer can use to develop project-specific solutions. The conceptual approaches shown in Figs. 7-2 and 7-3 are described in more detail in this section with listings of some of the manufacturers that provide useful products for developing details. Some of the ceiling designs shown can also be constructed with standard metal framing and gypsum wallboard or other materials, while some designs require a combination of proprietary products and generic construction materials. These are divided here into the two broad groups of closed- and open-ceiling systems.

Closed

PLANAR

A planar ceiling is often the simplest and least costly method of providing a finished ceiling and satisfying most of the functional needs of an overhead plane. In most cases, this is the standard 2 ft by 2 ft (600 mm by 600 mm) or 2 ft by 4 ft (600 mm by 1200 mm) lay-in acoustical ceiling. These ceilings have the advantages of simple installation, acoustical control, light reflectance, low cost, flexibility, accessibility to the plenum, and the ability to accommodate a wide variety of mechanical and electrical systems.

Since the development of suspended lay-in acoustical ceilings, designers have often objected to the finished appearance. Manufacturers have responded with a variety of grid types and panels to address the aesthetic objections as well as to provide specific system types of systems for specific building needs. Some of the varieties of grid profiles now available are shown in Fig. 7-8. Panels also come in hundreds of different styles, patterns, colors, and edge treatments. Many of the ceiling manufacturers are listed in Table 7-2. These include manufacturers of standard acoustical ceilings as well as specialty ceilings.

Planar ceilings may also be constructed with a concealed grid to eliminate the visible grid that many designers object to, while still maintaining acoustical control, accessibility to the plenum, and relatively low cost.

Figure 7-8 Types of ceiling grids

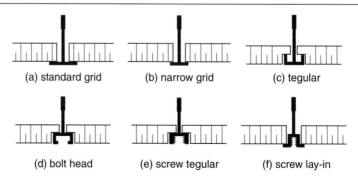

(a) standard grid   (b) narrow grid   (c) tegular

(d) bolt head   (e) screw tegular   (f) screw lay-in

Table 7-2   Suspended Ceiling Manufacturers

Manufacturer and Web site	Description
Alpro Acoustical Systems www.alproacoustics.com	Supplies corrugated, perforated metal acoustical panels of aluminum or steel in flat panels, curves, and floating sections.
American Decorative Ceilings www.americandecoativeceilings.com	Provides specialty ceilings including curved ceilings, tin ceiling replications, open grids, wood panels, corrugated, linear plank, linear metal ceilings, translucent panels for backlighting, metal panels, and floating "clouds."
Armstrong www.armstrong.com	One of the largest manufacturers of ceiling suspension systems, ceiling tiles, and specialty ceiling products including tiles, grids, specialty trim, curved ceilings. Provides drywall grid, wood panels, metal panels, open-grid ceilings, tin ceiling replications, coffers, floating "clouds," custom radial ceilings, and linear metal ceilings.
BPB America Inc. www.bpb-na.com	Standard ceiling tiles and grids.
Ceilings Plus, Inc. www.ceilingsplus.com	Offers a variety of specialty ceiling types including curved, serpentine, canted arc, corrugated, metal and wood open grid, linear metal, wood slat, wood panel, modular, and triangular grid shapes.
Chicago Metallic www.chicagometallic.com	Supplies a wide variety of grids and panels as well as specialty items such as curved grids for floating "clouds" curved ceiling sections, perforated panels, tin ceiling replications, linear metal ceilings, open grids, coffers, and drywall grid (including curved).
Gordon Grid www.gordongrid.com	Provides ceiling grid systems and aluminum, steel, or stainless steel panels in flat, curved, and custom configurations, as well as luminous ceilings and perforated panels. Also provides linear metal ceilings.
Hunter Douglas www.hunterdouglascontract.com	Techstyle® suspended ceilings consisting of 1-1/8 in. (28.6 mm) thick honeycomb panels snapped to concealed grid to provide thin reveals between panels up to 48 in. by 72 in. (1220 mm by 1830 mm) in size.
illbruck acoustic, inc. www.illbruck-archprod.com	Patterned, bevel-edged ceiling tiles with backer board for grid or adhesive installation. Also provides expanded metal ceiling panels.
Simplex Ceilings www.simplexceilings.com	Metal pan ceilings for flat or curved installation in addition to concealed plank panels, curved ceilings, linear metal ceilings, open grids, and custom designs.
Tectum www.tectum.com	Wood fiber ceiling panels, abuse resistant, paintable.
USG www.usg.com	Wide variety of ceiling grids and panels, including specialty systems such as curved, angles, floating "clouds," linear metal ceilings, open grid, tin ceiling replications, translucent panels, coffers, and fiber-reinforced gypsum systems.

Flat gypsum wallboard ceilings can also easily be constructed, but they usually require access panels to allow for maintenance of mechanical and electrical equipment above the ceiling. Gypsum wallboard ceilings can be constructed on a framework of metal furring channels on cold-rolled steel channels or with proprietary T-bar grids, as shown in Fig. 7-9(a) and (b). For small areas, such as corridors and restrooms, gypsum wallboard ceilings may also be installed on metal stud framing or wood framing if combustible materials are allowed by the local building code. See Fig. 7-9(c).

MODULATED

Modulated ceilings are those where the ceiling height varies. See Fig. 7-2(b). The ceiling may be continuous using the same material or may consist of one continuous closed portion with suspended "clouds."

Some of the methods used to make the transition between ceiling heights are shown in Fig. 7-10. These include using standard framing materials, as well as special manufactured accessories. Manufacturers of proprietary trim pieces are listed in Table 7-3.

Modulated ceilings are often used to create lighting coves for indirect lighting. Although such coves can be constructed with common metal framing and gypsum wallboard, premanufactured solutions are also available. Some of the methods of creating lighting coves are shown in Fig. 7-11.

Figure 7-9 Gypsum wallboard ceiling framing

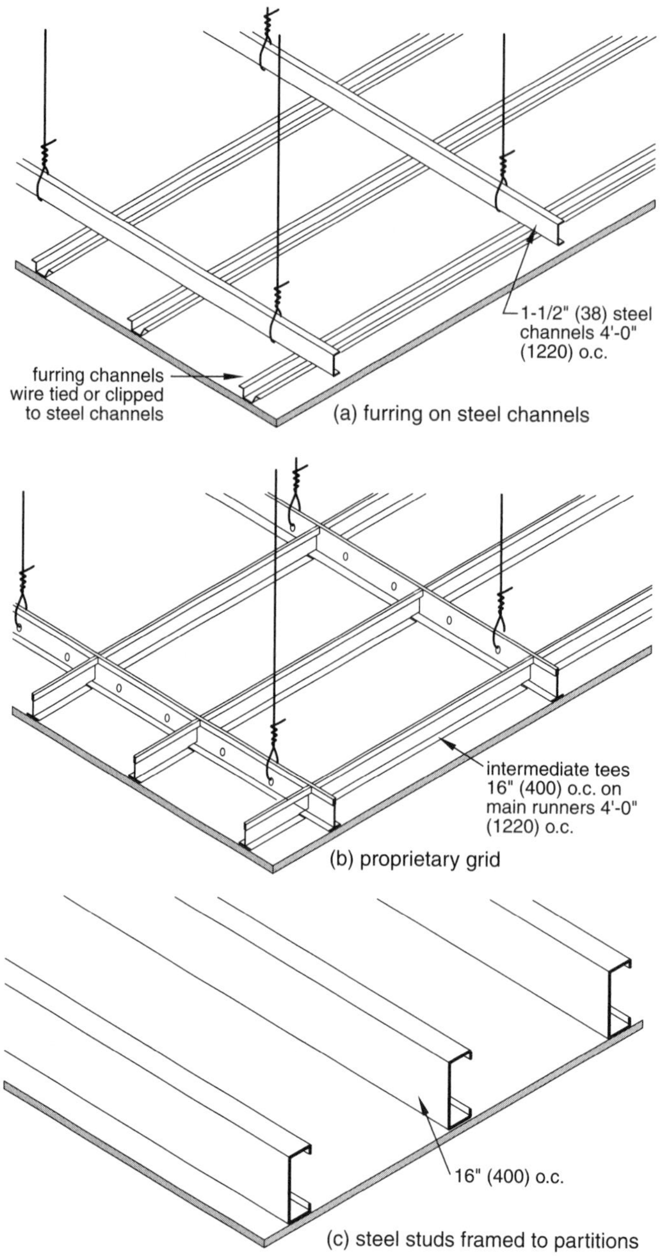

1-1/2" (38) steel channels 4'-0" (1220) o.c.

furring channels wire tied or clipped to steel channels

(a) furring on steel channels

intermediate tees 16" (400) o.c. on main runners 4'-0" (1220) o.c.

(b) proprietary grid

16" (400) o.c.

(c) steel studs framed to partitions

Lighting coves are also commonly incorporated into ceiling and wall transitions, as discussed in Chapter 10.

COORDINATED WITH GROUND PLANE

A variation of the modulated ceiling is one that is closely coordinated with a modulation of the ground plane as shown in Fig. 7-2(c). The ceiling may either be raised or lowered relative to the surrounding ceiling, depending on the effect the designer wants. Raising the ceiling maintains a constant ceiling height above a raised platform, while lowering the ceiling changes the scale of the space and makes a much more intimate area. The ceiling transition can be made with a vertical plane, as shown in Fig. 7-2(c) or with angled, stepped, or curved sides.

Figure 7-10 Ceiling height transitions

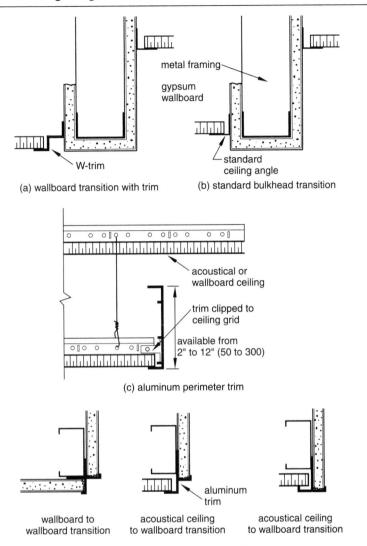

metal framing

gypsum
wallboard

W-trim

standard
ceiling angle

(a) wallboard transition with trim

(b) standard bulkhead transition

acoustical or
wallboard ceiling

trim clipped to
ceiling grid

available from
2" to 12" (50 to 300)

(c) aluminum perimeter trim

aluminum
trim

wallboard to
wallboard transition

acoustical ceiling
to wallboard transition

acoustical ceiling
to wallboard transition

(d) transitions with aluminum trim

Table 7-3	Ceiling Trim Manufacturers	
Manufacturer	**Web Site**	**Description**
Alpro Acoustical Systems	www.alproacoustics.com	Edge trim for T-bar systems in straight and curved sections
Armstrong	www.armstrong.com	Provides edge trim for floating ceilings, drapery pocket assemblies, panel transitions to drywall, and standard sized floating "clouds"
Chicago Metallic	www.chicagometallic.com	Metal ceiling grids in a variety of configurations as well as FRP grid sections
Fry Reglet	www.fryreglet.com	Aluminum ceiling grid and trim pieces for ceiling-to-ceiling transitions
Gordon Grid	www.gordongrid.com	Aluminum trim pieces for ceiling-to-ceiling transitions, as well as ceiling-to-wall transition moldings and perimeter pockets for drapery and cove lighting
Trim-tex	www.trim-tex.com	Vinyl wallboard trim in a variety of configurations for wallboard ceilings, vinyl crown molding, and some specialty ceiling trim

Figure 7-11 Lighting coves

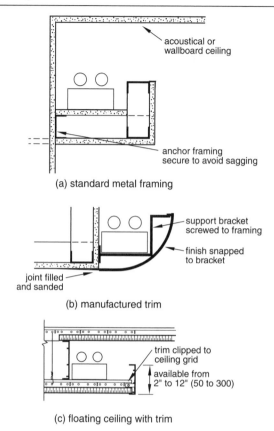

acoustical or
wallboard ceiling

anchor framing
secure to avoid sagging

(a) standard metal framing

support bracket
screwed to framing

finish snapped
to bracket

joint filled
and sanded

(b) manufactured trim

trim clipped to
ceiling grid

available from
2" to 12" (50 to 300)

(c) floating ceiling with trim

EMPHASIZED VOLUME

Another variation of the modulated ceiling is one that is raised or lowered to emphasize a given area. See Fig. 7-2(d). Here, the floor plane remains unchanged, while the ceiling is used to change the scale and spatial emphasis. This design can be used where mechanical and electrical services above the ceiling preclude an overall high ceiling height but where one area is available for special treatment. The designer may need to coordinate with the mechanical engineer to locate ducts, sprinkler piping, and other services in such a way that the ceiling can be raised.

ANGLED

Where space is available, the ceiling plane can be varied, creating different ceiling heights and a more dynamic spatial volume. See Fig. 7-2(e). The variations can be made over small distances such as 4 ft to 6 ft (1200 mm to 1800 mm) or with large areas, possibly sized to correspond to a functional area below the ceiling. Where the exterior window height is high, angled ceilings sloping down from the head of the window are a useful way to reflect natural light into a space, increasing daylighting efficiency.

CURVED

A curved ceiling plane, shown in Fig. 7-2(f), creates a different dynamic than an angled ceiling, suggesting a smoother transition from one space to another. As with angled or modulated ceiling planes, curves can be used selectively over certain areas of the space to provide a design contrast with flat ceiling planes or to emphasize special areas, such as a corridor, dining area, or retail space.

Large, sweeping areas of curved ceilings are difficult to build, but smaller, premanufactured curved sections are available from some manufacturers. See Table 7-2.

CHANGE OF MATERIAL

Different materials can be used in ceiling construction for a variety of reasons. The designer may want to control costs by using a less expensive material, such as a suspended acoustical ceiling, in most areas and reserving more of the budget for constructing a more expensive material in just special areas. For example, a gypsum wallboard modulated ceiling may be used in the reception area of an office space, while a standard suspended grid ceiling is used in the remainder of the area. See Fig. 7-2(g).

PLANAR WITH DROPS

A planar ceiling may be used to completely close the plenum for appearance or to minimize energy use, while still using separate elements below the plane of the ceiling. See Fig. 7-2(h). The suspended elements can be used to emphasize space, to modulate the scale of the space, or to contain special lighting. While the dropped elements can be any material or configuration, the limited heights in many interiors restrict the elements to flat, or nearly flat (angles or curved sections), suspended acoustical ceilings or pre-manufactured specialty ceilings, such as wood, metal, perforated metal, or glass. Several manufacturers offer floating "clouds" with edge trim that can easily be specified and installed. See Table 7-2.

Open

Open ceilings are those that expose all or a portion of the underside of the floor or roof above as well as mechanical and electrical services. Open ceilings are often used to save the cost of installing a separate suspended ceiling, to increase the size of space, or to use the esthetic of exposed structure and services as a design feature. However, eliminating a separate suspended ceiling to save costs should be carefully investigated with the assistance of the mechanical and electrical engineers. Although the first costs may be reduced, the life-cycle costs may higher. This is due to increased energy use without a suspended ceiling because larger HVAC systems are required to heat or cool additional space and to create required air movement. In addition, open ceilings generally require more maintenance for cleaning and painting and are not as efficient at reflecting both artificial and natural light.

ROOF AS CEILING

The first type of open ceiling, as shown diagrammatically in Fig. 7-3(a), is simply no ceiling at all. All the structure and building services are exposed. This approach generally only work in cases where no, or very little, partitioning is required, such as open plan offices, retail stores, manufacturing plants, and the like. The height of the floor above and the irregularity of lighting, pips, and ductwork, make it difficult to extend partitions to the structure above. In most cases, the pipes and ducts must be painted and the designer may want these element laid out in a particular way for aesthetic reasons, both of which increase the cost of using this approach. Usually, the designer specifies a light paint color to make the service visible and improve reflectance.

From a visual standpoint, the effect of this type of overhead plane is that of an irregular space, high and low points being defined by the size and position of the lights and mechanical services.

PLANE DEFINED BY LIGHTING

A variation of the totally open ceiling is to create a perceived ceiling plane with lighting. One hundred percent downlighting is used at a uniform elevation and all walls, structure, mechanical, and electrical services above the lights are painted black. The effect is a ceiling plane at the level of the luminaires. Although the services can be seen the eye adjusts to the higher light level and anything above the lights is not noticed. The main disadvantage to this ceiling design is the lack of light reflectance, for either improved daylighting or higher-efficiency artificial lighting. Generally, more luminaires are needed with this technique than with a continuous, high-reflectance ceiling.

SEMICLOSED WITH OPENINGS

A semiclosed ceiling with openings has the majority of the ceiling closed, with only portions open to the area above the ceiling. The closed portion can be a simple planar ceiling or it can be formed with angles or curves. Although this type of ceiling creates a strong overhead plane, there is still some sense of spatial modulation.

The openings may allow visibility to the structure and mechanical services above or vision may be blocked with a separate ceiling system above the surface of the lower ceiling. Return air is drawn into the plenum through the openings, eliminating the need for return air grilles.

FLOATING PLANAR ELEMENTS

A variation of the semiclosed ceiling design is one with separate planar elements that seem to float below the structure and mechanical services. With this type of overhead plane, more of the ceiling is open than with the semiclosed type and the suspended elements may be at various elevations and consist of varying shapes and sizes of construction. The sense of spatial modulation is greater with this type of ceiling than with the semiclosed one. Refer to Table 7-2 for manufacturers that supply specialty ceilings and trim that can be used to create this ceiling type.

OPEN GRID

An open grid ceiling, shown in Fig. 7-3(e), uses a suspended assembly of elements, usually of uniform size and spacing to create a strong visual plane, while allowing air to freely circulate between the occupied space and the volume above the ceiling. Most commonly, open grids consist of small, square grids or linear elements. A linear metal ceiling is a variety of this ceiling type. Refer to Table 7-4 for manufactures of open-grid ceilings.

Open-grid ceilings create an effect similar to a plane defined by lighting. The grid reflects ambient light, while the area above the grid is dark; the effect is that only the grid is visible, even when a person looks directly up.

SUSPENDED POINT ELEMENTS

A ceiling may be completely open, as with the *roof as ceiling* type illustrated in Fig. 7-3(a), but with visually prominent element suspended in the space. See Fig. 7-3(f). These elements

Table 7-4 Open Grid Ceiling Manufacturers

Manufacturer	Web Site	Description
Alpro Acoustical Systems	www.alproacoustics.com	Acoustical baffles
Armstrong	www.armstrong.com	Metalworks™ aluminum system
Ceilings Plus	www.ceilingsplus.com	Beamz retangular or square system in a variety of baffle sizes and grid sizes
Chicago Metallic	www.chicagometallic.com	Magna T-Cell™, Intaline™, CubeGrid™, BeamGrid™, and GraphGrid™ systems
Gordon Grid	www.gordongrid.com	Beam Mate wide open grid system and Fin Mate suspended fins in flat or curved configurations
Simplex Ceilings	www.simplexceilings.com	Aluminum grids from 1 in. to 6 in. (25 mm to 152 mm) square or custom sizes.
USG	www.usg.com	GridWare™, WireWorks™, and WireWorks™ Forms

may be luminaires, acoustic panels, banners, signs, air diffusers, or any combination to create a field of elements. The overhead plane is largely defined by the floor or roof structure above but modulated by the size, position, shape, color, and density of the suspended elements. With fewer elements, the structure and mechanical and electrical services are emphasized; with more elements the ceiling takes on the effect of floating planar elements or an open-grid ceiling.

CHAPTER 8

THE GROUND PLANE— FLOORS, STAIRS, AND RAMPS

8-1 INTRODUCTION

The ground plane is the most fundamental element of interior design. It is the surface that supports all the activities, construction, and furnishings that make up any interior space. As a basic enclosing surface, the ground plane, like the overhead plane, represents a significant percentage of the total surface area defining any room or space. It not only provides structural support and a walking surface but also contributes significantly to the character and definition of the interior environment.

The ground plane must remain flat and level. Unlike walls, ceilings, furniture, and other interior elements that can be angled, curved, and irregular, a floor must essentially be a smooth surface, with only occasional interruptions with ramps or stairs. The interior designer must express any design statement with material, color, pattern, shape, or a change in level.

Floors support two types of elements, fixed and movable. Fixed elements include construction such as partitions, cabinetry, and other raised floors. Movable elements include furniture, equipment, and temporary constructions. Fixed elements generally are perceived as part of the architecture of a space, while movable elements read as furnishings.

The ground plane can be a neutral background for furniture and other elements or it can be a major design statement in itself. The texture, color, and shapes of the flooring material can also change the scale and character of the space in which it is used.

The interior designer can use the ground plane as a major design element, while meeting all of the functional requirements of support, safety, durability, and accessibility. This chapter discusses some of the design concepts that the designer can use to begin thinking of the ground plane as a significant element and gives some practical starting points for detailing. Refer to Chapter 11 for more ideas on how to make transitions between ground planes.

8-2 ELEMENT CONCEPTS

Because of the planar nature of floors and the strict needs for safety, accessibility, and other functional requirements, there are fewer possible structural concepts that the designer can use than might be possible with the ceiling plane or with vertical barriers. However, even with these limitations, the designer can develop a strong design statement by using flooring creatively and in conjunction with the ceiling plane, vertical barriers, changes in level, and other built-in construction.

Flooring

When sufficient space is not available for changes in level, the designer can use the material, color, texture, and line of flooring materials as well as *changes* of these elements within a single plane to express the design intent of the space. Figure 8-1 shows some of these basic approaches.

Of course, the simplest approach is to use a single material as a background for the activities, furniture, and other construction within the space. The flooring material can be plain, textured, neutral, or boldly colored. The flooring can have a strong directional line, as shown in Figs. 8-1(b) and (c), which can affect the dynamic, proportion, and scale of a space. However, as with ceiling patterns, a strong directional pattern should be run perpendicular to the length of a space. Large patterns should generally be used with large spaces and small patterns with smaller spaces. Small patterns in a large space will sometimes be perceived as an overall tone rather than individual visual texture.

Changes in material can be used to define space or for functional reasons. For example, hard surface flooring may be required next to carpet for durability in a high-traffic area or for water resistance next to wet areas. The material changes may be made with a simple line or more complex patterns, as shown in Figs. 8-1(d)–(f).

Figure 8-1 Ground plane concepts

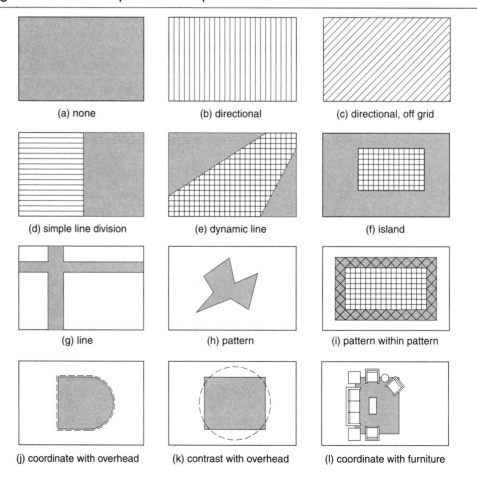

(a) none

(b) directional

(c) directional, off grid

(d) simple line division

(e) dynamic line

(f) island

(g) line

(h) pattern

(i) pattern within pattern

(j) coordinate with overhead

(k) contrast with overhead

(l) coordinate with furniture

Special patterns can also be designed as a design feature or to direct movement. See Fig. 8-1(g)–(i).

Flooring variations in a single plane are even more effective when coordinated with changes in ceiling plane or material or used in conjunction with furniture groupings as diagrammed in Fig. 8-1(j) and (l). Although islands of different flooring can also be created with area rugs, these may present a tripping hazard and may be difficult to maintain in commercial uses.

The ground plane can be used most effectively to define space when a level change is possible. Of course, this requires sufficient ceiling space, but even a slight rise is sufficient to create a noticeable difference and create the effect desired. In addition to the change in level itself, the line of transition can be treated in various ways as is shown in Figs. 11-7 and 11-10. The designer can use stairs or ramps alone to make the transition or simply have the change in level interrupted with railings or other features.

Stairs

Of course, when there is a change in level, the designer must provide a way to move from one level to the other. This requires steps and usually an adjacent ramp. Moving up and down just a few inches or a few feet within a space requires a different design response than moving from one floor level to another. Although there are some similar requirements of safety and comfort, floor-level changes often require stairs that meet egress requirements, while minor level changes are usually considered monumental stairs. This section only discusses small changes in level requiring one to five steps as might be used for a small level change.

One of the first decisions the designer must make is the height of the level change and the number of steps. Although a platform with a single step up is the easiest and least expensive to construct, single steps are inherently dangerous and should usually be avoided. However, with careful design and inclusion of handrails and visual clues identifying the level change, single-step level changes may be used.

Figure 8-2 illustrates some of the ways short runs of steps can placed relative to the level changes they serve. Straight, relatively narrow stairs are the most efficient and safest. See Figs. 8-2(a)–(c). Wide stairs, diagrammed in Fig. 8-2(d), extending the full length of the level change, create more of a design feature and allow movement over a wider area. Wide stairs may require intermediate handrails for safety. Refer to the later section in this chapter on constraints for a discussion of code requirements. These types of stairs can be made safer by extending the depth of the tread beyond the code minimum of 11 in. (279 mm).

Although stairs can be curved in plan or wrapped around an angle, these are inherently more dangerous and should be used carefully with sufficient handrails and nosing marking. See Figs. 8-2(e)–(g). Other variations can be used as shown in Figs. 8-2(h)–(l). These provide a variation in the straight run of stair but still provide for a walk path perpendicular to the width of the stairway, which is safer than walking at an angle to each tread. Splayed forms can be used to direct movement either at the top or bottom of the stair, as shown in Figs. 8-2(j)–(l).

Ramps

Accessibility codes generally require ramps be provided for any change in level. They may be used alone or in conjunction with steps. Because ramps require significant amounts of floor area, the designer typically limits the height of an optional platform created strictly for design reasons to minimize the length of ramp required. However, in some situations the length

Figure 8-2 Stair placement concepts

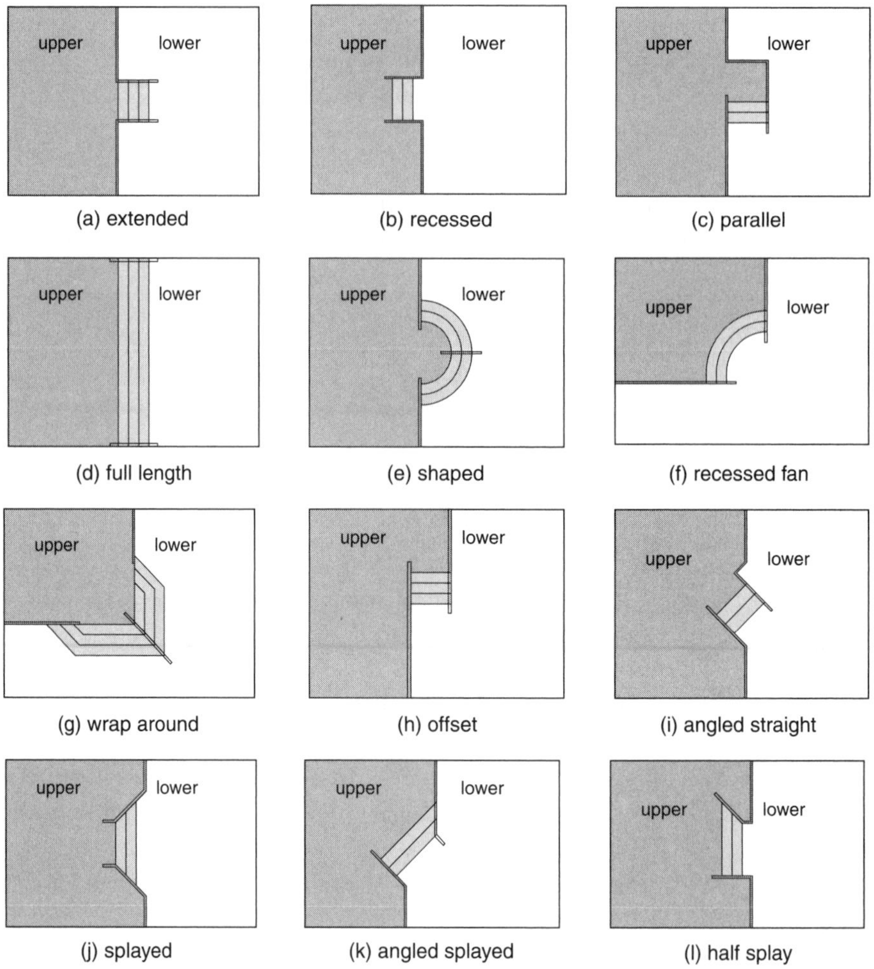

(a) extended

(b) recessed

(c) parallel

(d) full length

(e) shaped

(f) recessed fan

(g) wrap around

(h) offset

(i) angled straight

(j) splayed

(k) angled splayed

(l) half splay

along a ramp may be used for other purposes. For example, in a retail store, a display may be built next to one side of a ramp, so the ramp serves for both circulation and merchandising.

Figure 8-3 illustrates some of the conceptual ways ramps can be placed relative to level changes and in conjunction with steps. In most cases, especially in public areas, both stairs and ramps should be provided. Some people with mobility problems find it easier to use stairs than walk a longer distance along a ramp. Ideally, the starting and ending points of both stairs and adjacent ramps should be in the same area.

The designer should decide on how to place stairs and ramps based first on the height the ramp must serve. A 21 in. (533 mm) level change will require a much longer ramp than a 7 in. (178 mm) change, which may require a switchback configuration rather than a straight run.

8-3 FUNCTION

More than any other design element, the ground plane requires the most attention to its functional requirements. The floor of any space must provide a stable, safe means of movement for people and a structurally sound platform for furniture and other construction. Because of the amount of use the floor experiences, it must also be durable for the type of use it is put to and relatively easy to clean and otherwise maintain. The ground plane should also

Figure 8-3 Ramp placement concepts

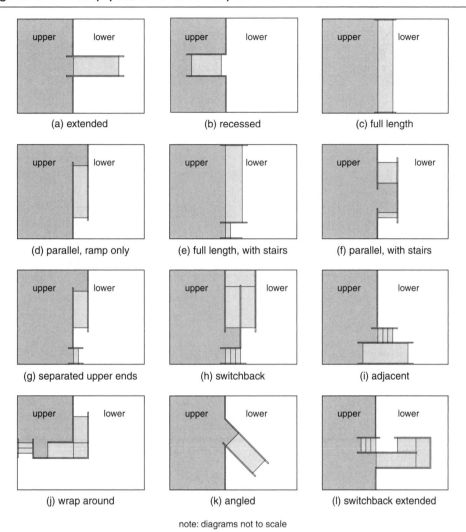

(a) extended

(b) recessed

(c) full length

(d) parallel, ramp only

(e) full length, with stairs

(f) parallel, with stairs

(g) separated upper ends

(h) switchback

(i) adjacent

(j) wrap around

(k) angled

(l) switchback extended

note: diagrams not to scale

provide the desired sense of movement and control of circulation. Some of the other functional requirements include accessibility for all users, comfort, water resistance, and sustainability. Regardless of the approach the designer may take with the ground plane, these functional requirements must be met. Refer to Chapters 2 and 3 for further discussion of basic constraints and functional requirements of details.

8-4 CONSTRAINTS

For the ground plane, constraints typically include the fire resistance of the finish floor material and its support as well as the structural integrity and safety of the floor. For changes in level, code requirements for safety and accessibility must also be considered.

Fire Resistance of Floor Finishes

The IBC regulates the use of some finish flooring materials. These include textile coverings or those composed of fibers, which is mainly carpet. The IBC specifically excludes traditional flooring such as wood, vinyl, linoleum, terrazzo, and other resilient floor coverings that are not composed of fibers.

The IBC requires textile or fiber floor coverings to be one of two classes as defined by NFPA 253, the *Flooring Radiant Panel Test*. The NFPA 253 test measures the flame spread in a corridor or exitway that is under the influence of a fully developed fire in an adjacent space. Class I materials are more resistant to flame spread than Class II materials.

In Groups I-1, I-2, and I-3 occupancies (such as assisted living facilities, hospitals, nursing homes, and jails) the flooring finishes in exit enclosures (stairways), exit passageways, and corridors must be Class I in a nonsprinklered building and at least a Class II in a sprinklered building. Practically, because the IBC also requires all I occupancies to be sprinklered, either Class I or Class II is permissible. In other areas of Groups I-1, I-2, and I-3 occupancies, the flooring must be a Class II material.

For all other occupancy groups, the IBC requires that textile floor coverings be a Class II material in nonsprinklered buildings. In sprinklered buildings, textile flooring must meet the requirements of 16 CFR Part 1630, *Standard for the Surface Flammability of Carpets and Rugs*. This is also known as the *methenamine pill test* or simply the pill test. It is also referred to by other designations, DOC FF-1, *Standard Test Method for Flammability of Finished Textile Floor Covering Materials* and ASTM D2859, *Standard Test Method for Ignition Characteristics of Finished Textile Floor Covering Materials*. All carpet sold and manufactured in the United States must pass the pill test.

Because all carpet in the United States must pass the pill test and because nearly all manufacturers of resilient and hard-surface materials provide products that meet a Class I or II classification, specifying finish flooring is usually not a problem when detailing platforms, stairs, and ramps.

Fire Resistance of Structural Flooring Components

In addition to finishes, the IBC regulates the types of materials that can be used to construct raised platforms, stairs, and ramps. These are classified generally as combustible or noncombustible. Combustible materials include wood, while noncombustible materials include steel framing, concrete, and masonry.

For the purposes of fire and life safety, buildings are classified into one of five categories, Type I, II, III, IV, or V. The classification is based on the fire resistance of certain building components such as the structural frame, bearing walls, floor construction, and roof construction. Type I construction is the most fire resistive, and Type V is the least fire resistive. For example, the structural frame of a Type I building must have a 3-hour rating, while the frame in a Type III building must only have a 1-hour rating. In combination with occupancy groups, building type limits the area and height of buildings. Homes and small, one to three-story buildings are typical of Type V construction.

In Type I and Type II construction, any subfloor framing must be noncombustible or the space between the fire-resistant floor of the building and the platform, stair, or ramp must be solidly filled with noncombustible materials or fireblocked in accordance the IBC. Refer to the IBC for more information on construction types and detailed requirements.

Some jurisdictions may allow the use of fire-retardant-treated wood to build low platforms or stairs in Types I and II buildings. In all cases, the interior designer should verify the type of construction and the requirements of the local authority that has jurisdiction before detailing level changes and stairs and ramps.

There are special requirements for wood finish flooring in Type I and Type II buildings. Wood flooring may be attached directly to embedded or fireblocked wood sleepers or directly cemented to the top of the fire-resistant structural floor. Wood flooring can also be attached to wood framing if it meets the requirements described in the preceding paragraph. For Types III, IV, and V buildings, wood framing may be used for any type of floor.

Refer to Chapter 2 for more information on fire tests for finish materials and construction assemblies.

Slip Resistance and Tripping

Two common safety problems with ground surfaces are slipping and tripping. All surfaces should have slip resistance appropriate for the use. For example, the floor of a public lobby where snow and water are tracked in should be more slip resistant than a private office. As discussed in Chapter 2, slip resistance is commonly measured by the coefficient of friction (COF) and is a number ranging from 0 to 1. A COF of 0.5 is considered a minimum value for floors. For accessible routes a COF of 0.6 is recommended for level interior surfaces and 0.8 for ramps. Refer to Chapter 2 for more information.

Tripping on level surfaces generally occurs because of a slight change in level between two different materials or between the same materials installed, so the edges are not flush. When two materials abut, the designer should detail the joint so that the two surfaces are as flush as possible. ADA requirements for accessibility limit any change in level with a vertical surface to 1/4 in. (6.4 mm). A change in level of up to 1/2 in. (13 mm) may be 1/4 in. (6.4 mm) vertical and 1/4 in. (6.4 mm) beveled with a slope not steeper than 1:2 (13 mm); that is, 1/4 in. (6.4 mm) high and 1/2 in. (13 mm) horizontal. Further, ADA requirements limit the pile height of carpet to a maximum of 1/2 in. (13 mm) measured from the top of the carpet to the backing. Ideally, there should be no vertical changes in level from one material to another with all changes made with sloped or beveled surfaces or transition materials. See Fig. 11-9 for details of some transitions.

Accessibility

In addition to the accessibility requirements for floor surfaces stated above, the designer must also consider other accessibility issues when detailing ramps and stairs.

Ramps cannot slope more than 1 unit in height for every 12 units in length. Thus, a ramp rising 14 in. (356 mm) must be at least 14 ft. (4267 mm) long in horizontal projection. However, whenever possible ramps should be designed with a slope less than 1:12, both to make it easier for people to use and also to allow for any construction tolerances when the ramp is constructed.

Ramps must be at least 36 in. (915 mm) wide between handrails. Handrails must be provided on both sides of the ramp when the rise is greater than 6 in. (150 mm). Level landings are required at the top and bottom of each ramp run. The landing must be at least as wide as the width of the ramp for straight runs and at least 60 in. (1525 mm) square when the ramp turns 90 degrees or at least 60 in. (1525 mm) deep at a switchback. Other requirements for accessible ramps are shown in Fig. 8-4.

Code Requirements

Building codes regulate the type, number, and width of egress stairways as well as detailed requirements for treads, risers, and handrails. Most of these are part of the architecture of a building. However, for the types of stairs described in this chapter that consist of only a few

Figure 8-4 Accessible ramps

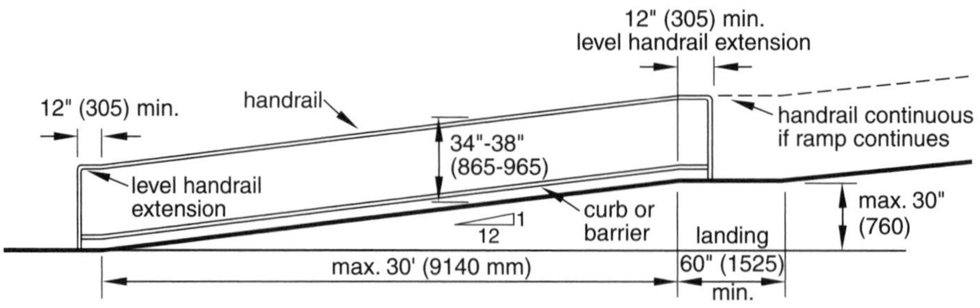

(a) schematic ramp elevation

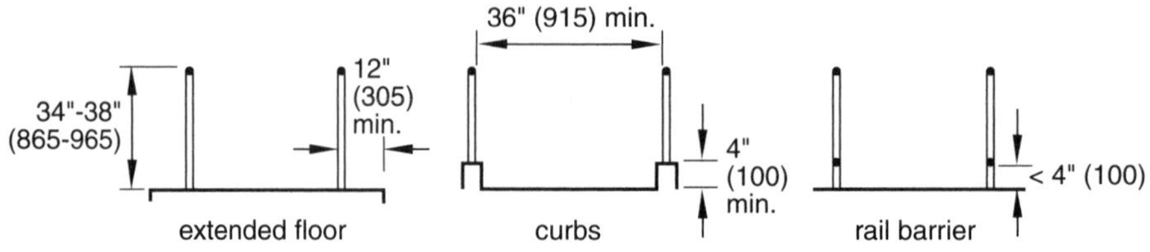

(b) edge protection options

risers and are often detailed by interior designers, the code requirements for step design and handrails still apply.

In most cases, the IBC requires handrails on both sides of stairs. The exceptions for interior use include the following:

- Aisle stairs in some situations
- Stairways in dwelling units
- Spiral stairways
- Single risers in Group R-3 occupancies
- Changes in room elevation of three or fewer risers within dwelling units and sleeping units in Group R-2 and R-3 occupancies (for example, apartments, dormitories, and nontransient hotels, and occupancies where the occupants are primarily permanent in nature not otherwise classified as R-1, R-2, or R-4)

However, even if handrails are not required, they should be provided for safety and convenience.

The basic requirements for stairways and handrails are shown in Fig. 8-5. The ends of handrails must return to a wall, guard, or the walking surface or be continuous to the handrail of an adjacent stair flight (or ramp run in the case of ramps). Refer to Chapter 3 for more guidelines on stair design.

On open stairways, the IBC requires that a separate guard or low wall, in addition to the handrail, be provided at 42 in. (1067 mm) above the height of the nosing. The guard must be solid or designed so that there are no openings that allow the passage of a sphere 4 in. (102 mm) in diameter. Refer to the IBC for exceptions to this requirement.

The issue of where handrails are required for monumental stairs (those not required for egress) can be confusing and sometimes contradictory. Of course, handrails should always be located on each side of any stairway. When the width of the stairway exceeds 60 in. (1524 mm), the IBC requires intermediate handrails such that all portions of the stairway width *required for egress capacity* are within 30 in. (762 mm) of a handrail. Thus, a wide stair that serves a small occupant load for egress purposes may not need intermediate handrails.

Figure 8-5 Stair requirements

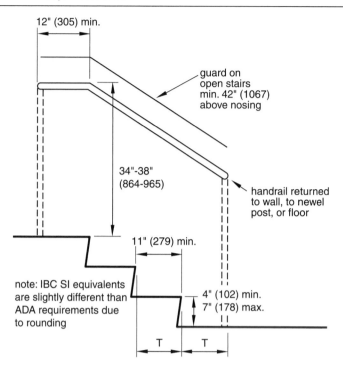

12" (305) min.

guard on
open stairs
min. 42" (1067)
above nosing

34"-38"
(864-965)

handrail returned
to wall, to newel
post, or floor

11" (279) min.

note: IBC SI equivalents
are slightly different than
ADA requirements due
to rounding

4" (102) min.
7" (178) max.

T   T

For example, assume that a wide monumental stair serves a raised platform on the first floor of a retail store and has handrails on both sides. Each handrail would be within 30 in. (762 mm) of egress width for a total of 60 in. (1524 mm). The IBC requires a minimum egress width for stairways of 0.3 in. (7.63 mm) per occupant served or,

$$\text{minimum width (in in.)} = \text{occupant load} \times 0.3 \text{ in.}$$

Knowing that 60 in. is available the maximum occupant load that can be served by these two handrails is,

$$60 \text{ in.} = \text{occupant load} \times 0.3 \text{ in./occupant}$$
$$\text{max. occupant load} = \frac{60 \text{ in.}}{0.3 \text{ in./occ.}}$$
$$\text{max. occupant load} = 200 \text{ occupants}$$

If the platform serves fewer than 200 occupants an intermediate handrail would not be required. For a mercantile occupancy on the first floor, the IBC states a maximum floor allowance per occupant of 30 sq. ft. In terms of a formula,

$$\text{occupant load} = \frac{\text{floorarea}}{30 \text{ sq. ft./occ.}}$$

If the maximum occupant load for the handrails is 200 then,

$$200 \text{ occupants} = \frac{\text{floorarea}}{30 \text{ sq. ft./occ.}}$$
$$\text{max. floor area} = 200 \times 30$$
$$\text{max. floor area} = 6000 \text{ sq. ft. } (557 \text{ m}^2).$$

Thus, the platform could be up to 6000 sq. ft. in area before intermediate handrails would be required. However, the IBC also requires that monumental stairs have handrails located along the most direct path of egress travel. The issue then would be whether the sides of the stairway are along the most direct path. This can be subject to interpretation. When the issue is questionable, the designer should consult with the authority having jurisdiction for the required location of intermediate handrails.

Handrails should be designed so that people can both grip them with maximum effect and hold them by friction when pulling up or descending. A circular shape with a diameter of 1-1/2 in. (38 mm) is generally the best, but other shapes are allowed. See Fig. 3-14 for the allowable limits on handrail profiles according to the IBC. The Type II handrail shown in Fig. 3-14(b) is allowed in private homes and in selective residential situations in commercial applications.

8-5   COORDINATION

Flooring design and detailing must be coordinated with flooring tolerances, light reflectance and acoustic requirements, durability needs, and desired circulation patterns. In addition, the design of the ground plane should be coordinated with the overhead plane and how the connections between the floor and the partitions are made. Refer to Chapters 7 and 10 for design ideas on overhead planes and how to make the floor-to-wall transition.

Tolerance Coordination

When carpet is used, the flatness tolerance of the subfloor is typically not a concern. However, when hard-surfaced finish flooring is specified, the subfloor on which it is placed must be within certain tolerances for a successful installation.

Some industry-standard tolerances for subflooring are given in Table 5-2. Table 8-1 lists some requirements for the installation of finish flooring. In many cases, existing subflooring may exceed the requirements for a successful installation and the interior designer will need

Table 8-1 Subfloor Tolerances Required for Finish Floors	
Finish Floor Material	**Required Subfloor Tolerance**
Wood flooring	
strip flooring and parquet flooring	wood subfloor: 1/4 in. in 10 ft. (6 mm in 3 m)
strip flooring and parquet flooring	concrete subfloor: 1/8 in. in 10 ft. (3 mm in 3 m)
cushioned flooring	concrete subfloor: 3/16 in. in 10 ft. (5 mm in 3 m)
laminated flooring	concrete subfloor: 1/8 in. in 10 ft. (3 mm in 3 m)
mastic cushioned	concrete subfloor: 1/4 in. in 10 ft. (6 mm in 3 m)
steel channel	concrete subfloor: 1/8 in. in 10 ft. (3 mm in 3 m)
Ceramic tile	
portland cement mortar bed	1/4 in. in 10 ft. (6 mm in 3 m)
dry-set or latex-portland cement mortar, thin set	1/4 in. in 10 ft. (6 mm in 3 m)
organic adhesive or epoxy adhesive	1/16 in. in 3 ft. (2 mm in 1 m) with no abrupt irregularities more than 1/32 in. (0.8 mm)
Stone flooring	
stone tile	wood subfloor: 1/16 in. in 3 ft. (1.6 mm in 900 mm)
stone tile on thin bed mortar	concrete subfloor: 1/8 in. in 10 ft. (3 mm in 3 m)
Terrazzo	concrete subfloor: 1/4 in. in 10 ft. (6 mm in 3 m)
Source: Handbook of Construction Tolerances, David Kent Ballast, John Wiley & Sons, Inc.	

to develop details or specifications to have the subflooring brought into compliance with finish flooring requirements. If this includes using a leveling compound, the finish surface may be raised higher than adjacent flooring. Grinding or patching existing subfloors will increase costs. In new construction, the interior designer may coordinate with the architect to create recessed areas for thick flooring material before the floor is constructed to minimize this problem.

Light Reflectance and Acoustic Coordination

For lighting design, the reflectance of the ground plane is generally the least important surface, coming after the ceiling and the walls. This allows the interior designer to specify nearly any color and texture for the floor finish without adversely affecting light quality.

The floor's sound absorption can significantly affect the overall acoustic quality of the space and should be selected with care. A hard-surface floor, such as wood or resilient tile, will both reflect sound and increase the sound transmission to the floor below, both of which may be undesirable. For example, the sound absorption average (SAA) (similar to the older NRC or noise reduction coefficient) of 1/2-in. pile carpet on padding is about 0.50, while the SAA of wood flooring is about 0.10. This means that carpet will absorb five times the sound of the wood flooring in certain frequency ranges. Likewise, footfalls on wood flooring can be easily transmitted to the floor below. If this is unacceptable, other detailing options (such as sound-deadening board) must be used to minimize the sound transmission, increasing cost and detailing complexity. Using carpet would be a simpler approach.

8-6   METHODS

Detailing flooring material on concrete or wood substrates is usually straightforward. The main detailing concerns for flooring other than carpet are accommodating the total thickness of the finish material, making transitions from one material to another, and allowing for tolerances and movement of the subfloor. If terrazzo or thick-set tile or stone is used the ability of the floor to carry the additional weight must be verified with a structural engineer.

Flooring

WOOD

For most commercial and residential applications either wood strip flooring or thin parquet or laminated flooring is used. Other types of wood flooring, such as plank, block, and resilient floor systems are not discussed in this chapter.

Wood strip flooring is installed over a suitable nailing base by blind nailing through the tongue of each strip of tongue-and-groove strip. Figure 8-6 shows the typical methods of detailing wood strip flooring over both wood and concrete floors. For wood structures, the subfloor should plywood, particleboard, or other suitable underlayment with a minimum thickness of 1/2 in. (13 mm). A layer of 15 lb. asphalt felt may be laid to prevent squeaking and act as a vapor barrier.

For concrete structures, either of the two methods shown in Fig. 8-6(b) and (c) may be used. Placing the floor on wood sleepers gives a more resilient floor and provides an air space

Figure 8-6 Wood strip flooring

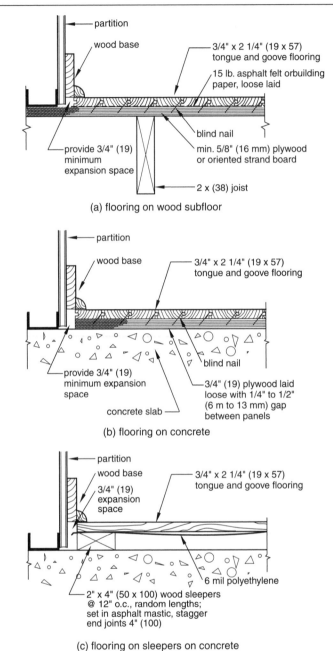

(a) flooring on wood subfloor

- partition
- wood base
- 3/4" x 2 1/4" (19 x 57) tongue and goove flooring
- 15 lb. asphalt felt or building paper, loose laid
- blind nail
- min. 5/8" (16 mm) plywood or oriented strand board
- provide 3/4" (19) minimum expansion space
- 2 x (38) joist

(b) flooring on concrete

- partition
- wood base
- 3/4" x 2 1/4" (19 x 57) tongue and goove flooring
- blind nail
- provide 3/4" (19) minimum expansion space
- concrete slab
- 3/4" (19) plywood laid loose with 1/4" to 1/2" (6 m to 13 mm) gap between panels

(c) flooring on sleepers on concrete

- partition
- wood base
- 3/4" (19) expansion space
- 3/4" x 2 1/4" (19 x 57) tongue and goove flooring
- 6 mil polyethylene
- 2" x 4" (50 x 100) wood sleepers @ 12" o.c., random lengths; set in asphalt mastic, stagger end joints 4" (100)

that allows excess moisture to escape. However, it requires more space and can be problematic when installing it next to a thinner floor. The method, using a 3/4 in. (19 mm) thick plywood or particleboard base, requires less total height but can still pose problems when abutted to much thinner flooring such as resilient tile. In all cases it is important to provide a minimum 3/4 in. (19 mm) expansion space at the perimeter of the room to allow for expansion and contraction of the flooring.

Parquet and laminated flooring can be glued or loose laid over wood or concrete subfloors, as shown in Fig. 8-7. However, when such flooring is placed on a concrete subfloor, especially a slab on grade, it is critical that moisture not be present and the slab be level to within 1/8 in. in 10 ft. (3 mm in 3 m).

Figure 8-7 Thin wood flooring

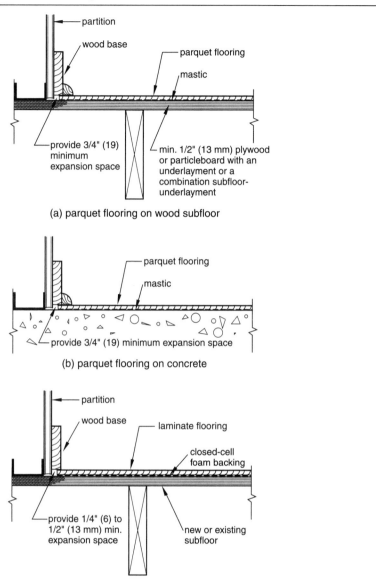

(a) parquet flooring on wood subfloor

(b) parquet flooring on concrete

(c) laminate flooring

CERAMIC TILE

Ceramic tile or quarry tile must be laid over a suitable substrate using one of several formulations of mortar, or with adhesive. The joints are filled with grout. Refer to *Ceramic Tile: The Installation Handbook* by the Tile Council of North America for a complete description of all the tile-setting methods. The two basic methods of detailing are the thin-set method and the full-mortar-bed method. Both of these are shown in Fig. 8-8.

With the thin-set method tile is laid on a suitable substrate, commonly a glass mesh mortar unit specifically manufactured for tile installation. This is a cementitious panel nailed to the subfloor. The tile is then laid on a thin coating of dry-set or latex-portland cement mortar. The subfloor must be rigid to prevent cracking.

When excessive deflection is expected (more than about 1/360 of the span) or on precast and post-tensioned concrete floors, a full-mortar-bed detail should be used. With this method,

Figure 8-8 Ceramic tile flooring

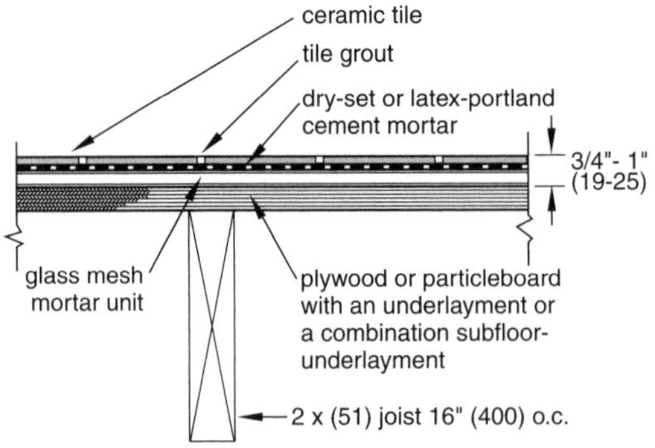

(a) tile on wood subfloor

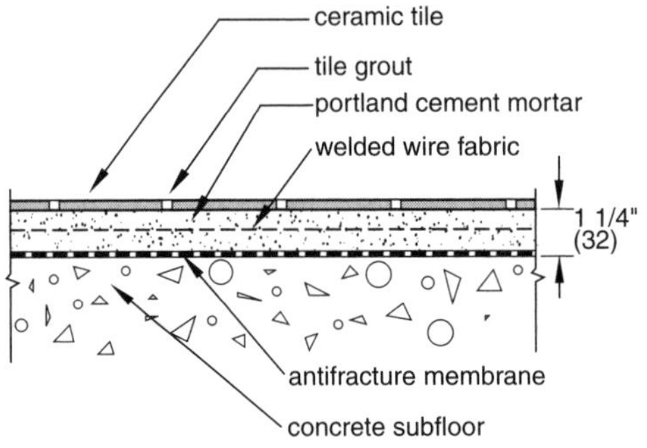

Labels: ceramic tile; tile grout; dry-set or latex-portland cement mortar; 3/4"- 1" (19-25); glass mesh mortar unit; plywood or particleboard with an underlayment or a combination subfloor-underlayment; 2 x (51) joist 16" (400) o.c.

(b) tile on full mortar bed over concrete

Labels: ceramic tile; tile grout; portland cement mortar; welded wire fabric; 1 1/4" (32); antifracture membrane; concrete subfloor

the tile and reinforced mortar bed are separated from the structural floor with an antifracture membrane to allow the two floor components to move independently. In addition to providing for movement, this system allows minor variations in the subfloor level to be corrected with the mortar. This is the preferred method (along with a waterproofing membrane) for tile floors in commercial showers or where continuous wetting will be present. Because of the overall thickness required, this is one finish flooring detail that should be placed on a subfloor depressed about 1-1/2 in. (38 mm), if possible.

With both the thin-set and full mortar bed methods of tile installation, it is important to provide for movement joints to prevent or control cracking. Movement joints (sometimes called expansion joints) are required for large expanses of tile and where the tile abuts restraining surfaces, such as at columns, walls, and pipes. They are also required where backing materials change and where dissimilar floors occur. They are not required in small rooms or corridors less than 12 ft. (3660 mm) wide. Figure 3-24 illustrates one type of tile movement joint, and Table 3-8 gives the recommended joint widths and spacing.

STONE

Like ceramic tile, stone flooring can be installed with either the thin-set method or the full-mortar-bed method. The full-mortar-bed method, while much heavier, is used when the subfloor is uneven, where excessive deflection or movement is expected, or when the stone varies in thickness, as with slate or sandstone. For most installations, current cutting and fabrication technology make it possible to use thin tiles of natural stone rather than the traditional 3/4 in. (19 mm) thick stone on a full mortar bed. However, for thin-set applications,

Figure 8-9 Stone flooring

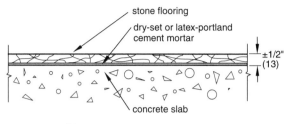

(a) thin set on concrete subfloor

stone flooring
dry-set or latex-portland cement mortar
±1/2" (13)
concrete slab

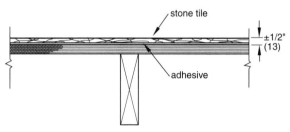

(b) thin set on wood frame subfloor

stone tile
±1/2" (13)
adhesive

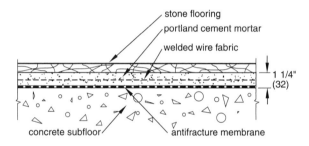

(c) full mortar bed on concrete subfloor

stone flooring
portland cement mortar
welded wire fabric
1 1/4" (32)
concrete subfloor
antifracture membrane

the floor must be level as given in Table 8-1 and not subject to deflection or movement more than about 1/720 of the span.

Figure 8-9 shows three methods of placing stone flooring on wood and concrete floors. With the thin-set method, a uniform thickness of stone is set on the subfloor with a special thin-set mortar or with an adhesive. The total thickness is about 1/2 in. (13 mm) depending on the thickness of the stone tile. The full-mortar bed method requires a layer of mortar from 3/4 in. to 1-1/4 in. (19 mm to 32 mm).

Stone floors can be set with the joints tightly butted together or with spaces between joints. If there is a gap in the joint, it must be filled with grout or a portland cement/sand mixture that can be color-coordinated with the stone. Several types of grout are available that are resistant to chemicals, fungi, and mildew. Latex grout is available and provides some flexibility when slight movement in the floor is expected.

TERRAZZO

Terrazzo is a composite material that consists of marble, quartz, granite, or other suitable stone chips in a matrix that is cementitious, modified cementitious, or resinous. It is typically poured in place but can also be precast. Terrazzo is generally not detailed and specified by interior designers as a finish material. Because of the additional weight and thickness required, it is usually part of the architecture of the building. It is also messy to install and requires time

Figure 8-10 Terrazzo flooring

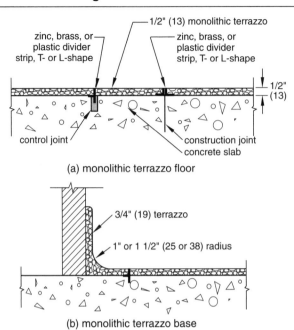

(a) monolithic terrazzo floor

(b) monolithic terrazzo base

for pouring, curing, and grinding to complete the process. However, terrazzo can be precast to avoid much of the on-site work required of standard installations. Terrazzo does provide a very durable floor and the colors and styles of the mixture can be varied between areas enclosed by the divider strips. It is also possible to design very ornate patterns using curved divider strips and different color stone matrices.

There are various types of terrazzo installation methods, including the sand cushion, bonded, monolithic, and thin-set methods. The sand cushion and bonded methods are very heavy and require total installation thicknesses up to 2-1/2 in. (64 mm) thick. These are usually designed as part of the original architecture of a building.

Monolithic terrazzo installations are applied directly to a concrete subfloor, as shown in Fig. 8-10. Terrazzo bases can be poured at the same time and provide a cove base, as shown in Fig. 8-10(b). This type of terrazzo installation is about 1/2 in. (13 mm) thick and weighs about 7 lb. per ft^2 (3.4 kg/m^2). The subfloor must be structurally capable of supporting the extra weight without excessive deflection. Divider strips must be placed to provide areas of approximately 200 ft^2 to 300 ft^2 (19 m^2 to 28 m^2) in rectangular areas. The area of each area should not be more than 50% longer than the width. Joint location should be coordinated with building joints.

Thin-set terrazzo is similar to monolithic but only requires from 1/4 in to 3/8 in. (6 mm to 10 mm) thickness and weighs about 3 lb. per ft^2 (1.5 kg/m^2). Thin-set terrazzo must use epoxy, polyester, or polyacrylate matrices with special types of divider strips.

TRANSITIONS

Whenever one flooring material abuts another on the same level, there must be some type of transition to prevent damage to the edges and to hold them secure. This is true whether they are the same type of material or different materials. As discussed in Chapter 11 and shown in Fig. 11-8 there are three basic ways of making floor transitions: by simply abutting the

Figure 8-11 Flooring transition strips

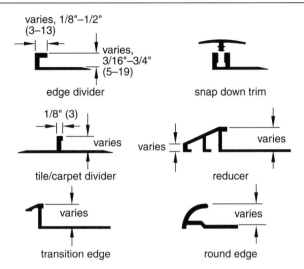

two materials, by placing a protective edge between them, and by using a third material as a transition strip.

Abutting two materials without an intermediate material usually only works when the two materials are the same type and are relatively hard. For example, two different types of stone flooring can be successfully abutted with a simple grout joint as long as the finish surfaces are flush. Stone can be placed next to ceramic tile with the same conditions. Conversely, the seam of two different types and pile heights of carpet is susceptible to damage unless a transition strip is placed over it.

Some type of protective edge is usually required when two materials abut. This can be as simple as a metal angle or a manufactured transition strip designed for specific types of flooring. Figure 11-9(a) shows the application of a protective edge angle. Refer to Tables 2-10 and 2-11 for common sizes of stainless steel and brass shapes that can be used to protect the edge of wood or stone flooring.

There are many types of manufactured wood, plastic, and metal transition strips made for various materials and material thicknesses. Figure 8-11 shows some common transition strips. Refer to Table 8-2 for a listing of some of the manufacturers of transition strips. Most resilient and wood flooring manufacturers supply their own line of transition strips.

The designer can also detail custom transition strips and make them a design feature between two flooring materials. These types of strips can be beveled to accommodate the thicknesses of the flooring and made any convenient width. See Fig. 11-9(b) and (c) for two different types of floor transition details using a separate transition strip. The details show a beveled stone strip but hardwood transition strips can also be used.

Handrails, Guards, and Stairways

As discussed in a previous section of this chapter, handrails are required on both sides of all stairways used for egress and on monumental stairs if they are used for egress. They should also be provided wherever needed for safety. Figure 8-5 shows the basic requirements for handrail design. In addition, the handrail design on an open stair as well as guards cannot allow the passage of a 4 in. (102 mm) sphere. Guards are only required if the change in elevation exceeds 30 in. (762 mm), but they should be used in all situations for safety.

Table 8-2 Transition Strip Manufacturers

Manufacturer	Web Site	Comments
Ceramic Tool Company	www.ceramictool.com	Edge, joint, bar, and carpet trim, and ramp transitions
Genotek	www.genotek.com	Wide variety of carpet trims, reducers, edge dividers, thresholds, movement joints, and transition edges, including adjustable transitions
Johnsonite	www.johnsonite.com	Transitions in a wide variety of colors for various thicknesses and material types, including reducers, edge guards, T molding, adaptors, wheeled traffic transitions, and expansion joint seals as well as stair treads and nosing strips
National Metal Shapes	www.nationalmetalshapes.com	Variety of trim shapes and styles in metal and vinyl for all flooring materials
Schluter Systems	www.schluter.com	Provides a wide variety of products for different materials and material thicknesses

Manufacturers of resilient flooring and wood flooring that also provide trim accessories are not listed.

When a change in level occurs the transition can be made in a number of ways as discussed in Chapter 11 and diagrammed in Fig. 11-10. The interior designer can detail custom railings and guards from wood, metal, or some combination of materials. However, in most cases, standard manufactured railing systems are used. These are available in a variety of styles and materials and are custom modified by the supplier to fit the exact requirements of the project. Table 8-3 lists some of the many manufacturers of railing systems while Table 5-6 lists manufacturers of cable rail systems.

Table 8-3 Interior Railing Manufacturers

Manufacturer	Web Site	Comments
American Railing Systems	www.americanrailing.com	Aluminum and stainless steel with standard selection of picket or glass infill
ATR Technologies, Inc.	www.ATR-Technologies.com	Aluminum tube railings with picket or glass infill; custom designs offered
Big D Metalworks	www.bigdmetal.com	Stainless steel and wood systems with glass and perforated metal infill panels
Blumcraft	www.blumcraft.com	Glass rail systems with metal and wood caps. including lighted rail systems and wall mounted handrails
Construction Services, Inc.	www.csialabama.com	Custom railing and handrail systems in a variety of materials and styles
C.R. Laurence Company	www.crlaurence.com	Glass railing systems
Hollaender Manufacturing	www.hollaender.com	Tube railing systems with pickets, wire mesh, and perforated metal infill
Livers Bronze Co.	www.liversbronze.com	Variety of railing systems with metal and wood with glass, picket, and rail infill; contemporary and traditional
Newman Brothers, Inc.	www.newmanbrothers.com	Metal and wood railing systems with glass infill
P&P Artec	www.artec-rail.com	Stainless steel railings with picket or glass infill
RamiDesigns	www.RamiDesigns.com	Stainless steel railing systems with picket, rail, and glass infill
The Wagner Companies	www.wagnercompanies.com	Variety of contemporary and traditional styles in all materials

Guards can be designed with wood or metal top rails and with infills of glass, pickets, horizontal rails, mesh, perforated metal, or solid panels. All-glass railings may be used with a top rail or without a rail for an open appearance while providing for safety. See Fig. 11-11 for one type of glass guard detail. This detail can also be used for stairways with the addition of a handrail.

Stairs must be provided for raised platforms more than 7 in. (178 mm) high. For most interior design work in spaces with low ceilings platform height is limited, requiring only two or three steps. These are easily constructed of wood or metal framing. Refer to Chapter 3 for guidelines on stair design.

CHAPTER 9

SPATIAL CONNECTION— OPENINGS, DOORS, AND GLAZING

9-1 INTRODUCTION

Like partitions and ceilings, the way two spaces are connected is a fundamental component of interior design and architecture. This spatial connection can be made with clear openings in the barrier between the two spaces and with doors and glazing. Both barriers and the openings in them are important for their own reasons; barriers separate and openings reconnect.

The way this connection is made is important for two reasons. Of course, the connection must allow the passage of people, goods, vision, and light while providing for physical separation needed for privacy, fire separation, acoustics, and security. On a more fundamental level, the connection either makes the separation complete or it unifies the various spaces and celebrates the passage between one and another. Openings make otherwise disconnected rooms and spaces into a complete design composition.

Unfortunately, in contemporary construction openings have been mostly reduced to functional necessities. Openings are often just punched holes. Doors are simply used to let people and goods get from one room to another while providing the fundamental requirements of fire separation, security, and privacy. Only in some instances, such as residential front doors and store entrances, do designers utilize the full design potential of door openings as a creative design element. Likewise, glazing is often not used to its full potential, simply being a way to provide basic views and admit daylight.

While a simple approach to providing openings in much of interior construction is often justified based on function and cost, the interior designer should recognize the value of the design of openings to contribute to the overall design intent of the project. Passage, views, and light are all important aspects of the human experience of space. This expanded vision of opening design can be realized while satisfying functional needs and specific constraints.

This chapter discusses some ideas the interior designer can use to develop design concepts for clear openings as well as door and glazed openings and gives some guidelines to begin detailing. Refer to Chapter 5 for other ideas on vertical barriers that allow some degree of opening between spaces.

9-2 ELEMENT CONCEPTS

Viewed individually, all types of openings can be designed in hundreds, if not thousands, of ways. When combined, as they often are, the number of possibilities increases significantly. For openings, the basic components are size, shape, and trim. For both door and glazed openings, the basic components are the material and opening configuration, the frame, and their relationship with the surrounding construction.

Openings

Openings are clear areas within an otherwise solid barrier. They may extend to the floor to allow people to walk through or they may be above floor level to allow vision, sound penetration, light, or the transfer of objects. They are sized to meet the requirements of the project and may be configured in hundreds of different ways with a variety of trim styles. Opening design is limited only by the designer's imagination. Figure 9-1 shows just a few of the possibilities.

Openings can frame views, direct movement, and modulate the connection between two spaces. They can be used singly or grouped. Openings can be placed in pairs, creating a vestibule or intermediary space to serve as a transition from one type of space to another that can heighten the experience of passage.

Doors

The interior designer can meet functional requirements and make a strong spatial connection with doors through their size, material, hardware, method of operation, and relationship to the surrounding partition, as well with the doorframe's configuration, material, size, and finish. Doors can also direct movement, control views, and maintain privacy when partially open by their placement and direction of swing.

Figure 9-1 Openings

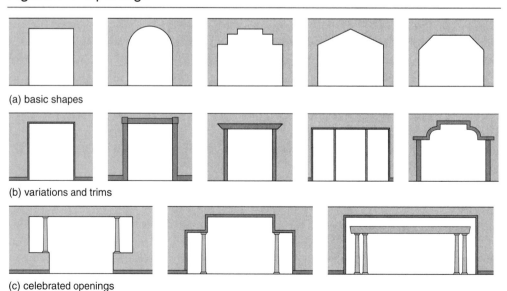

(a) basic shapes

(b) variations and trims

(c) celebrated openings

One of the simplest ways to give a door and entrance emphasis is with door size and a material. Most door types can be made larger than a standard 3-ft (900 mm) width and a 7-ft or 8-ft height 2100 mm or 2440 mm). This can usually be done without a significant increase in cost. The designer can vary the material by using a different base material or simply a different veneer. For example, any number of distinctive laminates can be specified instead of a standard wood veneer finish. Alternately, a stainless steel or bronze door can be used instead of a simple painted hollow metal door. Which approach is used depends on the effect desired and limitations on cost and code requirements. However, even with the constraints of egress requirements and budget restrictions, the interior designer can use size and material options to create distinctive openings.

As with door material, available hardware offers the designer a wide choice of effects. The type, shape, and finish of handles, locksets, hinges and other hardware can be varied in hundreds of ways. For example, brightly finished, surface mounted hardware can emphasize the traditional connection of movable door attached to fixed construction. Conversely, using door pivots and concealing closers instead of hinges and surface-mounted closers can deemphasize the hardware, if that is the desired effect.

In addition to size, material, and hardware, the way a door operates creates a particular type of experience of entrance and passage. Figure 9-2 illustrates some of the many ways doors can be configured based on their method of operation. For example, a pair of doors pivoted at the midpoints of the doors, as shown in Fig. 9-2(h), creates a unique entry, entirely different from a simple side-swinging door. Of course, code-mandated egress requirements and ease of use may preclude using some of them in certain circumstances.

The design of the surrounding construction can affect the overall impression of the entry as much as the door opening itself. The method by which a door is placed within a partition can greatly affect the sense of entrance and passage, including those design elements and principles of form, scale, balance, harmony, focus, contrast, variety, and proportion. Figure 9-3 diagrams some of the many ways a door can be configured in relationship to the partitions,

Figure 9-2 Types of door operation

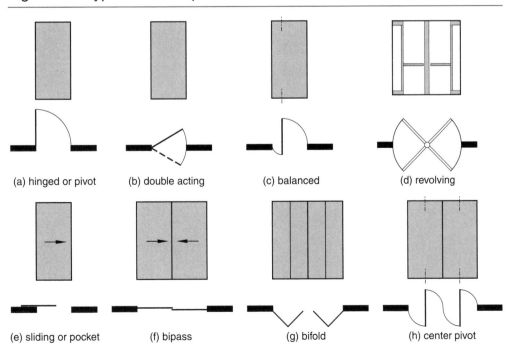

(a) hinged or pivot   (b) double acting   (c) balanced   (d) revolving

(e) sliding or pocket   (f) bipass   (g) bifold   (h) center pivot

Figure 9-3 Doors with surrounding construction

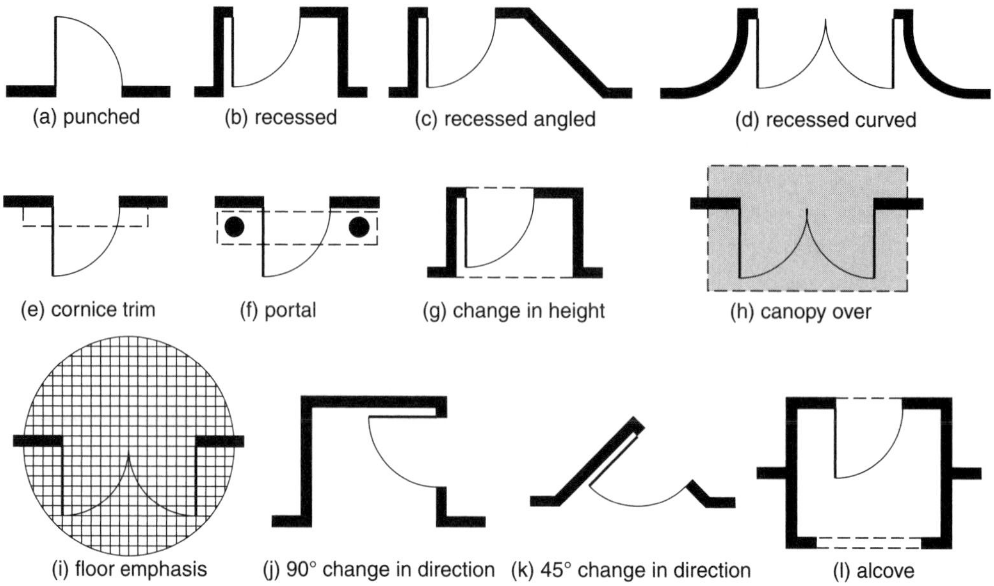

(a) punched	(b) recessed	(c) recessed angled	(d) recessed curved

(e) cornice trim	(f) portal	(g) change in height	(h) canopy over

(i) floor emphasis	(j) 90° change in direction	(k) 45° change in direction	(l) alcove

floor, and ceiling. Most of the options shown can be constructed without a significant increase in cost or without compromising function, code requirements, or accessibility. In some cases, such as a recessed doorway, the placement of the door even helps satisfy other needs, such as preventing swing into the required path of egress travel.

A simple punched opening, diagrammed in Fig. 9-3(a), in a partition depends on the door and frame alone to provide any design emphasis. Recessed openings, shown in Figs. 9-3(b)–(d) create a separate area for the doors, while addressing the problem of door swing into a path of travel. Recesses can be made any width or depth and can be combined with glazing to develop an entrance with varying degrees of transparency as required by the design intent of the project. Recesses must provide for maneuvering clearances as required for accessibility.

Doors can also be coordinated with overhead construction, whether that is a simple piece of cornice trim or a separate canopy below the height of the adjacent ceilings. See Figs. 9-3(e)–(h). Floor finishes can also be designed with door openings to emphasize the transition from one space into another as long as the transition is detailed to avoid any tripping hazard or accessibility problem. See Fig. 9-3(i). Doorways also provide an appropriate place to make a change in direction of movement, as shown in Figs. 9-3(j) and (k), or to mark a transition space between two different spaces, as shown in Fig. 9-3(l).

Lastly, the interior designer can use frames to create a design feature of doors as well as to solve practical problems of connection to the adjacent partition, protection, and finish. Frames can vary in their size, material, finish, and color. They can be complementary with the door or contrast with it. Frames can be underplayed or emphasized. Some of the many approaches to frames are diagrammed in Fig. 9-4. Some of these concepts can also be used to frame clear openings.

Glazing

Glazed openings provide the interior designer with a multitude of design options to modulate the visual connection between two spaces. Glazing can be used to affect the sense of enclosure, direct views, and allow daylight deep into buildings while satisfying functional requirements

Figure 9-4 Frame concepts

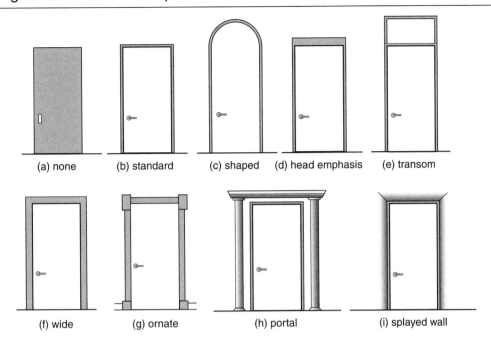

(a) none	(b) standard	(c) shaped	(d) head emphasis	(e) transom

(f) wide	(g) ornate	(h) portal	(i) splayed wall

of security, acoustic control, and fire separation. Glazing can even become a design feature in itself with the use of art or etched glass, or any of the many new glazing products available. While Chapter 5 discusses the use of glazing for entire translucent barriers, this section focuses on the use of glazing for smaller openings within a partition.

As with doors, the interior designer can use glazing material, shape, placement, framing, and the relationship of the glazing to the surrounding construction to make the desired connection between two spaces. Table 9-1 lists many of the types of glazing available. Refer to Table 5-5 for a listing of some of the many specialty glazing material manufacturers.

Figure 9-5 illustrates some of the many window opening shape and placement concepts the designer can employ. Some can be used for both views and daylight penetration, while some, such as a high or low strip of glass, can allow some daylight penetration while maintaining privacy. Frames can be configured the same way as described in the previous section and shown in Fig. 9-4.

Because glazing is also commonly used both in doors and adjacent to doors, the interior designer can combine solid partitions, doors, and glazing in a nearly unlimited number of ways to develop the precise type of connection required for any programmatic need. Figure 9-6 shows some of the basic conceptual ways to use glass in and adjacent to doors.

Window Covering

In many cases, the transparency of an interior glazed opening must be adjustable to meet the need for privacy or adjustment of light transmission, either to control glare or to temporarily darken a room. This can be done with a variety of window coverings, including vertical blinds, horizontal blinds, shades, draperies, solid sliding covers, and electrochromic glazing. These coverings may be side closing, top closing, or bottom closing. Some, such as solid sliding covers, offer only two states, open or opaque, while others, such as vertical blinds can provide a range of closure and translucency or be completely pulled out of the opening. Window coverings

Table 9-1   Glass Types

Type	Description
Float	Most common type of glass available in thicknesses from 1/8 in. to 3/4 in. (3 to 19 mm).
Tempered	Float glass that has been heat treated. About four times stronger than float glass and it qualifies as safety glazing.
Laminated	Two or more layers of glass bonded with plastic interlayer. Used for safety glazing, security glazing, and for acoustic control.
Wired	Mesh of wire embedded in 1/4 in. (6 mm) thick glass used for 3/4-hr. fire protection rated glazing.
Fire-rated	Broad term to include several types that qualify as fire-resistance-rated glazing. See text.
Electrochromic	General term for glazing that changes translucency when electric current is applied, changing from clear to either dark tint or opaque milky white.
Mirrored	Reflective glazing available on float or tempered glass. Also includes one-way glass.
Tinted	Float glass modified with various colorants for solar shading and privacy.
Patterned	Float glass given a surface texture by passing molten glass through rollers.
Beveled	Glass with a beveled edge that is commonly flat but can also be made in multiple bevels or curves. Beveled portion may be smooth or etched.
Etched	Also called carved glass, etched glass is given a pattern or image by removing some of the glass with sandblasting or acid. Can be used on float, tempered (before tempering), and laminated glass.
Stained	Classic type of decorative glass using colored pieces of glass.
Cathedral	Similar to patterned but transparent with one side smooth.
Opalescent	Machine formed with one or more colors to produce translucent, marbleized appearance.
Painted	Vitreous paints applied to clear class and fired to fuse paint to the glass.
Dichroic	Thin layers of metal oxides applied to glass in a special process to act as selective color mirror to reflect different colors depending on angle viewed.
Cast	Molten glass poured into a mold to produce three-dimensional product.
Kiln-formed	Sheet glass heated to slump into a mold to produce sculptural relief. Larger panels are possible than with cast glass.
Bent	Float or tempered glass formed into curved shapes.
Low-iron	Glass with low-iron content for clarity and to avoid greenish cast for showroom windows, display cabinets, control rooms and similar uses.
Antireflective	Low-reflective coating applied to float glass to produce glass that does not reflect light and obstruct vision as much as standard glass.
X-ray protective	Glass with large lead content for medical and radiology facilities.

Figure 9-5 Types of glazed openings

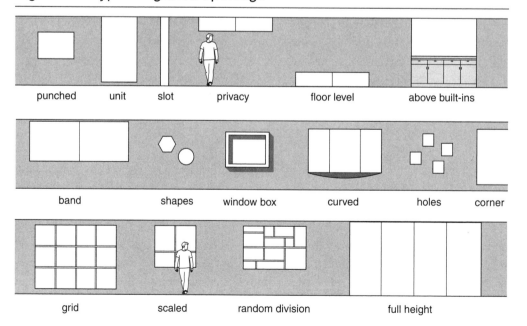

punched   unit   slot   privacy   floor level   above built-ins

band   shapes   window box   curved   holes   corner

grid   scaled   random division   full height

Figure 9-6 Door relationship to glazing

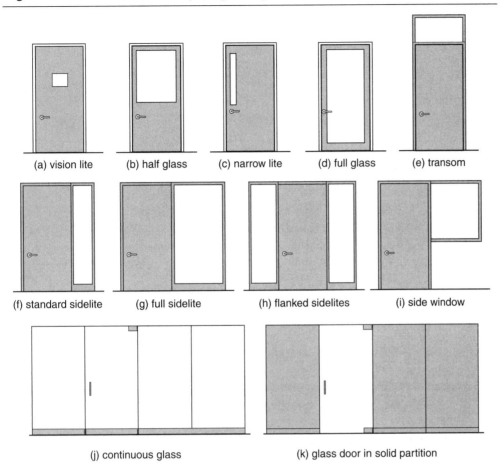

| (a) vision lite | (b) half glass | (c) narrow lite | (d) full glass | (e) transom |

| (f) standard sidelite | (g) full sidelite | (h) flanked sidelites | (i) side window |

| (j) continuous glass | (k) glass door in solid partition |

can be surface mounted so that they are visible when open or the construction surrounding the glazing may be detailed to provide pockets to conceal the coverings. Methods of window covering are discussed in more detail later in this chapter.

9-3 FUNCTION

Because openings serve many purposes, which can sometimes conflict with each other, the interior designer should have a clear understanding of what functions an opening must satisfy. Clear openings, doors, and glazed openings generally provide one or more of the following functions:

    Connecting two spaces while defining each

    Framing views

    Directing movement

    Controlling physical passage

    Providing variable visual privacy

    Controlling sound transmission

Providing security

Providing fire and smoke resistance

Providing for the control of light

Allowing for the use of daylighting

Providing radiation shielding

Providing for the passage of goods

Allowing views to the outside

Serving as a design feature

Only by understanding the specific functions an opening must perform can the designer select the best combination of opening type, size, configuration, material, frame, and connection to the surrounding construction and develop appropriate details.

To the extent possible, door and glazed openings and the materials used to create them should contribute to the overall sustainability of the design. Refer to the sidebar for suggestions on how sustainability issues can be addressed through the design and detailing of openings.

Sustainability Issues Related to Openings

Sustainability issues related to openings include the following:

- Specify doors, trim, glazing materials, and frames that use as much recycled content as possible.
- Specify and detail door openings such that the frame and door can be relocated or reused.
- Use glazing as much as practical to maximize daylight and views to the outside. This includes line of sight between 30 in. (762 mm) and 90 in. (2286 mm) above the floor and a direct line of sight from a point 42 in. (1067 mm) above the floor to perimeter vision glazing.
- Consider using regional materials to the maximum extent possible.
- Select window coverings for exterior windows to minimize heat gain, while allowing daylight and views. Consider the type of window glass used in a building constructed within the last five to ten years may have glazing that has the required properties. Consider using automated window shade control based on daylight conditions.
- Specify window coverings with recycled content and that do not adversely affect indoor air quality.

9-4 CONSTRAINTS

For clear opening connections between two spaces there are very few constraints limiting how the interior designer creates the connection. The existing ceiling height may be the only factor limiting the overall configuration and scale. Because interior opening are non-load-bearing, there usually is no limitation on the width of the opening; most can be detailed with metal or wood stud framing to span the opening. When wide openings are present, standard metal or wood headers can be used or that portion over the opening can be suspended from the structure above. When additional loads are present, framing can be reinforced with structural steel supports as required by the detail.

For doors, constraints most often include the levelness of the floor, cost, and the code requirements for egress and fire resistance. Accessibility requirements dictate minimum clear opening width, hardware types, opening force, and limits on threshold height, as well as maneuvering space adjacent to the door.

For glazed openings, constraints include code-mandated fire resistance (if any), acoustic requirements, and potential building movement when very large sections of glazing are used. Fortunately, fire-resistive-rated glazing is available for nearly all situations, in both doors and interior windows. Acoustic requirements can be addressed through the use of laminated glass and spaced glazing. These are discussed in the later section in this chapter on methods.

9-5 COORDINATION

For clear openings, there is little coordination required with other buildings elements or details. The designer should consider the size, shape, and height of openings relative to the desired amount of connection or separation between two spaces. Further, the designer should consider the position of the opening relative to furniture placement, views, and the number of people moving through the opening or the size of objects being moved through the opening.

Door opening design must be coordinated with the type of partition in which the door is located; different partition types and thicknesses may require different types of frames and frame anchorages. Door swings must be coordinated with sight lines, furniture location, and the required direction of travel as well as the clear space required to remain unobstructed in an egress path. Provide sufficient maneuvering space at the strike side of a door for accessibility. Generally, 12 in. (305 mm) is required on the push side of a door and a minimum of 18 in. (455 mm) is required on the pull side. Door locations should be positioned in a room to maintain good circulation and provide room for furniture placement.

Glazing must be coordinated with the amount and direction of views needed, both between adjacent spaces and with views to the outside. This also relates to the amount of glazing required to maximize daylighting. Lighting must also be placed relative to glass to avoid unwanted reflections. Detail coordination includes provisions for window covering pockets, allowances for building movement, and safety glazing requirements.

9-6 METHODS

There are innumerable ways to detail clear openings, doors, and glazed openings shown conceptually in Figs. 9-1 through 9-6. Some of the possible ways to develop openings in barriers were discussed in Chapter 5 and shown in Fig. 5-10. Standard frame details can be used to develop many of these. This section provides some starting points for developing opening details.

Doors

Most doors can be detailed with one of the three standard frame materials, shown in Fig. 9-7(a), (b), and (c), or with a minor modification of one of these. For example, Fig. 9-7(d) shows a wood framed door without a casing trim. Single- or double-rabbeted steel frames are available

Figure 9-7 Types of Doorframes

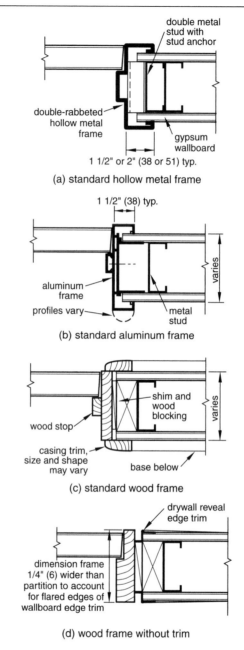

double metal stud with stud anchor

double-rabbeted hollow metal frame

gypsum wallboard

1 1/2" or 2" (38 or 51) typ.

(a) standard hollow metal frame

1 1/2" (38) typ.

varies

aluminum frame

profiles vary

metal stud

(b) standard aluminum frame

varies

shim and wood blocking

wood stop

casing trim, size and shape may vary

base below

(c) standard wood frame

drywall reveal edge trim

dimension frame 1/4" (6) wider than partition to account for flared edges of wallboard edge trim

(d) wood frame without trim

in a number of depths and face configurations. Aluminum frames are available in a number of shapes, sizes, and finishes. Wood frames can be modified by varying the size and shape of the casing trim and by varying the size and configuration of the stop.

However, when custom wood frames are detailed the designer should use industry-standard dimensions for the placement of hinges and positioning of the door within the frame. These are shown in Fig. 9-8. Maintaining standard dimensions simplifies detailing and minimizes the cost and difficulty of building the detail.

When fire-rated doors are required the necessary fire rating of the door depends on the use and the fire rating of the partition in which the door is located. Part of Table 9-3 summarizes these requirements. For example, in a 1-hour-rated corridor partition in a nonsprinklered

Figure 9-8 Standard doorframe and hinge settings

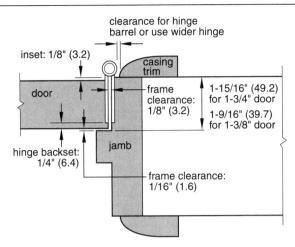

building, a 20-minute-rated door is necessary, while in a 1-hour- rated occupancy separation partition, a 3/4-hour-rated door is required.

Glazed Openings

STANDARD GLAZED OPENINGS

Standard glazed openings using float, tempered, laminated, or nearly any type of decorative glass can be set in standard wood or metal frames, as shown in Fig. 9-9. These standard frames can be modified in many ways to create details consistent with the design intent and specific needs of the project. When detailing glazed openings, certain dimensions should be maintained to hold the glass in place. These are shown in Fig. 2-4 and given in Table 2-7.

Hollow metal frames can be single or double rabbeted with face frames from 1 in. (25 mm) wide, although 2 in. (52 mm) is standard. Custom hollow metal frames can be ordered within the limitations of the presses used to form the frames. Aluminum frames can also be ordered in a wide variety of sizes, profiles, and finishes.

If the design intent is to minimize the appearance of the glazed opening, the designer can use frameless glazing, which makes the glass seems to float within the opening. The details can be configured to make the finish materials appear to continue uninterrupted from one side of the glass to the other. Figure 9-10(a) shows one method of detailing the sill and head of a full-height piece of glass. This detail shows the necessary glass framing recessed completely into the structure. Jamb framing can be completely eliminated with the edge of the glass held away from the wall a fraction of an inch as shown in Fig. 9-10(b). The gap can be left open or sealed with silicone sealant. If more than one panel of glass is required, the edges are butted together, and the joint either left open or filled with silicone sealant if sound control is required. Silicone sealant can be either clear or black, but clear sealant can show bubbles and may be more visually objectionable than black. The recommended joint width based on glass thickness is given in Table 2-9.

The thickness of the glass used depends on the size of the opening and the rigidity required. Interior glazed partitions must meet seismic requirements of 10 psf (0.48 kPa). The IBC also requires that when two adjacent panels of glass are unsupported (butt jointed with no sealant) the differential deflection cannot be greater than the thickness of the glass when a force of 50 lb per ft (730 N/m) is applied horizontally to one panel 42 in. (1067 mm) above

Figure 9-9 Types of glass frames

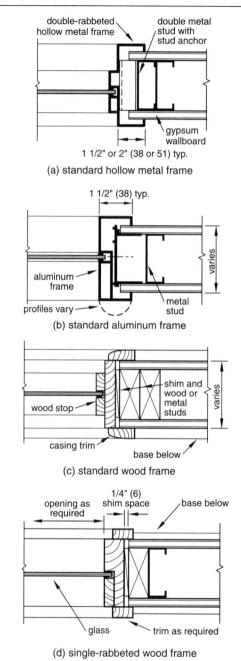

double-rabbeted hollow metal frame

double metal stud with stud anchor

gypsum wallboard

1 1/2" or 2" (38 or 51) typ.

(a) standard hollow metal frame

1 1/2" (38) typ.

aluminum frame

profiles vary

metal stud

varies

(b) standard aluminum frame

wood stop

shim and wood or metal studs

varies

casing trim

base below

(c) standard wood frame

opening as required

1/4" (6) shim space

base below

glass

trim as required

(d) single-rabbeted wood frame

the walking surface. Table 9-2 gives the recommended glass thicknesses based on the two conditions of full-height glass panels that have open or sealed joints. Glass thickness should be verified with the glass installer and local codes.

When full-glass doors are used with frameless glazing, the door can extend to the ceiling. The door may have a continuous bottom fitting to hold the pivot and lock as shown in Fig. 9-6(j) or simply have a fitting at one corner to hold the pivot, as shown in Fig. 9-6(k). Details must accommodate the floor pivot or floor closer and anchorage for the top pivot and a door stop. One way of doing this is shown in Fig. 9-11. If the concrete floor is not thick enough to accommodate a floor closer, overhead closers can be used, but they are more difficult to anchor.

Figure 9-10 Frameless glazed opening

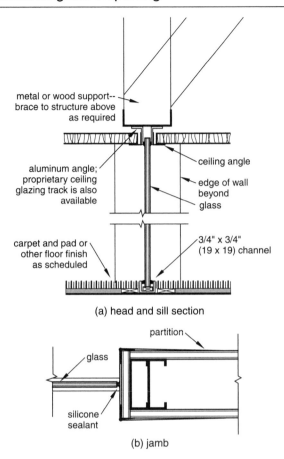

(a) head and sill section

(b) jamb

FIRE-RATED GLAZED OPENINGS

When the building code allows the use of glazing in a fire-rated partition, the glazing (in conjunction with the frame as a total assembly) must also have a fire rating, which is confirmed by standard fire tests of the glazed assembly. The required fire rating of the glazed assembly depends on the use and fire rating of the partition in which the glazing is located. Table 9-3 summarizes these requirements for window glazing as well as glazing in doors. The maximum

| | Top and Bottom Support Only | |
Panel Height	Single Panel or Attached Adjacent Panels, in. (mm)	To Meet Deflection Requirements When Adjacent Panels Have Open Joints, in. (mm)
Up to 5 ft. (1.5 m)	1/4 (6)	1/2 (12)
Over 5 ft. up to 8 ft. (over 1.5 m to 2.4 m)	3/8 (10)	5/8 (16)
Over 8 ft. up to 10 ft. (over 2.4 m up to 3 m)	1/2 (12)	5/8 (16)
Over 10 ft. up to 12 ft. (over 3 m up to 3.6 m)	5/8 (16)	3/4 (19)
Over 12 ft. up to 14 ft. (over 3.6 m up to 4.2 m)	3/4 (19)	7/8 (22)

Table 9-2   Minimum Interior Glass Thicknesses

Source: Glass Association of North American

Figure 9-11 All glass interior entrance door

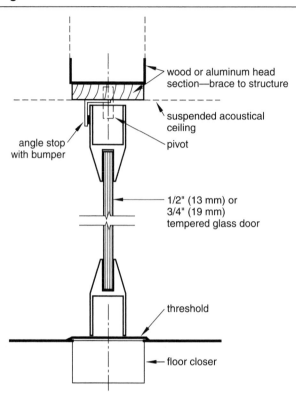

wood or aluminum head section—brace to structure

suspended acoustical ceiling

angle stop with bumper

pivot

1/2" (13 mm) or 3/4" (19 mm) tempered glass door

threshold

floor closer

glazed sizes given in this table are for wired glass. Fire-resistance-rated glazing may be used in larger sizes, which vary with each manufacturer.

Historically, wired glass was the only type of glazing that was acceptable for use in fire-rated doors and for windows in fire-rated partitions. Wired glass has traditionally had a 45-minute rating and was allowed in hazardous locations, such as a door or a sidelite next to a door, even though it is not considered safety glazing. New developments in glazing products now make it possible to replace traditional wired glass with other products that meet both fire rating and safety glazing requirements. These new products also have fire-resistance ratings greater than 45 minutes.

The IBC now does not allow the use of wired glass in hazardous locations as described in the next section of this chapter. The IBC does allow the use of two types of glazing that can be used in fire-resistance-rated partitions: fire-protection-rated glazing and fire-resistance-rated glazing.

Fire-protection-rated glazing is 1/4 in. (6 mm) thick wired glass in steel frames, or other types of glazing that meet the requirements of NFPA 252, *Standard Methods for Fire Tests of Door Assemblies,* or NFPA 257, *Standard for Fire Test for Window and Glass Block Assemblies.* Such glazing must have a 45-minute rating and is limited to 1-hour-rated fire partitions or fire barriers when the fire barrier is used to separate occupancies or to separate incidental accessory occupancies. The amount of such glazing is limited to 25% of the area of the common wall within any room using the glazing. This limitation applies to partitions separating two rooms as well as to a partition separating a room and a corridor. Individual lites of fire-protection-rated glazing cannot exceed 1296 in.^{2} (0.84 m^2) in area, and any one dimension cannot be more than 54 in. (1372). The IBC still accepts 1/4 in. (25 mm) wired glass (if not in a hazardous location) as meeting the requirements for a 45-minute rating without specific testing, but other glazing must meet the NFPA 252 or 257 test requirements for a 45-minute rating.

Table 9-3 Opening Protective Requirements for Interior Partitions

(Dimensions and Sizes Are for Wired Glass Only)

Use of Partition	Assembly Type*	Fire Rating	Doors—Limiting Dimensions for fire-Protection Glazing or Wired Glass					Window Glazing—Cannot Exceed 25% of the Area of the Common Wall between Rooms[a]			Notes
			Fire Rating, hrs.	Glass Area, sq. in. (m²)	Max. Width, in. (mm)	Max. Height, in. (mm)	Glass Fire Rating—hrs.	Glass Area, sq. in. (m²)	Max. Width, in. (mm)	Max. Height, in. (mm)	
Corridor wall, nonsprinklered (occupant load>30)	FP	1	0.33	not limited	not limited	not limited	3/4	1,296 (0.84)	54 (1372)	54 (1372)	1-hr. FRRG allowed
Corridor wall, sprinklered A, B, E, F, M, S, U, I-2[b], I-4	FP²	0	0	not limited	not limited	not limited	Not limited				
Walls separating dwelling units	FP	1	3/4	1,296 (0.84)	54 (1372)	54 (1372)	Not applicable				
Same, Types IIB, IIIB, VB[c]	FP	½	0.33	1,296 (0.84)	54 (1372)	54 (1372)	Not applicable				
Walls separating guestrooms, R-1, R-2, I-1	FP	1	3/4	1,296 (0.84)	54 (1372)	54 (1372)	Not applicable				
Same, Types IIB, IIIB, VB[c]	FP	1/2	0.33	1,296 (0.84)	54 (1372)	54 (1372)	Not applicable				
Party walls in covered malls	FP	1	3/4	1,296 (0.84)	54 (1372)	54 (1372)	3/4	1,296 (0.84)	54 (1372)	54 (1372)	1-hr. FRRG allowed
Stairway walls, < 4 stories	FB	1	1	100 (0.06)	10 (254)	33 (838)	Not allowed				1-hr. FRRG allowed
Stairway walls, >= 4 stories	FB	2	1 1/2	100 (0.06)	10 (254)	33 (838)					2-hr. FRRG allowed
Exit passageways, 1-hr.	FB	1	1	100 (0.06)	10 (254)	33 (838)	Not allowed				1-hr. FRRG allowed
Exit passageways, 2-hr.	FB	2	1 1/2	100 (0.06)	10 (254)	33 (838)					2-hr. FRRG allowed
Separate incidental accessory occupancies[d]	FB	1[d]	3/4	1,296 (0.84)	54 (1372)	54 (1372)	3/4	1,296 (0.84)	54 (1372)	54 (1372)	1-hr. FRRG allowed
Occupancy separation	FB	1[e]	3/4[f]	1,296 (0.84)	54 (1372)	54 (1372)	3/4	1,296 (0.84)	54 (1372)	54 (1372)	1-hr. FRRG allowed
Occupancy separation	FB	2[e]	1 1/2	100 (0.06)	10 (254)	33 (838)	Not allowed				

*Assembly types:
FP = Fire partition
FB = Fire barrier
FW = Fire wall
FRRG = Fire-resistance-rated glazing

See IBC for definitions of assembly types
[a] Based on the 2009 International Building Code.
Figures in these columns are for wired glass. Larger sizes are possible with fire-resistance-rated glazing. See manufacturer's data for size limitations for fire-resistance-rated glazing.
[b] I-2 occupancies also require smoke barrier.
[c] Must be sprinklered in these construction types.
[d] See the IBC for four instances where 2-hour separation may be required. In most, but not all, cases sprinkler system may substitute for 1-hour rating.
[e] See the IBC for required hourly ratings, sprinkler use, and other exceptions.
[f] 1-hour occupancy separation requires 3/4-hr. door and is most common for most interior design situations.

Fire-resistance-rated glazing is glass or other glazing material that has been tested as part of a fire-resistance-rated wall assembly according to ASTM E119, *Fire Tests of Building Construction and Materials*. This glazing definition allows the use of special fire-rated glazing that can have fire-resistive ratings of up to 2 hours.

There are four types of fire-resistance-rated glazing. The first is a clear ceramic that has a higher impact resistance than wire glass and a low expansion coefficient. It is available with a 1-hour rating in sizes up to 1296 in.^{2} (0.84 m^2) and with a 3-hour rating in sizes up to 100 in.^{2} (0.0645 m^2). Although some forms of ceramic glass do not meet safety glazing requirements, there are laminated assemblies that are rated up to 2 hours and are impact safety rated.

The second type is a special, tempered fire-protective glass. It is rated at a maximum of 30 minutes because it cannot pass the hose-stream test, but it does meet the impact safety standards of both ANSI Z97.1, *Safety Glazing Materials Used in Buildings—Safety Performance Specifications and Methods of Test*, and 16 CFR 1201, *Safety Standard for Architectural Glazing Materials*.

The third type consists of two or three layers of tempered glass with a clear polymer gel between them. Under normal conditions, the glass is transparent, but when subjected to fire, the gel foams and turns opaque, thus retarding the passage of heat. This product is available with 30-, 60-, 90-, and 120-minute ratings, depending on the thickness and number of glass panes used as well as how the product is tested by each manufacturer. There are restrictions on the maximum size of lites and the type of permitted framing. This glazing may be used in partitions that must have a rating higher than one hour, although the glazing must have the same rating as the partition in which it is used. There are no limitations on the total area of glass, but there are limitations on the size of individual framed units. These limitations vary with each manufacturer.

The fourth type of glazing is glass block. However, not all glass block is rated. The glass block must have been specifically tested for use in fire-rated openings and approved by the local authority having jurisdiction.

In all cases, the type and detailing of the frame is critical to the rating of the glazed assembly. Frames must be of the type required by the manufacturer of the glazing material and approved with the ASTM E119 test. Typically, framing is larger than for standard window glass. Figure 9-12 shows one type of frame.

SAFETY GLAZED OPENINGS

The IBC requires safety glazing in hazardous locations. Hazardous locations are those subject to human impact such as glass in doors, shower and bath enclosures, and certain locations in walls. The typical places where safety glazing is and is not required according to the IBC are shown in Fig. 9-13. The exact requirements are given in the *Code of Federal Regulations*, 16 CFR Part 1201. The IBC also allows glazing materials to comply with ANSI Z97.1 in all applications other than storm doors, entrance-exit doors, sliding patio doors, closet doors, or in doors and enclosures for hot tubs, bathtubs, saunas, whirlpools, and showers. Technically, safety glazing is any product that passes one of these two tests for the specific applications allowed. Practically, safety glazing is tempered or laminated glass, although plastic glazing would also qualify if it met the requirements of the tests.

Details for safety glazing must hold the glass in place and are typically the same as for standard glazing, as shown in Figs. 9-9 and 9-10. If a crash bar is used in place of safety glazing as diagrammed in Fig. 9-13, it must be able to withstand a horizontal load of 50 lb per ft (730 N/m).

Figure 9-12 Typical fire-resistance-rated glazing detail

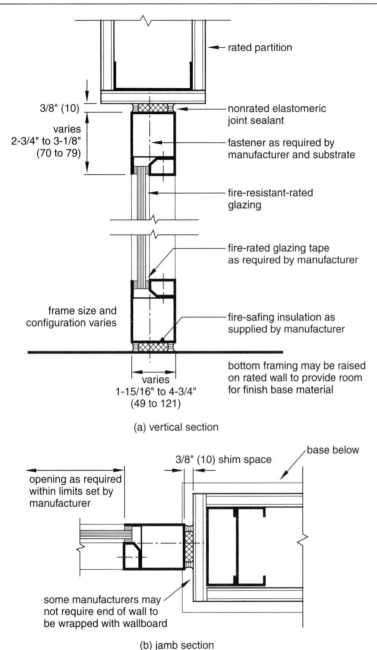

rated partition

3/8" (10)

varies
2-3/4" to 3-1/8"
(70 to 79)

nonrated elastomeric
joint sealant

fastener as required by
manufacturer and substrate

fire-resistant-rated
glazing

fire-rated glazing tape
as required by manufacturer

frame size and
configuration varies

fire-safing insulation as
supplied by manufacturer

bottom framing may be raised
on rated wall to provide room
for finish base material

varies
1-15/16" to 4-3/4"
(49 to 121)

(a) vertical section

3/8" (10) shim space

base below

opening as required
within limits set by
manufacturer

some manufacturers may
not require end of wall to
be wrapped with wallboard

(b) jamb section

ACOUSTIC CONTROL GLAZED OPENINGS

When a partition with a glazed opening must minimize sound transmission, special details must be used. A single thickness of glass provides only limited sound transmission loss. For example, a 1/4 in (6 mm) thick sheet of float glass only provides an STC rating of about 29 dB. When higher STC ratings are required, a combination of detailing strategies must be used. Refer to Chapter 3 for a discussion of methods of controlling sound transmission for both doors and glazed openings. Figure 3-20 shows one detail for a glazed opening with acoustical control.

Figure 9-13 Safety glazing locations

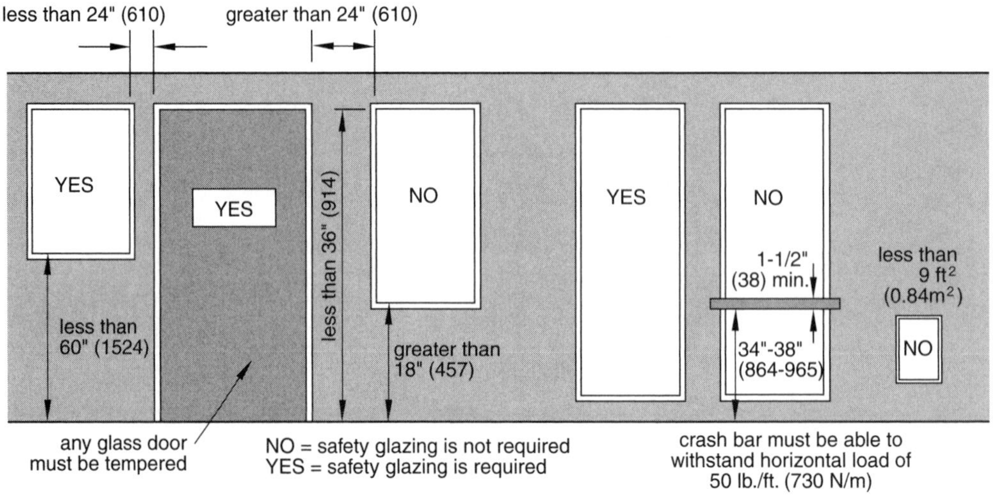

less than 24" (610)   greater than 24" (610)

YES

YES

NO

YES

NO

less than 36" (914)

1-1/2"
(38) min.

less than
9 ft²
(0.84m²)

NO

less than
60" (1524)

greater than
18" (457)

34"-38"
(864-965)

any glass door
must be tempered

NO = safety glazing is not required
YES = safety glazing is required

crash bar must be able to
withstand horizontal load of
50 lb./ft. (730 N/m)

Figure 9-14 Recessed blind pocket

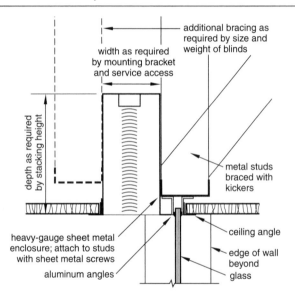

additional bracing as
required by size and
weight of blinds

width as required
by mounting bracket
and service access

depth as required
by stacking height

metal studs
braced with
kickers

heavy-gauge sheet metal
enclosure; attach to studs
with sheet metal screws

aluminum angles

ceiling angle

edge of wall
beyond

glass

Window Coverings

In most situations, interior glazed openings are intended to remain uncovered to allow views and daylight to penetrate interior spaces. However, in some cases, the opening must be temporarily closed off for privacy or light control. Blinds and shades can be surface mounted to the ceiling or the wall as with any window covering, but this requires stacking space and the covering is always visible. The designer can detail side pockets recessed into the wall space for vertical blinds or drapes. Horizontal blinds can be recessed into a pocket that is recessed above the ceiling. Figure 9-14 shows one way of doing this for a full-height glazed opening.

Alternately, electrochromic glazing can be used. Electrochromic glazing is a general term for a type of glazing that changes, when electric current is applied, from either a dark tint or an opaque milky white to clear. When the current is on, the glass is transparent; when the current is turned off, the glass darkens or turns white (depending on its type). Manufacturers of electrochromic glass are given in Table 5-5.

PART 3

TRANSITIONS

CHAPTER 10

WALL TRANSITIONS

10-1   INTRODUCTION

In addition to contributing to the overall design concept as discussed in Chapter 1, details also resolve aesthetic problems of connection or transition between two or more materials or architectural elements.

The shape and character of interior space is determined by many individual architectural elements, including things such as walls, ceilings, floors and free-standing components like furniture and accessories. Even more amorphous characteristics, like light, views, and acoustics can shape the character of an interior space. The fixed, architectural elements either connect with each other or form part of a larger architectural element. The way in which elements connect or transition from one to another is an important part of the overall design and aesthetic impact of a space. If done well, the connection contributes to the function and design impact of a space. If done poorly, the space appears disjointed and badly designed.

Sometimes the problem is more a technical one of how to physically make the connection and solve functional problems without being detrimental to the intended design concept. Other times the problem is more an aesthetic one of deciding how to change from one material to another or how to change from one architectural element to another out of a vast range of possible choices. Usually, the problem is a combination of both technical and aesthetic questions; a left brain and right brain solution is required. The best details solve technical problems in the most functional, economical way while elegantly enhancing the design of the project.

Detailing questions of connection or transition generally fall into two broad categories: those that occur when interior architectural elements connect, either in the same plane or in different planes, and those that occur when elements are placed on or are a part of other elements. This chapter discusses ways to make the transition of walls to either the ceiling plane or the floor plane.

10-2   CONNECTIONS OF MAJOR ELEMENTS

Interior space is created by combining many individual elements that define space and give it a particular character. Floor, wall, and ceiling planes are the obvious major architectural elements that define space, but other elements, such as columns, beams, pilasters, dropped ceilings, recesses, and projections, can also be used to shape the quality of space. Technically, there are generally only a few ways to connect major elements so that the functional and constructability needs are satisfied within the given constraints. However, there are often hundreds of ways to make the same connection from a strictly aesthetic standpoint.

How these elements connect is a detailing problem. While there are innumerable ways of connecting elements, they all tend to fall into one of the general types discussed in this chapter.

10-3 WALL TO FLOOR

Wall-to-floor connections are one of the most basic types, and usually little design attention is given to the junction. The floor supports the load of the partition, and generally each plane is finished with different materials with the joint between the two planes covered with some type of trim. Some of the general types of wall-to-floor connections are shown in Fig. 10-1. Which detailing approach is used depends on whether the designer wants to give equal weight to both the floor and partition or whether the goal is to visually separate the two planes.

Each produces a unique design effect useful for different design goals. For example, continuing the flooring material partially up the wall increases the apparent area of the floor. The types of transitions can be grouped into three general categories: standard bases, featured bases, and component bases.

Figure 10-1 Wall-to-floor transition concepts

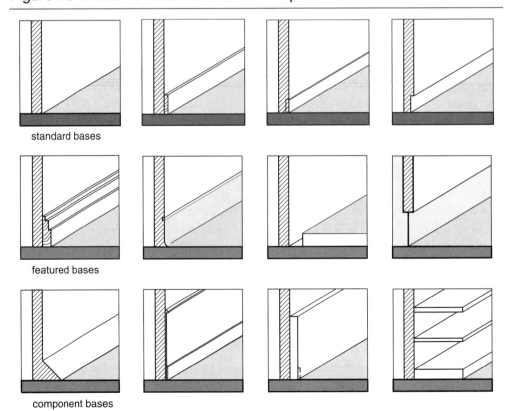

standard bases

featured bases

component bases

Standard Bases

NO BASE

In the most basic form, the partition simply rests directly on the floor with no trim, as shown in Fig. 10-2(a). The effect is plain, stark, and contemporary and may be appropriate in some situations. For practical reasons of construction and maintenance, a durable base should be provided, but this can be done by detailing the base flush with the partition surface and finishing it with the same color and texture as the wall. If the partition finish is durable itself, it may be extended to the floor.

How the bottom edge of the wall material is finished depends on the type of flooring. For example, if the floor will be carpeted, gypsum wallboard can be carried to the floor with

Figure 10-2 Standard wall-to-floor connections

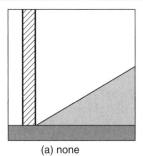

(a) none

A plain, flat wall with no base presents a clean, contemporary appearance. However, many finishes will not withstand normal wear and cleaning. In addition, any irregular floor surface or slope must be taken into account when deciding on the wall material and how the bottom edge of the wall will be detailed.

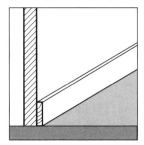

(b) applied

An applied base is the most common and works with any base material including wood, vinyl, rubber, stone, metal, and laminated products. This type of base can cover the joint between the bottom edge of the wall material and the floor and in most cases, can accommodate out of level floors.

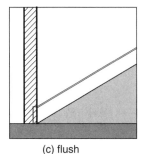

(c) flush

Flush bases combine the advantages of a clean, contemporary appearance with the retension of the functional requirements of a durable base that can withstand cleaning and other abuse. The size of the reveal can be very small to minimize the appearance of the base or can be larger to highlight the separation or make it easier to construct. To minimize the visual impact of the base it can be the same color and texture as the wall finish.

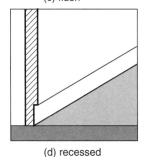

(d) recessed

A recessed base emphasizes the partition surface as a separate plane from the floor surface. It is a contemporary look and can mask minor damage to the base material in the reveal. However, it is more difficult and expensive to construct, generally requiring an additional layer of gypsum wallboard or a second, furred wall.

a slight gap as is normal for wallboard installation. Carpet and pad would then cover the gap. For a hard-surfaced floor, such as wood or resilient tile, the bottom edge of gypsum wallboard would need to be finished with a standard wallboard L-trim or J-trim, as shown in Fig. 5-4(a) and (b). Alternately, an aluminum reveal trim similar to that shown in Fig. 10-11(a) can be used. Generally, omitting a base is not advisable, especially where frequent cleaning of the floor is required. This base treatment is difficult to use when the floors are not level because each piece of wallboard or other wall finish must be cut to fit the floor line.

APPLIED BASE

Figure 10-2(b) shows the standard method of treating a wall-to-floor detail with a piece of applied base. The base covers the joint, while providing protection from cleaning equipment and kicking. This approach is inexpensive and easy to construct, while providing a wide choice of sizes, and configurations, and base materials, including resilient materials, wood, stone, or metal. Applied bases are fairly easy to remove and replace for remodeling or recycling.

FLUSH

Flush bases, shown in Fig. 10-2(c), provide the functional requirements of protection and joint concealment, while minimizing the visual impact of the base and giving a more contemporary appearance than an applied base. The base may be a contrasting material and color or one that matches the wall finish. As with any detail involving more than one material, it is difficult to construct a perfectly flush joint in the field, especially when one of the materials is gypsum wallboard. Three ways to create a flush base are shown in Fig. 10-3. To accommodate unleveled floors, the designer must decide whether to have the base and trim follow the line of the floor, scribe the base to fit the line of the floor, or have the trim set level and allow the reveal to vary in size as the base follows the floor line.

RECESSED

A recessed base emphasizes the separation between the ground plane and the wall plane. See Fig. 10-2(d). One of the practical advantages of a recessed base is that minor damage or soiling from cleaning operations is not as noticeable as with a flush or applied base. However, in most cases, a flush base requires a double-layer application of wallboard, especially if the partition requires a fire rating or if acoustical separation is needed.

Several of the ways to detail a recessed base are shown in Fig. 10-4. The simplest method, Fig. 10-4(a), uses a second layer of gypsum wallboard stopped short of the floor and trimmed with standard J-trim or L-trim. A base thinner than the thickness of the wallboard is used to finish the recessed portion. The wallboard trim can be set level, with the applied base following the line of the floor. In this case, the gap between the top of the base and the wallboard trim will vary as the irregularities of the floor vary. Alternately, the trim can be set at a constant distance from the floor and follow the line of the floor, in which case the edge of the trim may appear out of level. The designer must determine or estimate how much the floor will be out of level and decide which approach to use.

If a deeper recess is wanted, a second furred wall can be built out from the primary partition, as shown in Fig. 10-4(b). Standard furring strips can be used or a J-runner can be used with 2-1/2 in. (63.5 mm) metal studs. In this detail or the one shown in Fig. 10-4(a), the designer can determine whatever height of recess is wanted. This detail allows for a thicker

Figure 10-3 Flush base details

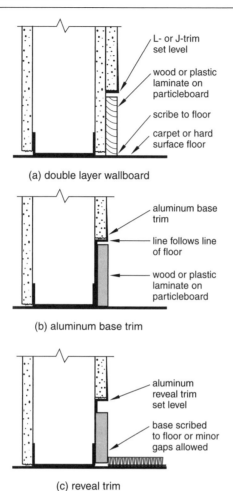

(a) double layer wallboard

L- or J-trim set level

wood or plastic laminate on particleboard

scribe to floor

carpet or hard surface floor

(b) aluminum base trim

aluminum base trim

line follows line of floor

wood or plastic laminate on particleboard

(c) reveal trim

aluminum reveal trim set level

base scribed to floor or minor gaps allowed

base (such as wood or stone), while still retaining a recessed appearance. The disadvantages are the additional cost and construction time.

A third way to create a recessed base is by using a proprietary aluminum trim piece, as shown in Fig. 10-4(c). This detail can be used with a single layer of gypsum wallboard because the aluminum closes off the stud space. The trim can be painted or another material adhesive-applied to the trim. However, this detail is limited to the manufacturer's 4-in. (102-mm) height, and because there is no wallboard, a fire rating is not possible and acoustical separation is compromised.

Featured Bases

EMPHASIZED

Emphasized bases, as shown in Fig. 10-5(a), are a type of applied base but larger and/or more ornate than standard base treatments. Emphasized bases are usually higher than the standard height of 4 in. (100 mm) of most resilient or wood bases. Emphasized bases are used to complement the scale of larger spaces or when the designer wants to emphasize or strengthen the transition between ground plane and wall plane.

Figure 10-4 Recessed base details

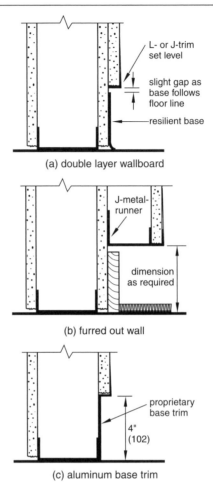

L- or J-trim set level

slight gap as base follows floor line

resilient base

(a) double layer wallboard

J-metal-runner

dimension as required

(b) furred out wall

proprietary base trim

4" (102)

(c) aluminum base trim

Emphasized bases can be formed in a number of ways. The size can simply be increased over standard bases; for example, by using a 9 in. (229 mm) high wood base instead of a 4-in. (102 mm) high one. The designer can also emphasize the base by building up its complexity as with a multipiece wood base composed of a base, base shoe, and base cap. Other materials can be used in the same way. The base may also be detailed with more than one material to highlight it or add emphasis.

COVE

Cove bases are those with a noticeable curve as a transition between the vertical plane and the horizontal plane. The curve must be larger than just the small cove built into some resilient base. See Fig. 10-5(b). While the cove base is most commonly used for sanitary reasons, coves may also be used to create a smooth visual transition between the floor and the wall, in some cases making them seem to be one surface. For this type of base to be visually effective, the cove must have a radius of at least 2 in. (50 mm) or more; greater sizes are required if the scale of the room is large.

Cove bases are more difficult and expensive to form than other types. One of the most common materials used for cove bases is terrazzo. When used with a terrazzo floor, it provides an easy-to-clean base, suitable for hospitals and other high-maintenance uses. See Fig. 8-10(b).

Figure 10-5 Wall-to-floor connections with featured bases

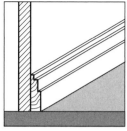

(a) emphasized

Emphasized bases celebrate the transition between the floor plane and the partition plane. They are also appropriate to increase the scale of the base for large rooms or spaces with high ceilings.

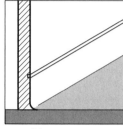

(b) cove

Cove bases smooth the transition between floor and partition. They are also an excellent way to provide a sanitary base that is easy to clean. In order to be effective the radius of the cove must be large enough to easily perceive and in scale with the room in which it is used.

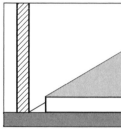

(c) floating floor

A floating floor is physically separated from the partition plane at the finish level of the floor. The reveal created may be shallow or deep, depending on the how it is detailed. A floating floor creates a very distinct separation between the horizontal plane and the vertical plane, although it does create a potential tripping hazard.

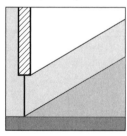

(d) floating wall

Like the floating floor, a floating wall physically separates the vertical plane from the horizontal plane with glass filling the gap. If carefully detailed it makes the floor finish appear to continue uninterruped into the next space and creates a greater sense of space, making the rooms appear larger. To be effective, this detail requires clear floor space, so the glass is not blocked by furniture.

A large cove base can present a safety hazard if people walk close to the wall and step on the curved portion.

Floating Floor

A floating floor has a gap, or reveal, between the edge of the flooring and the wall, making the floor appear to hover within the space. See Fig. 10-5(c). Of all the types of base detailing, the floating floor is the one that is most effective in physically and visually separating the ground plane from the wall plane. This type of floor can be used in retail stores, galleries, restaurants, lobbies, and anyplace where furniture does not need to be placed near the wall. To be most visually effective, this type of base needs to be visible along its entire length.

Although it makes a dramatic design statement, the floating floor presents obvious tripping hazards and can be dangerous for visually impaired people. However, if the width of the reveal

Figure 10-6 Floating floors

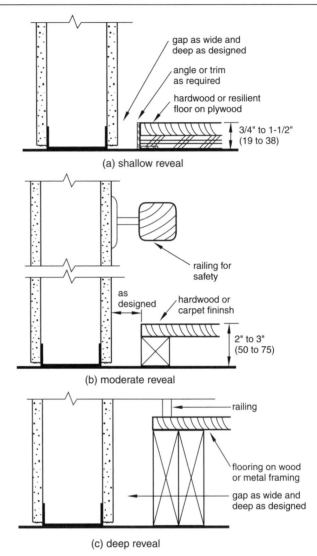

gap as wide and
deep as designed

angle or trim
as required

hardwood or resilient
floor on plywood

3/4" to 1-1/2"
(19 to 38)

(a) shallow reveal

railing for
safety

as
designed

hardwood or
carpet fininsh

2" to 3"
(50 to 75)

(b) moderate reveal

railing

flooring on wood
or metal framing

gap as wide and
deep as designed

(c) deep reveal

is minimized, these hazards can be mitigated. A railing attached to the floor or to the wall may also be used to prevent people from walking too close to the gap. The gap may also create cleaning problems if used in an environment where there are large amounts of debris.

Some of the methods of detailing this type of floor are shown in Fig. 10-6. In most cases, the depth of the reveal is created by the structure of the finish flooring; both the partition and the flooring rest on the same elevation of subfloor. Figure 10-6(a) shows a minimal depth of reveal with the finish flooring applied to a thickness of plywood or underlayment. Depending on the type of finish floor, a protective angle may be required to prevent the edge of the flooring from damage. For deeper reveals, the floor can be raised on a platform structure, as shown in Figs. 10-6(b) and (c). In all cases, the partition must be constructed and finished before the floor is installed, which may affect the construction schedule.

FLOATING WALL

A floating wall consists of the solid portion of the partition raised an obvious distance above the ground plane with the space between the ground plane and the bottom of the partition open or filled with glazing. This type of detail has the effect of creating the partition as a screen with the floor continuing uninterrupted below it. It creates a strong visual and actual separation between horizontal and vertical planes. Combined with an opening or glazing along the ceiling line, this design provides an open feeling and allows natural light to penetrate a partition line while maintaining visual privacy.

This design is one of the more difficult details to implement, especially if glazing is used to close the opening. One way of detailing this is shown in Fig. 10-7. This detail shows the use of a heavy-gauge metal runner to support the studs. Because most manufacturers supply runners in 10-ft. (3048 mm) lengths this limits the maximum space between supports. For longer spans or heavier walls, a structural steel channel can be used. In either case, a structural engineer should be consulted for recommendations on the exact type, size, and thickness of the member used to support the studs based on the span distance, the height of the wall, and its weight, as well as the type and size of the vertical support member.

In addition to structural considerations, electrical and data wiring must be coordinated. Electrical service can be supplied from the ceiling plenum and run horizontally through the studs as with any partition. The steel support member must be punched with holes prior to installation to allow the electrical conduit to pass through them.

Figure 10-7 Floating wall

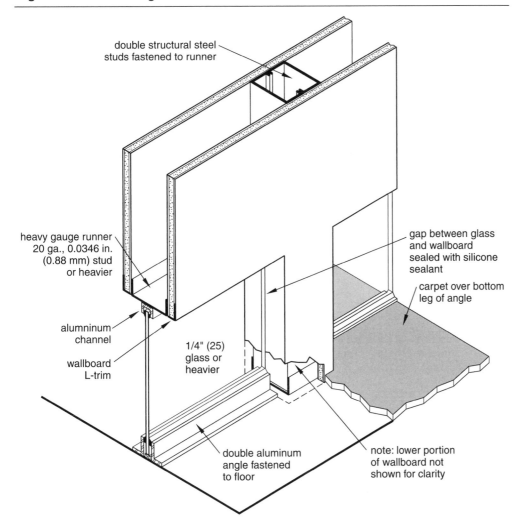

Component Bases

THIRD PLANE

Instead of a standard base, a third plane distinct from the horizontal ground plane and the vertical partition plane can be used to emphasize the transition and create a unique detail. See Fig. 10-8(a). Lighting can be incorporated into this type of detail to give a strong directional sense that may be appropriate in a corridor. The angle can be repeated and the intersection of the wall and the ceiling. Although this detail can be employed for emphasis, this detail can also make the two planes seem to merge, as with a large cove base, if the finish is the same as the partition and ceiling.

As with a cove base, a large third plane can create a tripping hazard, so its use is limited to appropriate situations. If the plane is finished with the same material as the partition, there

Figure 10-8 Component wall-to-floor connections

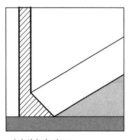

(a) third plane

A third plane transition between the floor and partition emphasizes the line of the base. The plane can be any size or angle and may be finished the same as the floor or partition or may be a different finish. It may incorporate lighting or other features to further emphasize the transition.

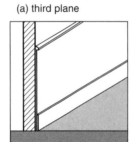

(b) wainscoting

Wainscoting is the traditional method of finishing the lower portion of a partition. In addition to providing protection from abuse, it can modulate the scale of the room and add visual interest to a space. The portion of the wainscoting near the floor can be detailed with a traditional applied base or with other methods.

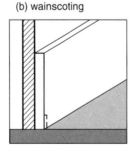

(c) parallel second plane

A parallel second plane is built out from the primary partition a significant distance. This treatment can both modulate the vertical scale of the space and provide a sense of added depth to an otherwise flat vertical surface. The portion of the plane near the floor can be detailed with a traditional applied base or with other methods. Functionally, this base treatment can conceal services or heating.

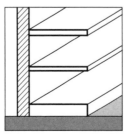

(d) base as storage

When the base transition is made very large, it can be used for storage. As with a parallel second plane, this detail can modulate the scale of the space as well as provide functional storage space. This detail adds significant depth to the vertical surface.

is the issue of durability and maintenance. If the flooring material is carried onto the third plane, it becomes less visible and may be a safety hazard. Both of these potential problems can be mitigated by functionally treating the third plane as a standard base, using a durable, easily maintained material such as plastic laminate or stone.

WAINSCOTING

Wainscoting is a traditional, practical way to treat the transition between the ground plane and the wall plane, while providing a durable surface as protection from furniture and other activities. See Fig. 10-8(b). From a design standpoint, wainscoting can also be used to change the scale of a room. While traditional wainscoting uses a standard wood base with wood paneling above, material can be selected and detailed so that there is no separate base with the wainscoting being the base. Plastic laminate panels, stone, metal, or wood panels can be used that extend to the floor without a separate base.

A trim cap of some type is required at the top of the panel to make the transition between wainscoting and the wall finish above.

PARALLEL SECOND PLANE

As an extension of the wainscoting concept, a separate plane can be built out from the primary partition, emphasizing not only the height of the transition but also its thickness. See Fig. 10-8(c). This type of detail can be used to modulate the scale of the space, provide a band of durable material, and, if necessary, conceal mechanical or electrical services such as large pipes or heating units. The top of the surface can also be used as a shelf, if necessary. At the floor line, the second plane can be extended to the floor with no separate base as shown in Fig. 10-2(a) or the transition can be treated in any of the other ways discussed in this chapter.

This type of design can be most easily constructed as a furred wall, using a stud depth as required for the functional and aesthetic requirements. If a depth greater than the depth of a stud is required, horizontal and vertical metal framing can be used to build out the third plane to the required dimension.

BASE AS STORAGE

Finally, the transition between horizontal and vertical planes can be filled with built-in storage, as shown in Fig. 10-8(d). This type of base design is useful where a great deal of storage is required. Because the partition finish above the storage is physically separated from activity within the room, more delicate finish materials may be used on the partition, protected from damage. As with wainscoting and a parallel second plane, this treatment is also useful for modulating the scale of the space.

At the floor line, the storage can be extended nearly to the floor with no separate base or the lowest storage shelf can be located a few inches above the floor and the bases at that point treated in any of the other ways discussed in this chapter.

10-4 WALL TO CEILING

The connection of the wall plane to the ceiling plane is one of the most important in interior design because it joins two of the most prominent architectural features and because it is always within view of a room's occupants. In contemporary construction, it is also one of the least

Figure 10-9 Wall-to-ceiling transition concepts

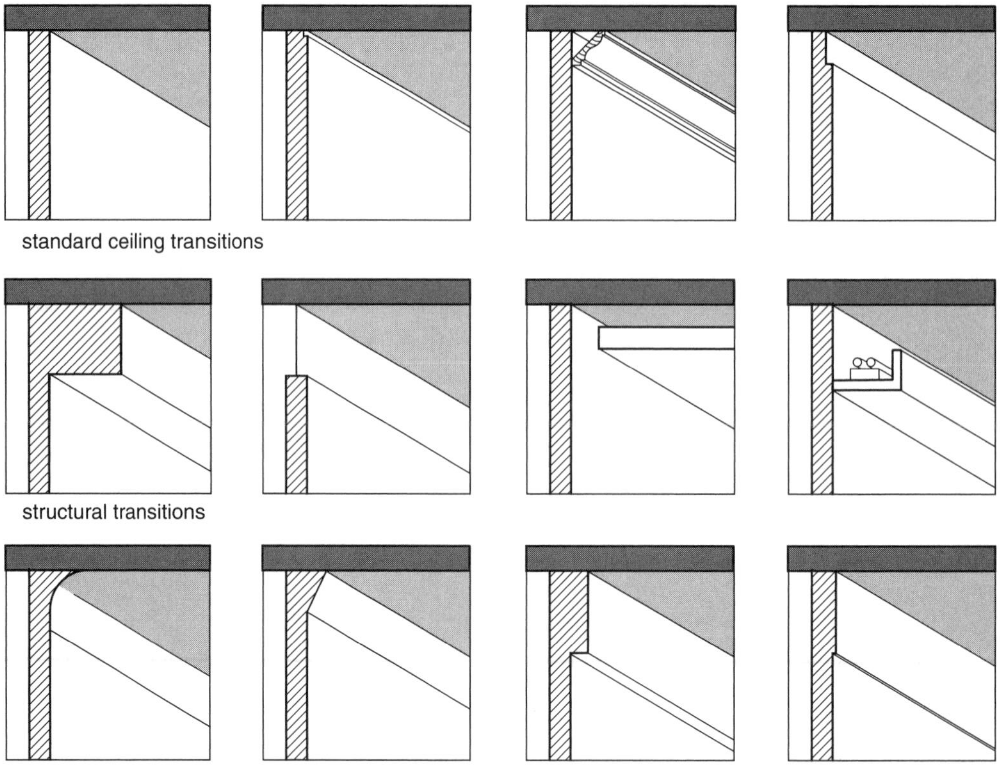

standard ceiling transitions

structural transitions

planar transitions

considered, which is unfortunate because the way the vertical and horizontal ceiling planes are connected can affect the scale and feeling of a space as well as solving many functional problems such as material transition, support, and lighting.

Some of the general types of wall-to-ceiling connection are shown in Fig. 10-9. Which detailing approach is used depends on whether the designer wants to give equal weight to both the ceiling and partition or whether the goal is to visually separate the two planes. Each of these is discussed in more detail in the following sections.

As with the wall-to-floor transition, each detailing approach produces a unique design effect useful for different design goals. For example, continuing the ceiling material partially down the wall increases the apparent area of the ceiling and lowers the apparent height of the wall. The types of transitions can be grouped into three general categories: standard ceiling transitions, structural transitions, and planar transitions.

Standard Ceiling Transitions

Standard ceiling transitions are those that are commonly used and are the traditional methods of treating the junction of the wall and ceiling plane. They are generally small in scale, simple to construct, and resolve the typical functional problems of ceiling construction. See Fig. 10-10.

No Transition

No detailing connection, as shown in Fig. 10-10(a), is, of course, the simplest and least expensive to construct, which is why it is used so often. However, a simple 90-degree joint

Figure 10-10 Standard wall-to-ceiling connections

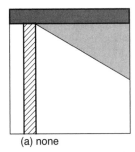

(a) none

A flat wall with an applied base and no trim at the ceiling is the most common type of partition. It is easy to build, inexpensive, and provides a good base for a wide variety of smooth interior finishes. Most commonly such partitions are gypsum wallboard applied to wood or metal studs.

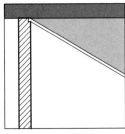

(b) minor trim or reveal

Minor trims or reveals are small in relation to the area of the partition or ceiling. They serve to provide a clear differentiation between the two planes. Reveals create a shadow line and separation between different materials, while small trim can conceal minor irregularities in the joint or at the edges of the ceiling or partition material.

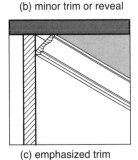

(c) emphasized trim

Emphasized trim makes a bolder statement than minor trim and celebrates the transition between vertical and horizontal planes. In most cases, the size of the trim should be adjusted to coordinate with the height of the ceiling and the overall scale of the room. Emphasized trim can be built in the traditional way with standard moldings or be built up of more contemporary square-edged elements.

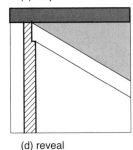

(d) reveal

A reveal transition provides a major separation between the ceiling plane and the partition. It is larger than a minor reveal and makes a bold, contemporary statement. The reveal may be finished the same as the partition or it may be a contrasting color or finish.

can also minimize the visual importance of the connection, giving equal visual weight to both planes. It also is generally viewed as contemporary in style and imparts a feeling of simplicity.

In residential construction and commercial construction where the partition and ceiling are both finished with gypsum wallboard, the joint is simply a continuation of the wallboard. Only the final finish of paint or wallcovering may differentiate the two planes. In commercial construction when the ceiling is a suspended acoustical ceiling, the transition may simply be a standard ceiling angle if the partition continues through the ceiling or there may be no trim at all if the ceiling continues over the top of the partition.

MINOR TRIM OR REVEAL

Small trim is sometimes used to conceal the joint between the partition and ceiling or to provide a minor shadow line for visual interest. A reveal may also be used to differentiate

Figure 10-11 Vertical ceiling reveals

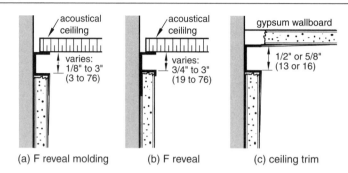

(a) F reveal molding   (b) F reveal   (c) ceiling trim

between the two planes or for strictly functional reasons, such as to make painting or finishing easier, to accommodate irregular surfaces, or to eliminate the need for a standard ceiling angel for acoustical ceilings. A reveal can be created by using standard gypsum wallboard trim and a standard ceiling angle, but there are proprietary aluminum trim pieces that can accommodate different conditions and ceiling materials. See Fig. 10-11. Refer to Table 5-3 for a list of trim manufacturers. However, if a fire-rated or acoustical partition is required, a second layer of wallboard is necessary.

EMPHASIZED TRIM

Emphasized trim is molding or other material used to highlight the intersection of the wall and ceiling planes, as shown in Fig. 10-10(c). Traditionally, this has been accomplished with crown molding or wood molding built up of individual pieces. The appearance of wood can also be created with traditional plaster molding, medium-density fiberboard, or high-density polyurethane molding with the same profiles as traditional wood molding.

Emphasized trims such as cornice molding reflect a more traditional approach to this transition of surfaces without giving more weight to either plane. For contemporary designs, a profile other than one of the traditional shapes can be used to accomplish the same design goals.

REVEAL

As with floor-to-wall connections, using reveals, or physically separating the two planes as shown in Fig. 10-10(d) tend to emphasize the ceiling plane, depending on what materials, finishes, and colors are used. Like recessed bases, this type of detail generally requires a double-layer application of wallboard or the second layer of framing and wallboard, as shown in Fig. 10-4. If a ceiling reveal is used with a matching recessed base (and possible reveals at the wall-to-wall intersection), the partition takes on the appearance of a separate vertical plane floating away from another surface.

Structural Transitions

Structural transitions between the partition and the ceiling have a distinct and significant piece of construction at the intersection of vertical and horizontal planes. In most cases, these types of transitions are made for practical reasons as well as to modify the scale or appearance of the space. For example, coves provide a way to provide indirect, ambient lighting in a room.

SOFFIT

A soffit is an area built down from the ceiling and away from the wall. See Fig. 10-12(a). In most cases, a soffit is constructed with wood or metal framing and covered with gypsum

Figure 10-12 Structural wall-to-ceiling connections

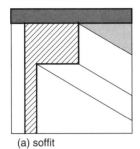

(a) soffit

Soffits are small areas of the total ceiling area built down from the elevation of the main ceiling plane. Soffits can be used to emphasize high areas of a ceiling, to conceal mechanical services, or to fill an area above cabinets.

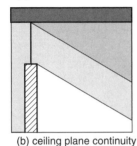

(b) ceiling plane continuity

The intersection between the ceiling plane and the partition plane can be virtually eliminated by continuing the ceiling across a partition and filling the gap with glazing or by leaving it open. In most cases, the gap is filled with glazing that provides acoustical separation, while allowing light to flow from one space to another.

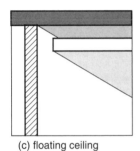

(c) floating ceiling

Floating ceilings create a definite separtion between the partition plane and the overhead plane. If the ceiling is carried close to the partitions, it seems that the partition disappears behind the ceiling. If the floating ceiling is composed of separate "clouds" of overhead elements the ceiling has additional depth with the space above flowing between several heights.

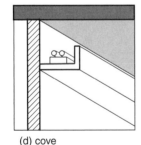

(d) cove

Coves are often used to conceal indirect lighting, but they can also be used to modulate the scale of a room and conceal air supply and return grilles. Coves can be constructed with simple, rectangular shapes or be finished in more traditional molding profiles.

wallboard. One of the common uses of a soffit is to fill the space above wall cabinets that do not extend to the ceiling. However, soffits can also be used to conceal structural elements or mechanical services, contain lighting, emphasize a wall area, or modulate the scale of a space.

CEILING PLANE CONTINUITY

Ceiling plane continuity refers to the use of glazing at the top of the partition so that the ceiling appears to continue from one space to another. See Fig. 10-12(b). This detail is an excellent way to make spaces appear larger and to allow daylight to penetrate into interior spaces while maintaining visual privacy.

If the intent is to allow daylight penetration, any type of framing can be used, from standard wood or metal frames to frameless glazing. However, if the design intent is also to minimize framing and make it appear that the ceiling continues uninterrupted, a detail like that shown in Fig. 10-13 can be used. With this type of frameless glazing, the vertical joints

Figure 10-13 Ceiling continuity over glazing

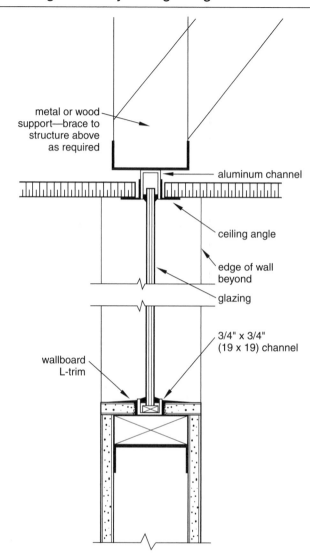

metal or wood
support—brace to
structure above
as required

aluminum channel

ceiling angle

edge of wall
beyond

glazing

3/4" x 3/4"
(19 x 19) channel

wallboard
L-trim

between glazing can be sealed with silicone sealant if acoustical control is required or left open. If the partition must be fire rated, fire-resistance-rated glazing and framing can be used, but the size of the framing can be significant.

FLOATING CEILING

Floating ceilings, shown diagrammatically in Fig. 10-12(c), physically and visually separate the ceiling plane from the partition. The effect can be used with a continuous, planar ceiling, as discussed in Chap. 7 and shown in Fig. 7-2(a) or with semiclosed or floating planar ceilings illustrated in Fig. 7-3(c) and (d). This type of transition emphasizes the overhead plane by separating it from the partitions and treating it as a unique construction element. Three ways to detail this are shown in Fig. 10-14.

To create indirect lighting washing down the wall, fluorescent lamps or other types of luminaires can be placed at the edge of the ceiling. Not only is this an interesting indirect lighting method but it also further emphasizes the separation of the horizontal and vertical planes. Floating ceilings can be created in a number of ways. Some of these are shown in

Figure 10-14 Horizontal ceiling reveals

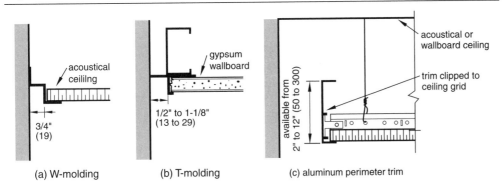

(a) W-molding

acoustical ceililng

3/4"
(19)

(b) T-molding

gypsum wallboard

1/2" to 1-1/8"
(13 to 29)

(c) aluminum perimeter trim

available from 2" to 12" (50 to 300)

acoustical or wallboard ceiling

trim clipped to ceiling grid

Figs. 7-10 and 7-11. Standard gypsum wallboard ceilings can be used with metal framing to trim the edges or a prefabricated edge treatment can be used. Refer to Tables 7-2 and 7-3 for manufacturers that supply edge trim as well as complete floating ceiling assemblies.

COVE

A cove is a separate molding or construction assembly running horizontally near the ceiling line. In addition to its decorative uses and as a way to modulate the scale of the room, coves can be used to provide indirect lighting onto the ceiling. See Fig. 10-12(d). Coves can be as small as standard cornice molding installed away from the ceiling plane or as large as required for the visual effect and lighting needed by the designer.

In addition to making the transition between wall and ceiling planes less abrupt, coves can solve practical problems such as providing lighting or concealing air supply registers and exhausts. Coves that are constructed of wood or metal framing or prefabricated aluminum sections can be used to support luminaires, as shown in Fig. 10-15. The aluminum cove sections are available in a variety of profiles and are screwed to the studs with flanges on a support bracket. The finish profile is then secured to the bracket. Wallboard flanges provide for taping and finishing, making a smooth transition between the trim and the gypsum wallboard.

Planar Transitions

Planar transitions are those that provide a change of plane from the ceiling to the partition with a single surface. There are four general types of such transitions.

CONTINUITY OF MATERIAL

With continuity of material, the finish of either the ceiling or the partition is continued onto the other plane with a smooth, uninterrupted surface. This is most often done with a curve as shown in Fig. 10-16(a).

This design detail blends the two surfaces and deemphasizes the corner and the junction of the two planes. When the ceiling material is continued partially down the wall, this also tends to lower the partition's apparent height. However, for this design to work the curve must be sufficiently large to create the desired effect.

Small coves can be created with wood molding or plaster, but a more efficient method is to use aluminum trim, which is available in a variety of radii, from 3/4 in. (19 mm) to 6 in. (152 mm). This trim is attached to the framing and provides flanges for using wallboard joint

Figure 10-15 Lighting coves

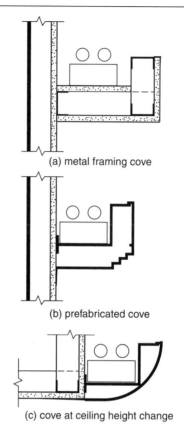

(a) metal framing cove

(b) prefabricated cove

(c) cove at ceiling height change

compound to smooth the curve into the gypsum wallboard. Larger radii can be created with curved wallboard, plaster, or gypsum-reinforced fiberglass.

THIRD PLANE

As with a floor-to-partition transition, a third plane tends to emphasize the transition between the ceiling plane and the partition plane, especially if it is finished differently than either the partition or the ceiling. See Fig. 10-16(b). When it is finished the same as either the partition or the ceiling, it may make the two planes appear to merge, but if this is the intent a cove transition works better.

Depending on the size needed for the third plane, it can be constructed with molding, veneer panels, or wallboard framed with wood or metal studs.

PARALLEL SECOND PLANE

A parallel second plane, shown diagrammatically in Fig. 10-16(c), creates a built-out wall section parallel to the partition with a noticeable height and thickness. As with a flooring transition, this detail can be used to modulate the scale of the space and create a three-dimensional interest. However, unlike a second plane at the floor level, this detail does not reduce the usable area at the floor. Because of the thickness, additional trim can be installed between the partition and the built-out section using other techniques described in this chapter.

The parallel second plane can be constructed using one of the methods of creating raised faces as shown in Fig. 5-3.

Figure 10-16 Planar wall-to-ceiling connections

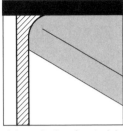

(a) continuity of material

Making a smooth transition between the vertical plane and the horizontal plane deemphasizes the joint between them. Most often created with a circular curve, a ceiling transition lowers the apparent height of the ceiling.

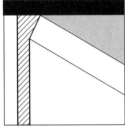

(b) third plane

A third plane transition between the partition and the ceiling tends to emphasize the intersection and creates an additional plane of interest. The plane can be finished the same way as the ceiling, in which case, it will also tend to lower the apparent height of the room, as with a cove, or it can be finished the same way as the partition. For added emphasis, the third plane can be finished with a different color or texture than the other two planes.

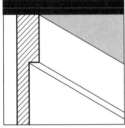

(c) parallel second plane

A second plane, parallel to the partition, modulates the height of the room and adds a third dimension to an otherwise flat wall surface. The plane can be finished the same way as the wall, but it also provides an opportunity to add a separate band of color or texture to the vertical surface.

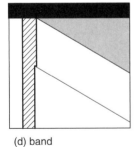

(d) band

A ceiling band is a small, but noticeable, thickness built out from the wall. It is similar to a wainscot but in reverse. Bands are useful for modulating the scale of a room, much like a parallel second plane, and provide a surface for decoration, signage, or other features.

BAND

A ceiling band, similar to wainscoting, is a separate, distinct edging built out slightly from the partition. This detail can be used to modulate the scale of a room and to emphasize the difference between the vertical and horizontal planes. It is less costly to construct than a parallel second plane but often creates the same type of effect. A ceiling band can be created by using an additional layer of gypsum wallboard with edge trim, with veneer paneling, thin stone, or other material, as appropriate. It can also be combined with other transition details as described in this chapter.

CHAPTER 11

PLANAR TRANSITIONS

In addition to the transition between different architectural planes in an interior space discussed in Chapter 10, there are also transitions between different materials, finishes, or levels in the same plane, including partitions, floors, and ceilings. These planar transitions are necessary to physically join different construction elements and resolve other functional requirements, but they can also contribute to the overall design concept.

As space dividers, walls and partitions serve the obvious functional purposes of visual and acoustical separation, security, and control of movement. Beyond this, however, they are one of the prime determinates in defining the character of interior space. Planar transitions provide design opportunities to differentiate materials, emphasize areas, modify scale, modulate space, and create visual interest.

11-1 PARTITION TO PARTITION

As discussed in Chapter 5, partitions both divide and create space as vertical barriers and can be treated and detailed in many ways. When two or more finish materials or construction elements join, the resulting transition must be detailed. This can be done so that the partition surfaces are in line with each other or slightly offset. There are nine basic ways these transitions can be made, as diagrammed in Fig. 11-1.

The type of partition transition that the designer selects is usually coordinated with the base or ceiling treatment, but it doesn't have to be. For example, a vertical reveal between sections of a partition may be combined with a reveal transition between the partition and the ceiling. Alternately, vertical corners could be created with 90-degree angles while ceilings could consist of curved forms.

In-Plane Transitions

BUTT JOINT

The simplest transition is a basic butt joint, shown in Fig. 11-2(a). In this detail the same substrate material is used and the finishes are joined in a straight, vertical line. Examples of this type of joint include two different adjacent paint colors, a vertical seam in vinyl wallcovering, or two wood panels touching along their vertical edges.

Butt joints provide a smooth, uniform appearance to a partition if that is the design intent. They are simple to construct and inexpensive and are necessary for most panelized materials

219

Figure 11-1 Partition-to-partition transition concepts

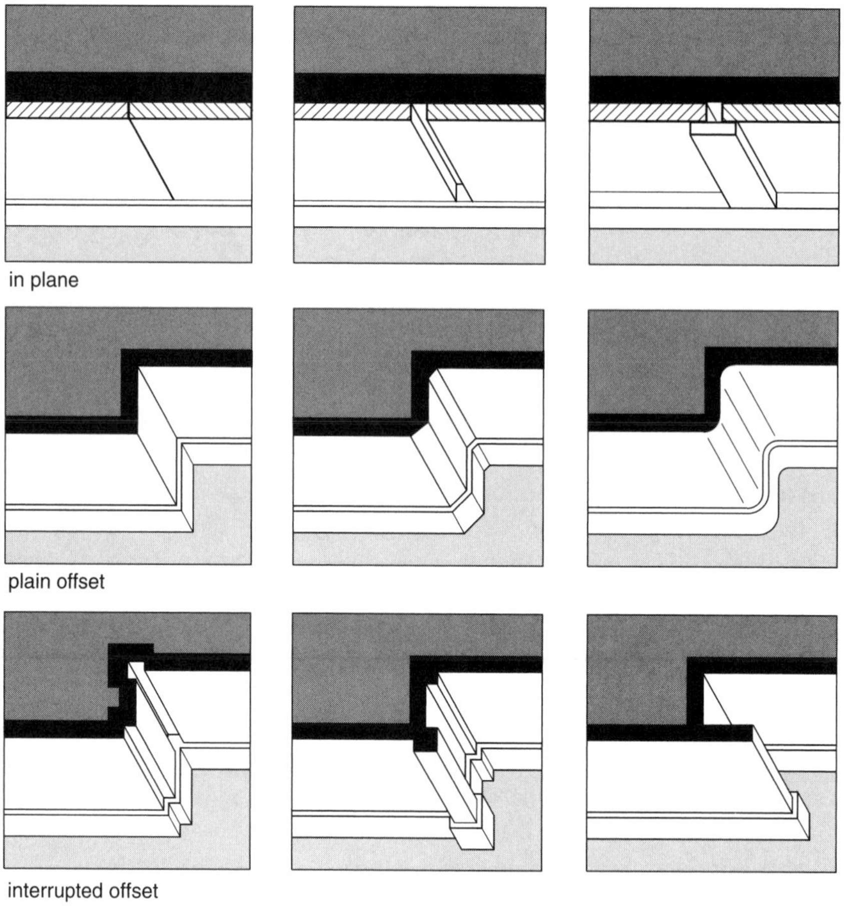

in plane

plain offset

interrupted offset

such as wood or stone. However, some materials, such as wallpaper or vinyl wallcovering may peel at the joint or two materials may shrink, causing an unsightly gap and defeating the design goal of a plain, uniform surface finish. The designer must choose to minimize the effect of a joint with a butt joint or celebrate it with one of the other transitions discussed in this chapter.

One variation of a butt joint is a butt joint with eased edge. An eased edge is a slight beveling of the edge of a material, generally a fraction of the total thickness, so the visible edge is not at a ninety-degree angle. For example, a wood panel can be given a 1/16 in. (1.6 mm) bevel. Although this shows the joint a little more, it is effective in concealing any slight, uneven shrinkage of the panels because the beveling was intentional.

REVEAL

Reveals are obvious separations between two materials with a joint that has an obvious depth to it. See Fig. 11-2(b). As discussed in Chapter 5, reveals are useful for concealing minor imperfections in joint width or alignment of adjacent surfaces. They also make painting or other finishing of different adjacent materials easier. Some of the ways reveals can be created are shown in Fig. 5-7.

BATTEN

A batten joint is one that is covered with another material extending from the face of two finished surfaces that are in the same plane. See Fig. 11-2(c). A batten may be the same

Figure 11-2 In-plane partition transitions

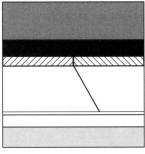

A butt joint minimizes the effect of the material transition and places more emphasis on the entire plane of the partition. Butt joints are typically used where the adjoining materials are identical.

(a) butt joint

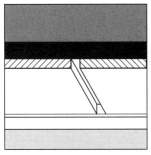

A reveal joint provides a distinct separation between materials and conceals any minor imperfections in alignment. Reveal joints also provide a good separation between different materials or finishes. These joints also make it easy to remove one portion of the partition for repair or replacement without disturbing adjacent panels.

(b) reveal

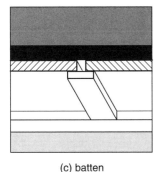

Batten joints are easy to construct and cover any imperfections in the edges or alignment of the surfaces underneath. Battens can be prefinished and when applied, give a neat, crisp edge to the materials.

(c) batten

material as the surfaces, such as wood, or a different material, such as metal over stone panels. In most cases, the batten is narrow relative to the exposed finished surfaces, but it may be as wide as the designer determines.

Battens are an easy, effective way to conceal joints because the finish materials do not have to be installed with their edges perfectly plumb or aligned. The batten hides minor imperfections. Because battens emphasize the joints, their locations should be carefully considered, in relation both to each other and to horizontal details. Battens are especially effective with wood detailing, coordinated with applied base and ceiling trim.

The method of attaching battens to the substrate should also be carefully considered. The connection may be concealed with adhesives or clips, or may be emphasized, with exposed screw heads, bolt covers, or other visible fasteners.

Plain Offsets

Offsets are used where two adjacent wall surfaces are not aligned, for aesthetic reasons, for functional reasons, or both. For example, one portion of an otherwise flat wall may need to be built out a few inches to conceal mechanical services or one portion of a wall may be recessed to highlight a large piece of art. Unlike outside corners of adjacent rooms that may extend

Figure 11-3 Plain offset partition transitions

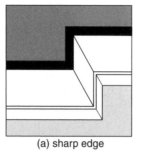

(a) sharp edge

Sharp edge wall transitions are the most common and simplest and least expensive to construct. They are what most people expect to see. Partition molding can easily be cut and fit to these types of transitions.

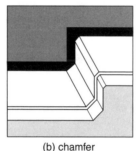

(b) chamfer

Chamfered corners soften the look of the corner and provide a safer edge. Both inside and outside corners shown here are chamfered, but typically only outside corners are chamfered.

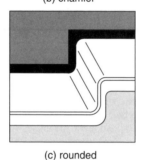

(c) rounded

Rounded transitions soften the corners even more than chamfered corners and deemphasize the change in plane. Rounded corners are also safer than square corners. As with chamfering, only the outside corners may be rounded, while inside corners can remain squared off.

for several feet or more, partition offsets are out of plane by only a few inches. The difference is that an offset is perceived as being part of the same partition plane, while an outside corner is clearly perceived as the inside corner of an adjacent space. Offsets can be treated in several ways, three of which are simple in their appearance and detailing, shown in Fig. 11-3, and three of which show an obviously interrupted change at the outside and inside of the offset, as shown in Fig. 11-5.

SHARP EDGE

A sharp edge offset is simply a 90-degree change in wall surface, as diagrammed in Fig. 11-3(a). This is a standard partition corner with the finish material, base, and any ceiling trim following the line of the partition. The offset may also be made with an angle other than 90 degrees. This detail provides the minimal amount of emphasis to the change in plane. However, if the offset is small, it may be difficult to construct it with some materials, such as wood paneling or propriety metal panels because these materials are sometimes difficult to fabricate in narrow pieces.

CHAMFER

A chamfer is a corner built with a slight angle as a transition between two other planes. Most commonly, a 45-degree chamfer is built between two planes at 90-degree angles to each other.

Figure 11-4 Methods of forming chamfers

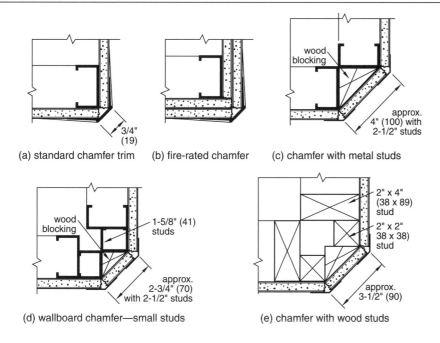

(a) standard chamfer trim   (b) fire-rated chamfer   (c) chamfer with metal studs

(d) wallboard chamfer—small studs   (e) chamfer with wood studs

See Fig. 11-3(b). In contrast with an angled offset, chamfers are small in relation to the height and area of the wall surfaces, most often in the range of a fraction of an inch to a few inches (approximately 15 mm to 100 mm).

Chamfers can be used to visually soften what would otherwise be a sharp angle and to minimize the sharp edge if safety is a concern. For gypsum wallboard partitions chamfers can be easily formed with proprietary aluminum trim pieces. Refer to Table 5-3 for some manufacturers of chamfer trim. However, premanufactured bevel trim usually requires that the wallboard be held back from the corner, so if fire-rating or acoustical performance is important, it may be necessary to use two layers of wallboard. See Fig. 11-4(a) and (b). There also may not be a corresponding premanufactured inside corner bevel, so small inside bevels would have to be framed with wood and finished with joint compound. For larger chamfers, an outside corner needs to be framed with wood, as shown in Fig. 11-4(c), (d), and (e).

For materials other than gypsum wallboard, the ease with which small chamfers can be detailed depends on the type of material. Wood is easy to form at an angle, but creating chamfers with some types of thick stone may be problematic.

ROUNDED

Like chamfers, rounded corner offsets are usually small relative the height and area of the wall planes. See Fig. 11-3(c). With gypsum wallboard, both outside and inside corners can be formed with proprietary aluminum trim. These trim pieces are available in radii from 5/8 in. (10 mm) to 6 in. (152 mm), depending on the manufacturer. Larger corners must be formed with curved wallboard or other means.

Although corners can be curved by various means, installing curved base, cornice molding, or chair molding can be problematic. Resilient straight base can be curved easily, but cove base is limited in the smallest radius that it can be curved without distorting. Wood base and other wood moldings can be curved using various means, such as lamination, machining to radius, segmenting, or steam bending, but these methods are sometimes difficult and more expensive than installing straight wood base.

Interrupted Offsets

Interrupted offsets are those planar offsets that have a significant piece of construction where the planes change direction. As shown in Fig. 11-5, there are three basic types of these offsets.

REENTRANT

A reentrant offset has an inside notch at the corner. These can occur at an outside corner as well as an inside corner, although their use is most often limited to outside corners. See Fig. 11-5(a). Reentrant corners are used to soften the abrupt turn of plane as well as to add emphasis and visual interest to the corner. For most types of reentrant corners, the primary partition construction of studs and gypsum wallboard cannot easily be formed into the reentrant shape and would leave an unusual shape on the opposite side of the partition.

Figure 11-5 Interrupted offset partition transitions

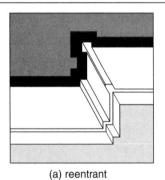

(a) reentrant

Reentrant corners have a small notch at the corner and are used to add visual interest and emphasis to an otherwise plain 90-degree corner. They may be used on inside corners, as shown here, but they are typically used on outside corners.

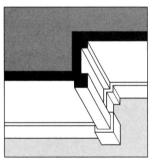

(b) trimmed

Trimmed corners also provide emphasis to a change in plane. They can also be used to conceal changes in material at the corner or hide irregularities in the joint. Trimmed corners are often used in conjunction with other trim molding.

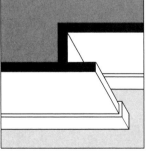

(c) overlap

Overlaps can be used to break up an otherwise long partition or to provide a more dynamic sense of enclosure to a space. Concealed lighting can be added to highlight one partition.

Figure 11-6 Reentrant corners

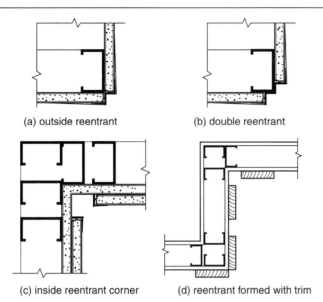

(a) outside reentrant	(b) double reentrant

(c) inside reentrant corner	(d) reentrant formed with trim

The shape itself must be formed with trim or other applied materials. Some of the ways of doing this are shown in Fig. 11-6(a) through (d).

However, larger reentrant corners may be formed by building a standard partition and building the reentrant shape with furring or added studs.

TRIMMED

Trimmed corners have an applied material on outside or inside corners that extends out from the finish surface of the partition, as shown in Fig. 11-5(b). Trimmed corners are used to conceal irregularities in the joint between adjoining planes, to make a transition from one finish material to another, or simply to emphasize the corner for aesthetic reasons.

There may or may not be a flat surface between the trims, as shown in Fig. 11-5(b), depending on the amount of offset. Applied trim corners are generally easy to build as the basic partition is constructed and then trim material applied by whatever means is appropriate.

OVERLAP

Overlapped partition transitions create an effect of one partition sliding past another without the connection being visible. See Fig. 11-5(c). These types of transitions can be used to create the effect of floating partitions, to modulate the scale of large expanses of walls, or to create a three-dimensional vertical plane. Functionally, they can also be used to conceal small open storage areas or to provide a space for indirect side lighting.

In addition to overlapping in just one place, an entire wall plane can be modulated in and out with multiple overlaps. The concept of overlapping partitions can be combined with the modulated barrier type discussed in Chapter 5.

Overlaps are easy to construct as one partition is simply extended past another. Base molding and other finishes are also easy to apply. As variations on this concept, the overlap can be curved or angled to suit the design requirements. The only limitation is that there must be enough distance between the partition planes to allow workers to apply finishes and moldings to the inside of the small space created.

11-2   FLOOR TO FLOOR

Floors are major design elements in interior spaces. They can be simple, single-plane functional surfaces or they can be raised or lowered to define space or set certain areas apart for specific functions. Levels can be varied to create dynamic spaces separated into visually distinct areas without the use of wall planes. Floor-level changes also create a strong sense of "here" and "there" within the same volume.

Floors direct movement horizontally as well as vertically. Changes in floor planes without steps or ramps automatically control and direct horizontal circulation without closing off space. The location and use of stairs or ramps determines the position and type of experience of moving from one plane to another. That experience can be purely functional or it can be made monumental, gradual, deliberate, or exciting to suit the design requirements of the space.

Floors are one of the few building elements that people actually touch. Therefore, the tactile qualities of the flooring and the transition from one floor to another can be a powerful tool for the designer to enhance the experience of a space.

Floors can also affect acoustic qualities by reflecting or absorbing room sounds and by absorbing or emphasizing the footfalls of people walking. This in itself can greatly influence people's perception of the size of a space as well as its liveliness, formality, and function. Noisy spaces, for example, generally seem more dynamic and exciting, while quiet spaces suggest formality.

Because most interior design involves working within existing buildings or with buildings that have already been designed and are under construction, most floor-level changes involve building up from a structural floor. Depending on the architectural limitations of the space or the existing ceiling height, the amount of floor level change that the interior designer may make can be limited. However, even minor changes can strongly enhance the interior design concept.

Floors transition to other floors in one of two ways, either in the same plane or in different planes. The various ways floor-to-floor transitions can be made are shown in Fig. 11-7. There are three basic types of transitions: in plane, plain offset, and interrupted offset. Refer to Chapter 8 for a discussion of the ground plane as a design element in itself.

In-Plane Transitions

In-plane transitions are those in which adjacent finishes are flush with each other or within 1/2 in. (13 mm) or each other. The planes must be within this distance to conform to accessibility regulations. Changes greater than this must be made with a ramp. There are three basic ways these types of transitions are made, as shown in Fig. 11-8.

ABUTTING MATERIALS

The simplest same-plane transition detail is butting two materials together. They are placed in direct contact with each other, as shown in Fig. 11-8(a). This is the simplest transition to make and may work well for some materials if they are perfectly flush with each other. However, without additional protection, some materials may be damaged along the edge as people walk across the joint. For example, a hard surface material like wood or stone may become chipped if installed slightly above another material such as carpet.

Figure 11-7 Floor-to-floor transitions

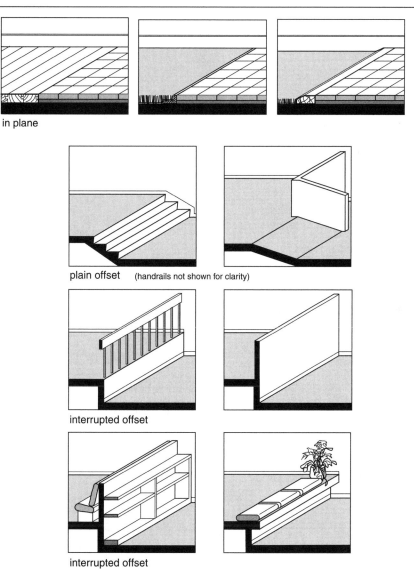

in plane

plain offset   (handrails not shown for clarity)

interrupted offset

interrupted offset

This type of flooring installation is used when the materials must change for functional reasons, but the designer does not want to emphasize or call attention to the change.

PROTECTIVE EDGE

To avoid the potential damage to materials, a thin protective edge should be placed between the materials, flush with the highest installed material. This is most commonly done with a metal edge angle, as shown in Fig. 11-9(a). This type of detail provides protections for the edge and minimizes maintenance issues while still minimizing the joint and transition. Carpet and tile accessory manufacturers provide a wide variety of edge strips for their respective materials to transition to other materials.

TRANSITION STRIP

A transition strip is a material placed between two adjacent floor surfaces both to protect the edges of the two materials and to highlight or emphasize the transition. A transition strip

Figure 11-8 In-plane floor transitions

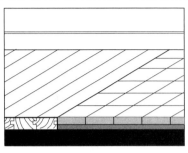

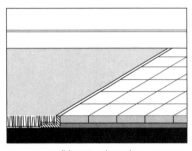

(a) abutting materials

Two materials can be butt-joined if they are approximately the same thickness and are self-edging. This detail minimizes the emphasis given to the joint. However, if one material is slightly higher than the other, damage may occur.

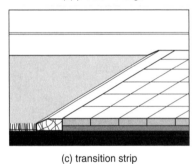

(b) protective edge

Using a metal angle, plastic edging, or similar protective edge prevents damage to both materials and can accomodate minor differences in height while minimizing the appearance of the joint.

(c) transition strip

A transition strip highlights the change in floor materials and can accommodate larger differences in material height while maintaining accessibility. The transition strip can be the same material as one of the floor surfaces or it can be a contrasting material.

can also be used to make minor changes in the finish elevation of the two surfaces. This is a practical safety feature to prevent tripping as well as being required for accessibility. Any change in elevation up to 1/2 in. (6 mm) must be made with a slope no greater than 1:2; that is, a 1/4 in (6.4 mm) high slope would need a horizontal run of 1/2 in. (13 mm). Changes in elevation up to 1/4 in. (6.4 mm) can be made vertical.

Figure 11-9 Floor transition details

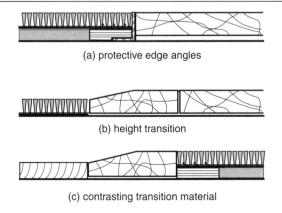

(a) protective edge angles

(b) height transition

(c) contrasting transition material

The designer also has the choice of placing an intermediate material to emphasize the transition or to make up for minor differences in level, as shown in Fig. 11-9(b). The intermediate material can be the same as one of the flooring materials or a third, contrasting material can be used, as shown in Fig. 11-9(c).

Plain Offset Floors

When adjacent floors are on different levels, one of two conditions is possible: either there is provision for convenient movement between levels at any location or the two floors are separated so that movement is possible only at selected locations.

Plain offset floors use either stairs or ramps, or both, to make the transition between levels. In these types of level transitions, the stair or ramp is the main design feature and continues across a wide portion of the level change, serving as both the method of making the transition and the physical means of movement. In most cases, when stairs are provided, an adjoining ramp is required for accessibility. Ramps cannot have a slope greater than 1 vertical unit for every 12 horizontal units, or 8.33%.

Refer to Chapter 8 for more information on the design and detailing of stairs and ramps.

PLANE CHANGE WITH STAIRS

Stairs can be used where the difference between floor levels is greater than about 12 in. (305 mm). This is because at least two steps should be used for safety; single steps should be avoided whenever possible. Stairs can occupy the majority of an opening with a minimal ramp provided only for accessibility. Handrails must be provided as required by the applicable building code.

PLANE CHANGE WITH RAMP

Ramps are best used for movement where the difference between the floor levels is less than about 12 in. (305 mm) because of the safety issues with single steps. Ramps can be used alone or with a stairway. Ramps allow for barrier-free design and generally create less of an impediment to the smooth flow of circulation. A ramp can occupy the majority of an opening with a stair of minimal width for those who prefer stairs or who cannot use ramps.

Interrupted Offset

Interrupted offsets occur when the majority of the level change is blocked to prevent movement up and down. Of course, at a selected location there is a stair and ramp to allow for physical movement between levels, but in this concept this is a minor part of the level transition. There are four basic methods for designing and detailing interrupted offsets: visible plane changes, concealed plane changes, functional transitions, and transitions in which the upper level becomes a usable surface. These are shown in Fig. 11-10.

VISIBLE PLANE CHANGE

A visible plane change occurs when occupants can see both the lower and upper levels. If a guard is needed, it is open so there is a clear sight line. See Fig. 11-10(a). Visible plane changes are used when the space must be kept as open as possible and when the designer wants to emphasize the change. The IBC does not require a guard if the change in level is less than

Figure 11-10 Interrupted offset floor transitions

The floor surfaces and the change in elevation of a visible plane change can be clearly seen from both the lower and upper levels. If a guard is needed it should be as open as possible while still meeting building code requirements.

(a) visible plane change

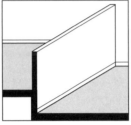

A concealed plane change looks like a low partition when viewed from the lower level. It is a simple, low-cost method of minimizing the appearance of the level change while providing a guard. The solid partition also hides furniture and other equipment placed against the wall.

(b) concealed plane change

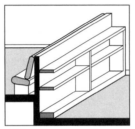

Like a concealed plane change, a functional transition provides usable area along the level change. Functions such as storage, counter space, seating, and display space can be built into the transition.

(c) functional transition

Using the upper level as a platform provides a visible plane change while making use of the edge. If the applicable building code does not require a guard, accessories along the edge can provide a visual cue for a moderate amount of safety.

(d) floor as bench or platform

30 in. (762 mm), but for safety reasons a guard should be used. For a completely open feeling a glass guard can be used. One way to detail this is shown in Fig. 11-11.

CONCEALED PLANE CHANGE

A concealed plane change uses a solid railing to limit the view from the lower level. This is used when the level change needs to be deemphasized or when there is furniture or other equipment near the edge. The simplest method of creating this type of concealment is to use a low partition, continuing the finish material of the level drop up the surface of the partition. The partition can be capped in any of the ways shown in Fig. 5-17.

FUNCTIONAL TRANSITION

A functional transition incorporates useful elements into the change in level. For example, as shown in Fig. 11-10(c), storage units face the lower level and built-in seating is located at

Figure 11-11 Glass guard and level change

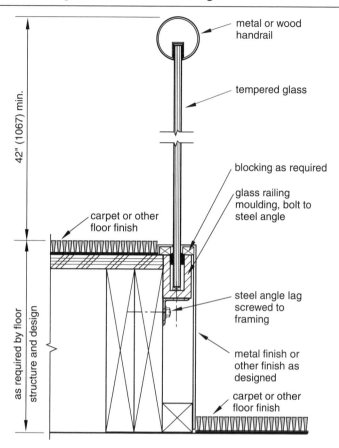

42" (1067) min.

carpet or other
floor finish

as required by floor
structure and design

metal or wood
handrail

tempered glass

blocking as required

glass railing
moulding, bolt to
steel angle

steel angle lag
screwed to
framing

metal finish or
other finish as
designed

carpet or other
floor finish

the upper level. This conceptual approach minimizes the effect of the level change, making it look more like a low partition, if this is the design intent. Whatever functional element is used also serves as a guard for safety.

FLOOR AS BENCH

The upper level of a floor transition can also be used as a bench or other type of work surface, as shown in Fig. 11-10(d). This maintains the open feeling of the space while providing an indication of a level change, providing some degree of safety if a guard is not otherwise needed by the applicable building code.

11-3   CEILING TO CEILING

As discussed in Chapter 7, the ceiling is a major design element because it is always in view and occupies a major percentage of the total planar elements that define a space. Because the ceiling must also contain a variety of other features such as lighting and mechanical equipment, its design is important.

A ceiling can express the structure of a building or completely conceal it with a suspended flat surface. Alternately, a ceiling can create an entirely new shape. If sufficient space is available, ceilings allow a great deal of flexibility in shaping space because they do not have to be flat or follow a particular configuration like floor and wall planes do.

Figure 11-12 Ceiling-to-ceiling transition concepts

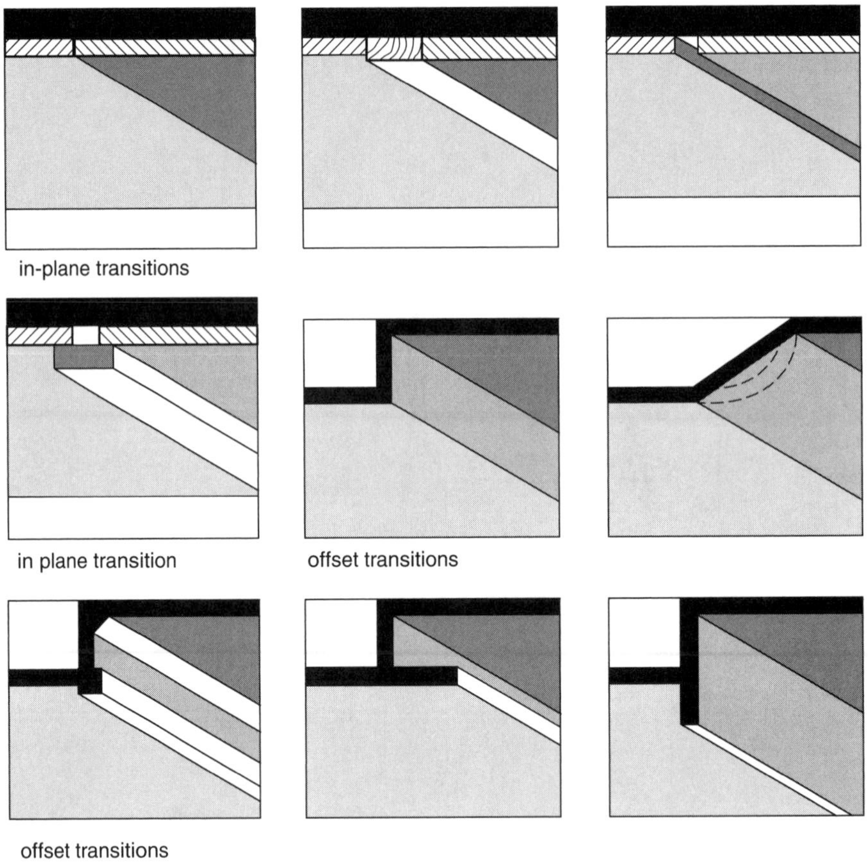

in-plane transitions

in plane transition   offset transitions

offset transitions

Because ceilings are nearly always out of physical reach, their effect must be a purely visual one. The type of material used for the ceilings and the amount of space above the ceiling determines what type of transition may be most appropriate.

There are basically two variations of transition from one ceiling to another: transitions that are in the same plane and transitions that are offset. See Fig. 11-12.

In-Plane Transitions

In-plane transitions occur when two adjacent ceilings are flush or nearly flush with each other, as shown in Fig. 11-13. There are four basic ways of designing this type of transition.

ABUTTING

Abutting ceilings are the same as abutting walls or floors. Two materials or finishes touch each other along a single line and are flush or nearly flush. See Fig. 11-13(a). Butt joints minimize the change in ceiling materials and keep the ceiling elevation constant. This is a simple joint to make, but as with other butt joints, it is sometimes difficult to get both materials to align perfectly and finishing may be difficult. Butt joints are also only appropriate for certain materials. Gypsum wallboard and acoustical ceiling tile, for example, may be aligned but require some type of trim between them to support the edges of both materials. As shown in Fig. 11-14(a), a white, aluminum extrusion can be used to serve this purpose without being obvious, but it is still not a true butt joint.

Figure 11-13 In-plane ceiling transitions

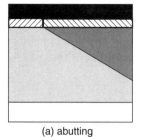

Butt joints provide a good in-plane match of finish materials if both finishes are placed on the same substrate or both substrates are the same thickness. These types of joints are simple and easy to make, but it is difficult to get two surfaces to align if they are on different substrates.

(a) abutting

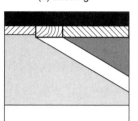

Transition strips can accommodate slightly different substrate thicknesses and disguise any minor problems with alignment. Because it is difficult to get two surfaces to be flush, it is best to make the transition strip at a different elevation than the two ceiling materials. Transition strips also highlight the change in ceiling finishes.

(b) transition strip

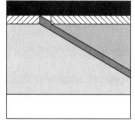

As with wall reveals, a ceiling reveal visually separates two different materials and provides an interesting shadow line. A reveal also disguises any minor misalignment between the two edges.

(c) reveal

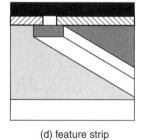

A feature strip is used when the ceiling finishes or substrates are the same thickness. It provides an easy, inexpensive way to conceal the joint thickness and any misalignment of the edges of the finish. Like a transition strip, a feature strip also highlights the change in ceiling materials or finishes.

(d) feature strip

TRANSITION STRIP

A transition strip, shown diagrammatically in Fig. 11-13(b), is a third material placed between two ceiling surfaces to emphasize the transition, to add visual interest to the ceiling, or to accommodate slightly different substrate thicknesses. The transition strip can be flush with one of the surfaces, both surfaces, or neither surface, depending on the design concept or the functional requirements of the detail. Transition strips are relatively easy to apply on gypsum wallboard ceilings but may be difficult to apply to acoustical ceilings. Fig. 11-14(b) shows one method of using a wood strip with a wallboard ceiling, while using it to support the ceiling angle for an acoustical ceiling.

REVEAL

A reveal is a noticeable gap between the two ceiling materials. See Fig. 11-13(c). As with wall reveals, a ceiling reveal conceals any slight misalignment of the surfaces, adds visual interest,

Figure 11-14 Planar transition details

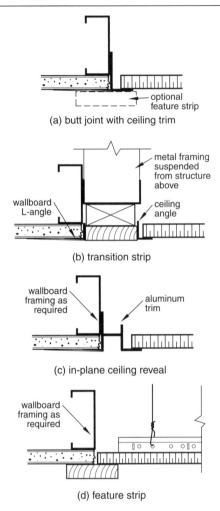

(a) butt joint with ceiling trim

(b) transition strip

(c) in-plane ceiling reveal

(d) feature strip

creates a clear separation between two materials, and may make finishing easier. A reveal may be created by simply separating the two materials by the desired amount if they have a finished edge, or by using a preformed aluminum trim, as shown in Fig. 11-14(c).

FEATURE STRIP

A feature strip is a third material placed over the joint of the two ceiling surfaces, much like a batten strip used for wall transitions. See Fig. 11-13(d). Featured strips provide a functional way to easily finish a joint, while emphasizing the transition between the two ceiling finishes. One way to detail this is shown in Fig. 11-14(d).

Offset Transitions

Offset transitions occur where the adjacent ceiling planes are at obviously different elevations. Offset transitions are required to create many of the ceiling concepts discussed in Chapter 7. There are five basic types of ceiling-to-ceiling transitions.

SHARP EDGE

A sharp edge is simply a 90-degree change from the lower horizontal ceiling plane to the upper plane, as diagrammed in Fig. 11-15(a). The vertical portion of this type of offset

Figure 11-15 Offset ceiling transitions

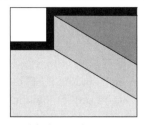

(a) sharp edge

A sharp edge is the most common type of ceiling transition and can be formed with almost any material, including acoustical ceiling systems. However, the vertical portion is most commonly gypsum wallboard.

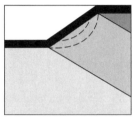

(b) angle or curve

An angle or curve gives a more gentle transition between two ceiling planes and can be an effective design, especially when combined with similar shapes used elsewhere in the space.

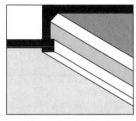

(c) emphasized edges

Emphasized edges are used to draw attention to the ceiling transition and to add interest the change in plane. The edges can be treated with any material and can be traditional wood trim or contemporary in feeling.

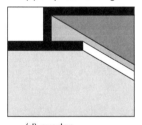

(d) overlap

An overlap gives a lighter feeling to a ceiling height transition than other types, making it appear that one ceiling floats below the other. The portion inside the overlap can conceal HVAC registers or indirect lighting.

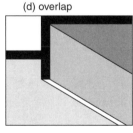

(e) bulkhead

A bulkhead creates a strong volumetric feeling to the space below the upper ceiling. Combined with a raised floor this design can strongly differentiate one space from another.

can be constructed of any material but gypsum wallboard is most commonly used whether the horizontal planes are wallboard, suspended acoustical tile, or other materials. Gypsum wallboard and its support framing allow a wide variety of trims and other construction elements to be attached to support any type of ceiling system. If acoustical tile is used for the two horizontal plans details such as those shown in Figs. 7-10(a), (b), and (d) can be used.

ANGLED OR CURVED EDGE

The transition between ceilings can also be made with a sloped plane set at any angle that is appropriate for the design concept. See Fig. 11-15(b). It may also be made with a curved profile. The transition may be made with the same material as the horizontal portions or a different material. For example, the curve or angle may be gypsum wallboard, while the two level portions can be wallboard, acoustical tile, or other ceiling finishes.

EDGES EMPHASIZED

Emphasized edges are used when the ceiling transition needs to be highlighted. The emphasis may be created with applied trim or, if the ceiling is gypsum wallboard, by building up the desired profile with wallboard. See Figs. 11-16(a) and (b).

Special aluminum trim may also be used to emphasize the edges. Three examples of proprietary trim are shown in Fig. 11-16(c) that combine emphasized edges with an angled transition.

OVERLAP

An overlap transition is one in which the lower ceiling plane is extended beyond the vertical connection so it appears the lower ceiling is floating below the upper ceiling, as shown in Fig. 11-15(d). The elevation difference is determined by the design concept, the desired ceiling height, and by the limitations of structure and mechanical services above the upper ceiling.

Figure 11-16 Emphasized edges

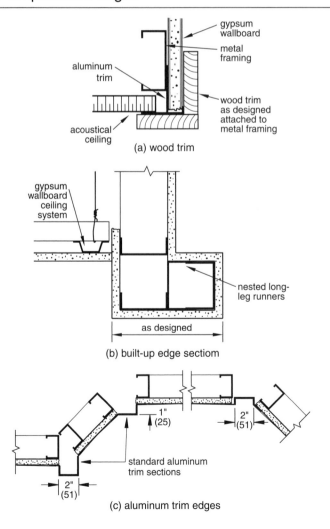

(a) wood trim

(b) built-up edge sectiom

(c) aluminum trim edges

The space between the two ceilings can be used for indirect lighting, to conceal air supply registers, or can be left open. See Figs. 7-10(c) and 7-11(c).

BULKHEAD

A bulkhead is a vertical construction element extending from the upper ceiling to well below the lower ceiling. See Fig. 11-15(e). This detail emphasizes the transition as well as creating a strong sense of spatial volume below the upper ceiling as diagrammed in Fig. 7-2(d). This design approach is especially effective when coordinated with a differentiated floor finish or a raised ground plane as shown in Fig. 7-2(c).

Bulkheads are easily constructed with gypsum wallboard framing suspended from the structure above similar to the detail shown in Fig. 7-10(b) except that the lower edge of the bulkhead is extended farther below the elevation of the lower ceiling.

CHAPTER 12

STRUCTURAL TRANSITIONS

12-1 INTRODUCTION

A sense of structure is basic to a person's perception of the environment. People live in a world of gravity, compression, tension, bending, twisting, and impact. Even without knowledge of the technical aspects of structural design, people have a sense of building elements responding to these basic structural forces. For example, people have an inherent sense of whether a column looks like it is adequate to support a beam or if a sign looks too heavy for the wires supporting it.

Every experience in architecture and interior design is judged, consciously or unconsciously, within the context of these structural forces. The result is conformation of structural forces being stable or a visual dissonance when what is visible runs counter to a person's normal experience and expectations. In most cases, the structural forces are perceived in terms of a structural transition from one component to another, such as a beam resting on a column. In this chapter *structural transition* refers to the connection of one element to another, whether the connection is a real, supportive link or whether the connection is simply a visual suggestion of a structural connection.

Of course, by law, interior designers cannot design the actual structure of a building or major structural elements. However, in the broadest sense, even the simplest interior detail has a structural component. For example, a countertop spanning an open area must support its own weight and any weight placed on it without bending or breaking. Interior designers are involved in structure-related design in the following ways:

- By covering the real structure of the building with finishes, either to emphasize the structure or conceal it
- By creating presumed structure with, for example, false beams and columns
- By detailing building elements governed by prescriptive codes in seismic zones
- By designing and detailing suspended elements that are not otherwise governed by building codes
- By detailing and specifying the anchorage of wall-mounted items
- By detailing architectural woodwork where minor forces are present
- By detailing other miscellaneous interior elements such as low partitions, openings, or panel supports, that have a real or presumed structural component

The ability to create structural expression provides the interior designer with a powerful tool to enhance design concepts, shape experience, and solve detailing problems. The designer can decide whether to express and celebrate structure, articulate an opposition to it, or to design independently of it. The designer can create a sense of stability, provoke dissonance, create interest, suggest wonder, or completely conceal structure. Any approach is not necessarily better than another; the interior designer must simply determine which structural expression best meets the design goals of the project.

Structure can also suggest and define spatial volume. Historically, structure has been the prime determinant of spatial character and has largely been lost as a design tool in much of current architecture and interior design. For example, the huge columns, vaulted ceilings, and massive walls of the great cathedrals are the main form givers of those interior spaces, not the detailed painting and carving on their surfaces. Contrast that approach with most any contemporary interior where flat ceilings, plain walls and nondescript openings give little clues as to what actually supports the spatial enclosure. If desired, the interior designer can articulate the structure of a building as a starting point for defining space and specific use areas.

This chapter discusses the conceptual ways to make transitions between major building elements as well as smaller building components. These transitions can be categorized into three broad areas: columns, beams, and suspended elements. Chapter 4 discussed some of the basic structural methods of detailing connections, while suggestions for specific structural connections have been given in various other chapters.

12-2 COLUMNS

Columns are one of the most common architectural structural elements that remain visible in interior design. They may appear freestanding in the middle of a room or may prominently extend out from an otherwise flat wall. Other structural building elements, such as beams, joists, and bearing walls, are generally concealed by other architectural or interior construction finishes. The interior designer may choose to minimize the appearance of columns within a space by applying a finish with the smallest possible dimensions while still retaining any required fire-resistive coatings or by hiding them within partition construction. In other instances, the designer may elect to emphasize the column by enlarging the dimensions of the finish or by changing the shape of the finish covering.

Regardless of the final size and configuration of the column itself, the design and detailing of the transition between the column and the ceiling, floor, or beam are important considerations in expressing the designer's approach to structure.

Column-to-Ceiling Transitions

The method by which a column supports a ceiling or a beam is a basic design archetype. Most fundamentally, a beam rests directly on a column. The beam, in turn, supports other secondary beams or the ceiling. All people intuitively understand this fundamental structural principle and use it to assess other structural conditions that they experience. However, in interior design most conditions present the intersection of a column with the ceiling directly, without an intermediate beam.

From a strictly design standpoint, it is sometimes difficult to design and detail an elegant column to ceiling transition because in much of contemporary construction the ceiling is a suspended acoustical ceiling whose grid may or may not be coordinated with the building structural grid or the functional layout of partitions is completely independent of the building's structure. However, when possible, the interior designer can consider some of the following approaches to structural expression. The first four suggest the column is actually supporting the ceiling, the ceiling being dependent on the column. The second group of four indicate that the ceiling is clearly independent from the interior column and, thus, the building structure itself.

NO TRANSITION

The most common method of making the transition between a column and a ceiling is no transition at all. See Fig. 12-1(a). This is the simplest and least costly and is one way to minimize the appearance and significance of the structure, if that is the designer's intent. If no fire-resistive coating is required, the structural column may even be left exposed to minimize the size of the column. This approach is the most tenuous in suggesting that the column is supporting the ceiling.

If a gypsum wallboard ceiling is used, the transition with a gypsum wallboard column will appear as a simple inside corner. The intersection with a suspended acoustical ceiling will

Figure 12-1 Dependent column-to-ceiling transitions

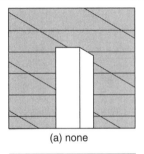

The simplest type of column-to-ceiling transition is to have none at all. This is common because of its low cost and quick and easy installation. When a suspended acoustical ceiling is used, a ceiling angle may be the only construction visible at the junction of the two elements.

(a) none

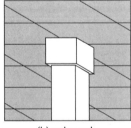

An enlarged column is a simple transition, acknowledging the meeting of column and ceiling without elaborate construction.

(b) enlarged

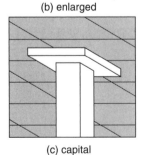

A capital is a major design feature between the column and the ceiling. The capital can be simple, as shown here, or more decorative. Traditionally, a capital was used to create a broader bearing area. It is best used when coordinated with the type and layout of the ceiling.

(c) capital

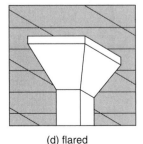

A flared capital appears to spread the weight from above and gives a sense of stability. As with other dependent column transitions, the location of the ceiling grid should be coordinated with the size and shape of the capital where it touches the ceiling.

(d) flared

only be interrupted with a simple ceiling angle. It appears like any other wall or penetration of the ceiling.

ENLARGED

The classic method of making a transition from column to ceiling is with a capital or other transition device or to have the column support a beam, which, in turn, supports the ceiling. If the column appears to support the ceiling directly, as is typical with interior construction, the transition may be made with a simple enlargement of the column. This is a slightly more elegant solution to the transition detail. It gives a suggestion of a traditional approach to column design but without elaborate construction or cost. It can be as simple as an extra layer of gypsum wallboard or plain wood trim. See Fig. 12-1(b). The trim is usually identical to other trim or crown molding used against the partitions.

CAPITAL

A transition with a capital uses a distinct and fairly large element between the top of the shaft of the column and the ceiling. It is the classical method of construction with the capital providing a larger bearing surface for two beams joining at the column than the column could provide alone. Intuitively, people see the capital collecting the weight of the structure above and placing it on the column.

Capitals can be designed in a wide variety of configurations, from the simple column cap, shown in Fig. 12-1(c) to ornate classical capitals. Of course, the detailing of the capital should be coordinated with the type and style of the ceiling and with the overall design concept of the space in which it is used. Figure 12-2 shows two variations of how to detail capitals with metal framing.

FLARED

A flared capital is one of many variations that can be used. Flared capitals make the obvious transition from the size and shape of the column shaft to the size of the upper portion of

Figure 12-2 Framed column capital

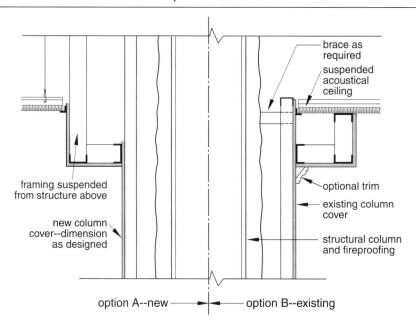

the capital, as shown in Fig. 12-1(d). Flared columns can easily be detailed by using metal framing.

REVEAL

The second broad group of column-to-ceiling transitions includes those that clearly and obviously treat the ceiling as a separate, distinct interior finish from the architectural structure of the building. A reveal provides a subtle separation between the column and the ceiling.

With a reveal, it appears that the column is penetrating the ceiling. See Fig. 12-3(a). It is one of the most honest expressions in contemporary construction because, in most cases, columns really do not support the ceiling. The ceiling is a separate and artificial plane, and the interior finish is separate from the architecture. Reveals can be constructed easily with the same gypsum wallboard trim discussed in Chapter 7 and shown in Fig. 7-10(a). Larger reveals can be detailed by using ceiling trim held away from the column by a few inches.

Figure 12-3 Independent column-to-ceiling transitions

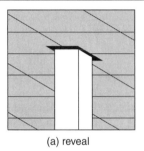

(a) reveal

A reveal transition may be created by using a simple W-trim supporting acoustical tile or with a deeper and wider reveal created by framing an opening around the column with trim accessories or gypsum wallboard.

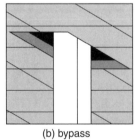

(b) bypass

A bypass installation distinctly separates the suspended ceiling from the column, which appears to extend untouched to the structure above. The distance between the column and the edge of the ceiling trim can be set at whatever value the designer wants.

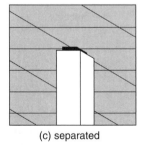

(c) separated

A separated column visually disconnects the column from the ceiling. Although the actual structural part of the column extends to the beam above, when viewed at eye level, the effect is that there is no connection between the column and the ceiling.

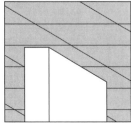

(d) column to wall

In this design, the column is enlarged to appear to be a thick partition or bearing wall. Portions not occupied by the actual column can be used for storage or other uses.

Bypass

To very clearly separate the column from the ceiling a bypass detail can be developed as shown in Fig. 12-3(b). With this detail, there is a large gap between the column and the edge of the suspended ceiling. The ceiling appears to float independently from the column and if the gap is large enough the building structure and mechanical services may be visible. Because the edge of the ceiling suspension system is visible some type of trim should be used, similar to that shown in Fig. 7-10(c).

Separated

A separated column appears to stop short of the ceiling line. See Fig. 12-3(c). To make this effect work the finish covering must be significantly larger than the actual structural column, which may be difficult if the column is concrete or steel with applied fire-resistive coating. The column cover must extend out from the actual column enough so that the sightline from most areas of the space prevents the actual column from being visible. To enhance this effect, the actual, smaller column that extends through the ceiling can be finished with a mirror to reflect the surrounding ceiling surface.

Column into Bearing Wall

A column can also be designed and detailed to be independent from the ceiling by transforming it into something other than a column. As diagrammed in Fig. 12-3(d), the column can be enlarged into what appears to be a thick partition. The final finish can be simply gypsum wallboard or any finish material that is consistent with the overall design concept of the space. To make more efficient use of the space, the portion of the enlarged partition that does not actually contain the column can be used for shelving or other functional needs.

Column-to-Floor Transitions

As with a column-to-ceiling transition, the intersection between the base of a column and the floor can be understated, emphasized as a normal structural condition, or the two elements can be clearly differentiated. However, unlike the top of a column, any additional construction at the floor line requires additional floor space and may present a tripping hazard if it exceeds the thickness of standard wall base. As with column-to-ceiling transitions the column at the base can appear to be dependent on the floor or independent from it.

None

The column can terminate directly on the floor, with no base or only the standard base used elsewhere in the room applied to the column. This is the easiest and least costly approach that requires the least amount of floor space and that minimizes the appearance of the column. See Fig. 12-4(a). This is the simplest type of dependent transition.

Enlarged Base

The second type of dependent column-to-floor transition is an enlarged base. As with columns supporting the ceiling or a beam, the most stable-looking transition is a column resting on a base larger than the column. Structurally and traditionally, this was a way to spread the weight of the column load over a larger area of the floor. Even though this is not actually the case in most instances in contemporary construction, the visual effect is the same. People perceive

Figure 12-4 Dependent column-to-floor transitions

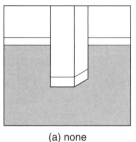

To deemphasize the column at the base, the designer may choose to provide no base at all or just a minimal base as used elsewhere in the room. This is the easiest and least costly approach and requires no elaborate detailing.

(a) none

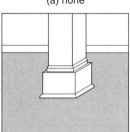

An enlarged base appears as the most stable and normal as this is the traditional way to treat columns so the weight appears to be spread out on the supporting floor. An enlarged base may be a simply applied wood trim or broader, built-up sections of wood, stone, or other materials.

(b) enlarged base

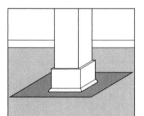

A distinct floor material placed around the column base calls attention to the transition without requiring any special base detailing and without presenting a tripping hazard, assuming the two floor materials are flush.

(c) floor material change

this type of transition as being inherently stable. The size of the base can be as large and complex as desired. See Fig. 12-4(b)

FLOOR MATERIAL CHANGE

As diagrammed in Fig. 12-4(c) the base condition can be emphasized by using a large base as well as by changing flooring materials around the base. This provides additional highlighting of the intersection without using additional floor space or creating a tripping hazard. The floor material around the column can be extended as far as the designer wants or, in large spaces, it can run continuously from one column to the next, suggesting the actual structural grid of the building.

FLOATING COLUMN

A floating column, diagrammed in Fig. 12-5(a), is one type of independent column-to-floor transition that visually separates the structure from the interior finish of the space. Because the actual structural column must continue to and through the floor, an additional thickness of finish material must be detailed that stops short of the finish floor line. This can be as simple as using a base reveal, such as shown in Fig. 10-4(c), or by furring out from the original finish covering to extend the finish several inches out from the actual column. One way this can be done is with a J-runner similar to Fig. 10-4(b). Whichever way this concept is detailed, it is most effective when the actual column cannot be seen at normal eye level and it so the column truly looks like it does not touch the floor.

Figure 12-5 Independent column-to-floor transitions

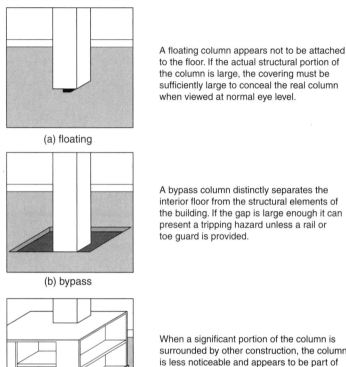

A floating column appears not to be attached to the floor. If the actual structural portion of the column is large, the covering must be sufficiently large to conceal the real column when viewed at normal eye level.

(a) floating

A bypass column distinctly separates the interior floor from the structural elements of the building. If the gap is large enough it can present a tripping hazard unless a rail or toe guard is provided.

(b) bypass

When a significant portion of the column is surrounded by other construction, the column is less noticeable and appears to be part of the other construction. This concept can be combined with the "column-to-wall" concept to completely conceal the column.

(c) surround

BYPASS

As with a bypass column-to-ceiling transition, a floor bypass distinctly separates the interior finish from the structure of the building. See Fig. 12-5(b). Although this can be an effective way to create an independent column-to-floor transition, it can present a tripping hazard if the reveal is too large. Some of the ways to create a bypass column at the floor line are the same as the partition conditions shown in Fig. 10-6.

SURROUND

A column surround uses the column as a position to create additional construction so that the column no longer appears as a structural support but as a functional element within the space. The surround can take on the appearance of a thick partition, as diagrammed in Fig. 12-3(d), or be surrounded by storage or other usable construction, as shown in Fig. 12-5(c).

Column-to-Beam Transitions

While a column-to-ceiling transition is the most common in interior design, there are three situations where the intersection of a column and a beam is visible or suggested. In the first instance, the structural column and beam may be exposed as part of the architecture of the building. The interior designer can elect to leave them exposed as part of the interior design or cover them. In the second instance, finish materials, such as gypsum wallboard, cover the actual structural column and beam, but the covering follows the same general line as the

Figure 12-6 Finish column-to-beam transitions

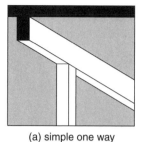

(a) simple one way

Simple beam to column connections are made by resting the beam directly on the top of the column. This approach can be used with typical structural materials, such as wood, or it can be created with gypsum wallboard to create one smooth surface.

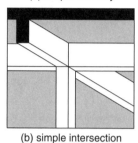

(b) simple intersection

A simple intersecting beam and column transition is typically used for columns in the middle of a space that supports structural beams that are enclosed with gypsum wallboard finish. In large spaces, this creates an interesting pattern of low beams and ceiling spaces that define the structural bays of the building.

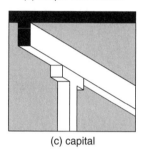

(c) capital

A capital used on top of a column that, in turn, supports a beam is a classical way of post-and-beam construction. It can be used with simple wallboard finishes or with false structures of wood or other materials that the interior designer may create. Normally, the capital is approximately the same width as the column.

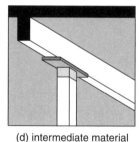

(d) intermediate material

An intermediate material may be used much like a capital but it may have a different size and shape and be constructed of a different material, at the designer's discretion. It generally is only effective if the column and beam are of materials that are normally associated with structural materials, such as wood.

structure. For example, a furred-out covering below the ceiling line indicates that there is an actual structural beam dropped below the ceiling. In the third case, the designer may create an artificial column-to-beam connection, either as a one-time instance in the space or to repeat an existing architectural connection.

There are several different conceptual approaches to finish column-to-beam transitions. These are shown diagrammatically in Fig. 12-6. In all these examples, gypsum wallboard construction is used.

SIMPLE ONE-WAY CONNECTION

In the one-way connection the actual structure of the building is covered with some type of finish material, most often gypsum wallboard on metal framing. See Fig. 12-6(a). The depth and width of the beam covering depends on the size of the structural element and, if the beam or column is steel, any fire-resistive coating that was applied during construction of the building. This type of detail minimizes the effect of the structure as much as is possible and is the least costly to create.

Quite often, the finish covering may have been applied as part of the base building construction and the interior designer may choose to keep what is there, change the shape or finish, or make the covering larger. In any case, any fire-resistive coating must not be disturbed or removed. Some architectural details incorporate the gypsum wallboard covering as the fire-resistant covering. In this situation, it should not be removed or disturbed, but additional construction can be built around it. Of course, if the columns or beams are concrete no additional fire-resistive coating will be present. The interior designer should review the architectural plans of the building or consult with the architect or building official if it is unclear what the column or beam material is or how it is fireproofed.

SIMPLE INTERSECTION

A variation of the one-way beam-to-column connection is the simple intersection in which a structural beam is framed into a girder on top of a column. All the structural elements are covered with gypsum wallboard, as diagrammed in Fig. 12-6(b). In large spaces, this type of simple transition can be used to express the structure as well as to create distinct spatial volumes within each structural bay. As a variation on the simple intersection, an enlarged capital may be used to give a sense of support between the column and the beams. The finish column covering may be smaller or larger than the width of the beam covering, at the discretion of the interior designer.

CAPITAL

Using a capital to distribute the weight from the beams to the column is a classic method of construction and can be suggested by simply enlarging the wallboard framing above the shaft of the column, as shown in Fig. 12-6(c). Painting or other finish materials can further enhance the effect.

INTERMEDIATE MATERIAL

An intermediate material used between the top of the column and the beam enclosure may be used to emphasize the structural transition and make it a more important detail. See Fig. 12-6(d). The intermediate material can be as simple as a different paint color or finish, or it may actually be a different material, such as wood trim or stone veneer around the column. It can be as simple or elaborate as the designer feels necessary to coordinate with the design concept of the space.

There are several different conceptual approaches to *architectural* column-to-beam transitions; that is, those that look like a true structural connection rather than just being a finish covering. The beams can bear on top of the column, on brackets or ledgers, or other types of connectors can support the beams as the column appears to continue upward. These are shown diagrammatically in Fig. 12-7.

BRACKET

A *bracket*, sometimes called a *knee brace*, projects out from the column to support or brace the beam. Brackets can be detailed in a wide variety of configurations, two of which are shown in Fig. 12-7(a). Brackets emphasize the connection between the column and beam to highlight the structural aspects of the construction. If two columns are close together the brackets can also give a strong sense of division between the spaces on either side of the beam. Brackets

Figure 12-7 Architectural column-to-beam transitions

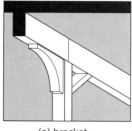

A bracket appears to support or brace the connection between the beam and the column. Brackets can be designed in a variety of ways and may or may not include visible fasteners, such as bolts or screws.

(a) bracket

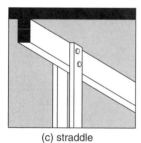

A ledger is attached to the column to provide support for the beam. For false beams and columns, the ledger may be designed in any configuration and any size. For wood construction the ledger is generally wood but may also be a steel angle or other type of connector.

(b) ledger

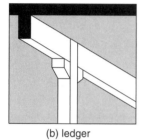

A pair of column members can straddle the beam as shown here or two horizontal members may straddle a single column. Bolts or other fasteners are used to connect the beam and column.

(c) straddle

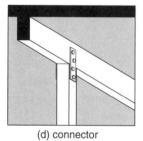

Connector transitions make a design feature of the joint between the beam and column. Steel plates or other types of metal connectors may be used and the fasteners and plates may even be sized larger than would normally be required for strictly structural reasons to bring them into scale with the structural elements and the space in which they are used.

(d) connector

can simply be a wallboard shape or the designer can detail them with wood, metal, or other materials as simply or elaborately as required to suit the design concept of the space.

LEDGER

In structural terms, a *ledger* is relatively small construction element attached to the column that supports a beam framing into the column instead of resting on top of it. Sometimes also called a *corbel*, a ledger can take on any configuration, from a simple rectangular block of wood to ornately carved woodwork. See Fig. 12-7(b).

STRADDLE

A straddle connection is one in which either two vertical members are placed on either side of the beam, as shown in Fig. 12-7(c), or one or two horizontal members are supported by a single column. In either case, the members are connected with nails, screws, pegs, or bolts to transfer the loads from the beam to the column. The beams and column are typically wood in this type of joint. This type of transition provides an interesting detail and emphasizes the structural nature of the connection. For a nonstructural, false connection that the interior designer may be detailing, the actual fasteners are not critical. However, in most cases, this type of joint expresses the structure the best when bolts are used.

CONNECTOR

A connector is a metal fabrication used with bolts or other fasteners to hold two or more structural components together and transfer loads. See Fig. 12-7(d). Generally, connectors are used for wood members. For example, a steel plate fastened between the column and the beam gives a stronger sense of structure than just showing the beam resting on the column as diagrammed in Fig. 12-6(a). Connectors come in a wide variety of shapes, sizes, and configurations. Of course, for the false structure the interior designer may be detailing, the actual size and configuration is not critical, so the designer may develop any type of detail that looks appropriate. In addition to the simple connection shown in Fig. 12-7(d), connectors are useful for making joints when several elements, such as wood beams and columns, intersect at odd angles.

12-3 BEAMS

Beams are major structural elements but are typically concealed in both commercial and residential construction. When they are exposed, they are usually designed as a major architectural feature of the building, and the interior designer may want to leave them exposed to respect the architectural design.

In some cases, structural beams encroach into the interior space and require an area to be furred down to conceal them and any fire-resistive coating material applied to them. This is especially true where the floor-to-floor dimension is small and the distance from the suspended ceiling and the floor above is not sufficient to conceal all the structural members. In other cases, the interior designer may want to express the location of beams and possibly add false beams to enhance the sense of the building's structure or to use the implied structural elements to define space.

There are three basic conditions that the interior designer must consider when designing the transition of beams to other building elements: between a beam and a partition, between a beam and the ceiling, and between a beam and another beam. These can be combined with the beam-to-column transitions discussed in the previous section to develop an overall design concept related to structural transitions.

As with other structural transitions, how the designer treats beams depends on the designer's overall philosophy of structure: whether to treat the interiors as completely independent from the architectural structure of the building, to emphasize the structure, or to minimize the appearance of the structure when it is an unavoidable feature.

Beam-to-Partition Transitions

NONE

The simplest transition is none at all. See Fig. 12-8(a). In this case, the structural beam or the finish covering simply disappears into the partition. As with other types of structural

Figure 12-8 Beam-to-partition transitions

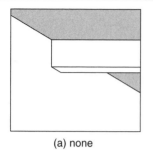

(a) none

The simplest transition is one in which the beam runs directly into the partition. The beam may be a wallboard covering or it may be any other material with the wallboard finished around it. This is the least accurate expression of structure because there appears to be nothing supporting the beam.

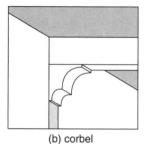

(b) corbel

A corbel provides a visible means of support for the beam framing into it. The corbel may be made simply from wallboard or it can be wood or some other material. The corbel can appear to be supported by a vertical member by applying another finish to the partition or by installing a thin layer of finish that extends to the floor as shown here.

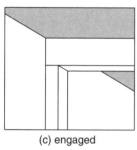

(c) engaged

An engaged column provides a simple post-and-beam connection that most people recognize as being structurally stable. The engaged column can be gypsum wallboard if the beam is enclosed in wallboard or it can be wood or some other material. A corbel may also be used to emphsize the structural nature of the transition.

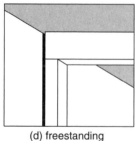

(d) freestanding

A freestanding beam-to-partition transition appears as if the beam and the column do not touch the partition at all. This may be constructed by actually holding the false structural members away from the partition or by using a simple wallboard reveal so it appears that the partition runs past the column and beam.

transitions, this approach minimizes the appearance of the beam and may even appear as an enclosure for ductwork or other mechanical equipment. If the structural beam is exposed, the designer may choose to cover it with gypsum wallboard or some other finish to disguise its appearance.

CORBEL

A *corbel* is a small projection from a wall designed to support a structural member. Traditionally, corbels were stone members projecting from stone walls to support stone arches but the concept can also be used for any material. Figure 12-8(b) shows one approach to creating a corbel. They can be constructed of gypsum wallboard on metal framing or by using a more traditional structural material such as wood or stone. However, wood or stone on a simple wallboard partition may look out of character, so the designer may want to use the same material as the corbel and extend it down the partition.

ENGAGED COLUMN

An *engaged column* is a column that is attached to a wall. In commercial design, it typically appears as a gypsum wallboard covering over an actual column, but an artificial one may be created simply by furring out from the partition. See Fig. 12-8(c). Using an engaged column to make the transition to an enclosed beam is a more honest representation of a structural connection and can create a visual interest along a partition, particularly a long one that would otherwise be uninterrupted. An engaged column may be combined with a corbel to create an even stronger sense of structure. While an engaged column emphasizes the structure, it requires very little floor space and generally does not interfere with the functional use of the space. If the beam is deep and the corbel relatively large, this approach is good for creating a strong definition of space on either side of the beam.

FREESTANDING COLUMN

A freestanding column visually separates the structure from the interior partition. The partition may be placed well away from the column so that there is actually open space behind the column or the partition can be constructed with a small reveal to make it appear that the column is freestanding. See Fig. 12-8(d). The column may either be covered with gypsum wallboard or wood or other materials can be used. Freestanding columns require more floor area to create and may interfere with furniture placement or other functional uses, but they do give a strong sense of structure to the space.

Beam-to-Ceiling Transitions

Beam-to-ceiling transitions occur when the interior designer is responsible for both the ceiling design and the treatment of any exposed beams. However, if the intent of the building architect was to leave the roof or ceiling structure exposed, the interior designer may elect to keep it exposed or just provide intermittent suspended ceiling elements as diagrammed in Fig. 7-3. This section discusses some of the alternate ways to design and detail the connection between a beam and the ceiling plane.

STANDARD ENCLOSURE

In most cases, in both commercial and residential construction, beams that drop below the finished ceiling are enclosed in gypsum wallboard or wood concealing the actual structural beam as diagrammed in Fig. 12-9(a). Metal or wood framing is suspended from the structure above to provide the base for the application of wallboard and finish.

If the designer wants to emphasize the structure of the building, additional false beams of gypsum wallboard, wood, or other materials may also be used. The enclosures and false beams can be detailed larger than actually required to conceal the structural beams to further emphasize the structural framework.

SUGGESTED ENCLOSURE

A suggested indication of structure may occur when the actual structural beam drops below the finished ceiling by only a small amount or when the designer wants to just give an indication of the structure but is limited in the distance the enclosure can be dropped below

Figure 12-9 Beam-to-ceiling transitions

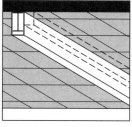

The simplest way to make a beam-to-ceiling transition is to use a simple gypsum wallboard enclosure regardless of what type of ceiling is used. To highlight the structure for additional interest, an additional step of wallboard framing can be applied, as indicated here with the dashed lines.

(a) standard

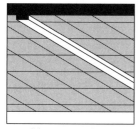

A smaller gypsum wallboard enclosure can be used when the actual structural beam only extends slightly past the ceiling or when the designer wants to indicate where the structural grid is but needs to maximize headroom.

(b) suggested

A trimmed beam transition uses some type of molding or intermediate material between the vertical portion of the beam and the horizontal plane of the ceiling. This is one of the traditional methods of finishing the beam and can create a distinct coffered ceiling when beams frame four sides of a space. This diagram shows a simple block trim on one side and a more ornate wood molding on the other side.

(c) trimmed

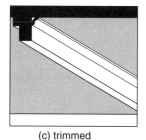

Planking or other fill material can be used between beams in a very traditional way to give a strong sense that one material supports the other.

(d) structural ceiling

the ceiling. See Fig. 12-9(b). As with standard enclosures, the beam can be indicated with simple wallboard framing, or wood or other materials may be applied directly to the ceiling or attached to framing above the ceiling.

TRIMMED

A trimmed beam transition is a more traditional way to treat the transition between a beam and the actual ceiling. In this detail some type of additional material is placed at the intersection of the beam and the column. As diagrammed in Fig. 12-9(c), the material may be as simple as an additional wallboard step or as elaborate as complex as wood cornice molding.

This design looks best when the ceiling is gypsum wallboard or other type of decorative ceiling other than an exposed grid acoustical ceiling. In large spaces where there are several structural bays, this design concept creates a strong coffered ceiling with a rhythm reflecting the structure of the building.

STRUCTURAL CEILING

A structural ceiling is one in which the intermediate fill between beams is exposed. In residential construction, it could be exposed wood decking, and in commercial construction it may be just a replication of decking or other finish material. See Fig. 12-9(d). This design approach emphasizes structure the most if the fill material is resting on beams, which, in turn, is resting on girders (as discussed in the next section), which are resting on exposed columns.

Beam-to-Beam Transitions

For interior design, beam-to-beam transitions are limited because of the limited ceiling height generally encountered in either commercial or residential construction. If the original building architect designed a high-ceiling space with the intent of leaving the structure exposed, the interior designer may want to keep the structural expression as it is. In other cases, the interior designer can consider the following structural concepts.

HIDDEN

A hidden beam-to-beam transition is one in which the actual structural beams are concealed with a finish material, commonly gypsum wallboard, and only give a suggestion of the structure. See Fig. 12-10(a). In some cases, only one enclosure may contain a real structural beam and the designer may add other intersecting enclosures to indicate where other structure is located or simply to create smaller structural bays. The bottom of the intersecting beams can be flush with the main beam or made smaller. As with beam-to-ceiling enclosures, the construction is detailed using gypsum wallboard on metal or wood framing.

CONNECTOR

A connector transition uses a steel angle or type of metal fabrication to physically join one bean with another as shown in Fig. 12-10(b). This connection is typically used with wood beams with bolts or other fasteners prominently exposed. A connector transition emphasizes the structural nature of the beams and can provide an interesting contrast with a finished ceiling. This type of structural connection may be part of the original architecture of the building or the interior designer can create a false grid of beams and girders using these types of connectors.

HANGER

A hanger is similar to a connector transition in that a metal fabrication is used to hang one wood beam from a wood girder to maximize height clearance. Girders are the primary structure, while beams are secondary members and frame into girders. See Fig. 12-10(c). Depending on the type of hanger used, the fasteners may not be as prominent as those used with an angle connector. The fasteners are usually nails or screws.

DIRECT BEARING

A direct bearing transition is seldom encountered in interior construction unless it is part of the original architectural design of the building. See Fig. 12-10(d). This is because it requires a significant amount of space below the elevation of the ceiling or roof. Direct bearing is a

Figure 12-10 Beam-to-beam transitions

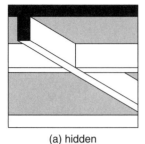

A hidden beam transition conceals any indication of the actual structural connection or even the type of beams that are connected. Instead, they are hidden with a gypsum wallboard covering. However, this type of transition can create a strong sense of the location of the structure.

(a) hidden

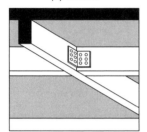

A connector is typically used with wood beams and makes a very clear statement of how one beam is supporting another. It may be part of the original architecture of the building or the interior designer may create a series of false beams and connectors.

(b) connector

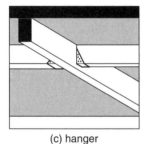

A hanger is a simple way to frame a beam into a girder. It is primarily a functional connection used in wood framing but can be replicated in interior construction. As with using connectors, this is a way to maximize headroom.

(c) hanger

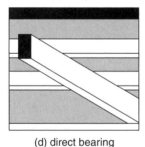

Direct bearing is the classic method of supporting beams on top of girders and gives a clear indication of how one part of the structure is supported by another.

(d) direct bearing

fundamental structural archetype and the most honest expression of structure because people can see beams resting on girders.

12-4   SUSPENDED OBJECTS

For interior design projects, suspended objects may include things such as signs, lighting, specialty ceilings, display systems, panels, HVAC equipment, and piping. In many cases, the designer wants to minimize the appearance of the suspension system and may specify the thinnest wire and smallest connectors possible. In other instances, the designer may want to make the transition between the ceiling and the suspended object a design feature in itself. The suspended objects discussed here assume that the construction element is distinctly separated from the ceiling or structure above rather than being directly attached to it. To meet accessibility requirements no suspended object can be less than 80 in. (2030 mm) above the floor level.

The basic design concept determines the general approach to detailing the suspension system. Which method is finally selected also depends on the following factors:

- Ceiling material and structure
- Weight of the suspended object
- Rigidity required
- Material of the suspended object (what kind of fastener is possible)
- Thickness of the suspended object
- Requirements for electrical power, if any
- Adjustability up and down, if any
- Ability to change out the suspended object without changing the support
- Ability to change the location of the suspended object

Figure 12-11 shows some of the possible conceptual approaches to detailing suspended objects. Some of the concepts shown can be used with either a thick or a thin suspension element, while some can only be used with a thick suspension element.

Thin Supports

Thin supports include cable, chain, double hooks, and rods as shown diagrammatically in Figs. 12-11(a)–(g). Cable is one of the simplest ways to hang most objects in the most unobtrusive way possible. It is flexible and can accommodate flat or three-dimensional objects and both light and heavy weights by varying the cable size and attachment methods. With loop or hook attachments cable-supported objects can be repositioned easily.

A variety of connectors are available to attach cable to both the ceiling and the object being suspended. Alternately, thin, threaded rods can also be used. Figures 12.11(a), (b), and (c) show three variations of this method assuming the wire is connected to the suspended object along the top of the object. Figures 12.11(d)–(g) show other variations when using thin cable or rods. Some of the basic connectors used with cable suspension are shown in Fig. 12-12. For light loads suspended from an acoustical ceiling T-bar clamps can be used with cable, hooks, or chains. Heavier loads can be supported with toggle bolts installed through the ceiling or with channels resting on the tops of the T-bars, as shown in Fig. 12-12(a). Some of the various methods for attaching cable to signs and thicker suspended objects are shown in Fig. 12-12(b).

Clamps

As shown in Fig. 12-11(h), clamps provide an easy way to hang thin panels with a relatively small connection between the wire and clamp. However, the clamps and fasteners can be oversized if the designer wants to emphasize the structural connection. Additional cables can be added to support heavy loads. In addition to the methods shown in Fig. 12-12(b), Figs. 5-9 and 5-13(d) illustrate two other methods for suspending panels with clamps.

Figure 12-11 Suspended object transitions

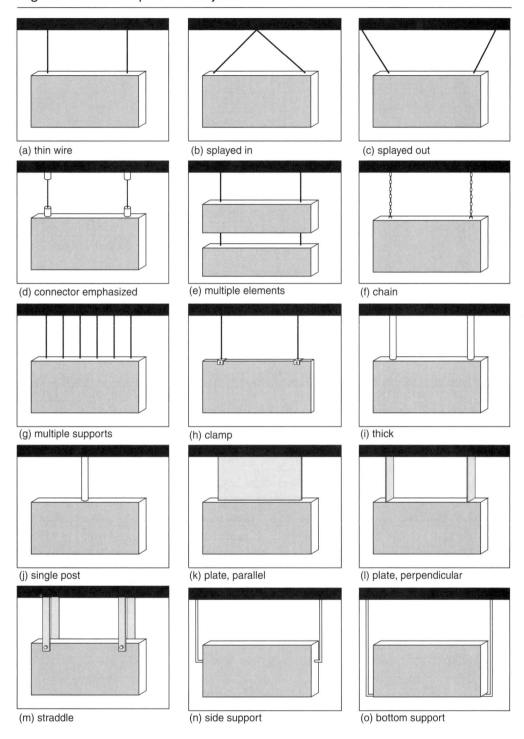

(a) thin wire

(b) splayed in

(c) splayed out

(d) connector emphasized

(e) multiple elements

(f) chain

(g) multiple supports

(h) clamp

(i) thick

(j) single post

(k) plate, parallel

(l) plate, perpendicular

(m) straddle

(n) side support

(o) bottom support

Thick Supports

Thick supports include round and square pipe as well as other tubular material, as diagrammed in Figs. 12-11(i) and (j). For heavy or large objects, thick suspension members give a greater sense of structure to the detail and create a significant architectural element.

Figure 12-12 Suspension hardware

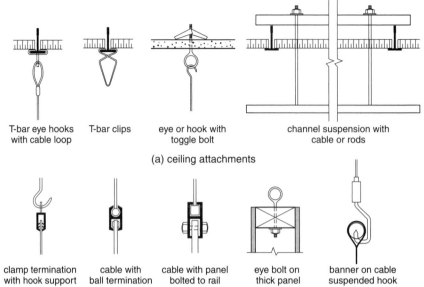

T-bar eye hooks with cable loop   T-bar clips   eye or hook with toggle bolt   channel suspension with cable or rods

(a) ceiling attachments

clamp termination with hook support   cable with ball termination   cable with panel bolted to rail   eye bolt on thick panel   banner on cable suspended hook

(b) suspended object attachments

If steel or aluminum pipe is used, it can be welded to plates that are screwed or bolted to the ceiling as well as the suspended object. Plastic pipe, if allowed by the local building code, can be slipped over cable or thin rod supports. Wood supports can be detailed in any size and configuration.

Rigid Supports

Rigid supports include panel products and other large connectors. See Figs. 12-11(k)–(o). Parallel plate suspension panels, as diagrammed in Fig. 12-11(k) add significant mass to the suspended object and, as with thick supports, create a larger architectural element than the suspended object alone. Panel products can be suspended from the ceiling and attached to the object with metal channels or angles. Side and bottom support systems can be detailed with aluminum or steel tubing or plates.

APPENDIX A
Resources

BOOKS AND PUBLICATIONS

Architectural Woodwork Institute. *AWI Quality Standards*. Potomac Falls, VA: Architectural Woodwork Institute, 2009.

Ballast, David Kent. *Handbook of Construction Tolerances, 2nd ed*. New York: New York: John Wiley & Sons, Inc., 2007.

Ballast, David Kent. *Interior Construction and Detailing for Designers and Architects, 4th ed*. Belmont, CA: Professional Publications, Inc., 2007.

Beylerian, George M., Jeffrey J. Osborne, and Elliot Kaufman. *Mondo Materials: Materials and Ideas for the Future*. New York: H. N. Abrams, 2000.

Binggeli, Corky, ed. *Interior Graphic Standards, 2nd ed*. New York: John Wiley & Sons, 2010.

Bonda, Penny, and Katie Sosnowchik. *Sustainable Commercial Interiors*. New York: John Wiley & Sons, 2007.

Brownell, Blaine, ed. *Transmaterial*. New York: Princeton Architectural Press, 2006.

Dell'Isola, Alphonse J., and Kirk, Stephen J. *Life Cycle Costing for Facilities*. Kingston, MA: RS Means, Reed Construction Data, 2003.

Egan, M. David. *Architectural Acoustics*. Fort Lauderdale, FL: J. Ross Publishing, 2007. (reprint of original McGraw-Hill edition, 1988) www.jrosspub.com.

Glass Association of North America *GANA Glazing Manual*. Topeka, KS: Glass Association of North America, 2008.

Gypsum Association. *Fire Resistance Design Manual, GA-600*. Washington: Gypsum Association, 2009.

Jones, J. Christopher. *Design Methods: Seeds of Human Futures*. New York: John Wiley & Sons, 1980.

Kirk, Stephen J., and Dell'Isola, Alphonse J. *Life Cycle Costing for Design Professionals, 2nd ed*. New York: McGraw-Hill Companies, 1995.

Lawson, Bryan. *How Designers Think, The Design Process Demystified, 4th ed*. Oxford: Architectural Press, 2006.

Marble Institute of America. *Interior Stone Wall Cladding Installation Guidelines*. Farmington, MI: Marble Institute of America, 2001.

Martin, Cat. *The Surface Texture Bible*. New York: Harry N. Abrams, Inc., 2005.

Panero, Julius, and Zelnik, Martin. *Human Dimension & Interior Space: A Source Book of Design Reference Standards*. New York: New York: Whitney Library of Design, 1998.

Ramsey/Sleeper. *Architectural Graphic Standards, 11th ed*. New York: John Wiley & Sons, 2007.

Spiegel, Ross, and Dru Meadows. *Green Building Materials: A Guide to Product Selection and Specification, 2nd ed*. New York: John Wiley & Sons, 2006.

Staebler, Wendy W. *Architectural Detailing in Contract Interiors*. New York: The Whitney Library of Design, 1988.

Templer, John. *The Staircase, Studies of Hazards, Falls, and Safer Design*. Cambridge, MA: The MIT Press, 1992.

Tilley, Alvin R., and Henry Dreyfuss Associates. *The Measure of Man and Woman: Human Factors in Design*. New York: New York: John Wiley & Sons, Inc., 2001.

Underwriters Laboratories. *Building Materials Directory*. Northbrook, IL: Underwriters Laboratories. 2010.

United States Gypsum. *Gypsum Construction Handbook*. Chicago, IL: United States Gypsum Company. 2008.

Wilson, Alex, et. al. eds. *GreenSpec® Directory: Product Listings & Guideline Specifications*. Brattleboro, VT: BuildingGreen, Inc., latest edition.

PRODUCT WEB SITES

www.aia.org/marketplace Online directory of latest product and service innovations from building product manufacturers

www.contractmagazine.com/products Directory of interior materials

www.construction.com McGraw-Hill Construction Network for Products (formerly Sweets). Can sort by green attributes

www.dezignare.com Online database of interior design products in a variety of categories

www.studio.bluebolt.com Tectonic Studio. an online resource library of over 100,000 commercial interior finishes representing more than 60 brands. Green Search feature looks for products by rating or certification systems or by area of environmental benefit.

www.todl.com Online, to the trade only, database of over 260,000 products with information including specifications and images of products

OTHER USEFUL WEB SITES

www.icc-es.org International Code Council Evaluation Service, which reviews submissions for new materials for compliance with code requirements. ICC also runs the SAVE program (Sustainable Attributes Verification and Evaluation), which provides a voluntary program where manufacturers can apply to have their products evaluated by for those seeking to build sustainably and qualify for points under major green rating systems.

www.greenguard.org Greenguard Environmental Institute.

www.holistic-interior-designs.com Provides information about sustainable building materials.

www.metalreference.com Gives standard stock metal forms of the five major metals groups commonly available in the United States, including hot-rolled steels, cold-finished steels, stainless steels, aluminum, and copper alloys.

www.nssn.org Search engine to database of industry standards from nearly all developers.

APPENDIX **B**

Industry Standards for Interior Materials and Products

PARTITIONS

Gypsum Wallboard Partitions

ASTM INTERNATIONAL:

ASTM A653 Specification for Sheet Steel, Zinc-Coated (Galvanized) or Zinc-Iron Alloy-coated (Galvannealed) by the Hot-Dip Process

ASTM C475 Specification for Joint Compound and Joint Tape for Finishing Gypsum Board

ASTM C514 Specification for Nails for the Application of Gypsum Wallboard

ASTM C645 Specification for Nonstructural Steel Framing Members

ASTM C754 Specification for Installation of Steel Framing Members to Receive Screw-Attached Gypsum Panel Products

ASTM C840 Specification for Application and Finishing of Gypsum Board

ASTM C955 Standard Specification for Load-Bearing (Transverse and Axial) Steel Studs, Runners (Tracks), and Bracing or Bridging for Screw Application of Gypsum Panel Products and Metal Plaster Bases

ASTM C1002 Specification for Steel Self-Piercing Tapping Screws for the Application of Gypsum Panel Products or Metal Plaster Bases to Wood Studs or Steel Studs

ASTM C1007 Specification for the Installation of Load Bearing (Transverse and Axial) Steel Studs and Related Accessories

ASTM C1178 Specification for Coated Glass Mat Water-Resistant Gypsum Backing Panel

ASTM C1278 Specification for Fiber Reinforced Gypsum Panel

ASTM C1396 Standard Specification for Gypsum Board

ASTM C1629 Standard Classification for Abuse-Resistant Nondecorated Gypsum Panel Products and Fiber Reinforced Cement Panels

GYPSUM ASSOCIATION (GA):

GA-214 Recommended Levels of Gypsum Board Finish

GA-216 Application and Finishing of Gypsum Board

GA-600 Fire Resistance Design Manual

Plaster Partitions

ASTM INTERNATIONAL:

ASTM C28 Specification for Gypsum Plasters

ASTM C35 Specification for Inorganic Aggregates for Use in Gypsum Plaster

ASTM C59 Specification for Gypsum Casting Plaster and Gypsum Molding Plaster

ASTM C61 Specification for Gypsum Keene's Cement

ASTM C150 Specification for Portland Cement

ASTM C206 Specification for Finishing Hydrated Lime

ASTM C207 Specification for Hydrated Lime for Masonry Purposes

ASTM C587 Specification for Gypsum Veneer Plaster

ASTM C631 Specification for Bonding Compounds for Interior Gypsum Plastering

ASTM C841 Specification for the Installation of Interior Lathing and Furring

ASTM C842 Specification for the Application of Interior Gypsum Plaster

ASTM C843 Specification for the Application of Gypsum Veneer Plaster

ASTM C844 Specification for the Application of Gypsum Base to Receive Gypsum Veneer Plaster

ASTM C847 Specification for Metal Lath

ASTM C897 Specification for Aggregate for Job-Mixed Portland Cement-Based Plasters

SUSPENDED ACOUSTICAL CEILINGS

ASTM INTERNATIONAL:

ASTM C423 Test Methods for Sound Absorption and Sound Absorption Coefficients by the Reverberation Room Method

ASTM C635 Standard Specification for the Manufacture, Performance, and Testing of Metal Suspension Systems for Acoustical Tile and Lay-in Panel Systems

ASTM C636 Standard Practice for Installation of Metal Ceiling Suspension Systems for Acoustical Tile and Lay-in Panels

ASTM D3273 Standard Test Method for Resistance to Growth of Mold on the Surface of Interior Coatings in an Environmental Chamber

ASTM E580 Standard Practice for Application of Ceiling Suspension Systems for Acoustical Tile and Lay-in Panels in Areas Subject to Earthquake Ground Motion

ASTM E1264 Standard Classification for Acoustical Ceiling Products

CEILINGS & INTERIOR SYSTEMS CONSTRUCTION ASSOCIATION (CISCA):

Recommendations for Direct-hung Acoustical Tile and Lay-in Panel Ceilings, Seismic Zones 0–2

Guidelines for Seismic Restraint for Direct-hung Suspended Ceiling Assemblies, Seismic Zones 3 & 4

NATIONAL FIRE PROTECTION ASSOCIATION (NFPA):

NFPA 13 Installation of Sprinkler Systems

NFPA 13D Installation of Sprinkler Systems in One- and Two-family Dwellings and Manufactured Homes

NFPA 13R Installation of Sprinkler Systems in Residential Occupancies Up to and Including Four Stories in Height

DOORS

Wood Doors and Frames

AMERICAN NATIONAL STANDARDS INSTITUTE (ANSI):

ANSI A117.1 Specifications for Making Buildings and Facilities Accessible to and Usable by Physically Handicapped People

ARCHITECTURAL WOODWORK INSTITUTE (AWI):

Architectural Woodwork Standards, Section 6, Doors, and Section 9, Interior and Exterior Millwork and Doors

ASTM INTERNATIONAL:

ASTM E119 Fire Tests of Building Construction and Materials

DOOR AND HARDWARE INSTITUTE (DHI):

DHI-WDHS-3 Recommended Hardware Locations for Wood Flush Doors

NATIONAL FIRE PROTECTION ASSOCIATION (NFPA):

NFPA 80 Standard for Fire Doors and Windows

NFPA 105 Standard for the Smoke Door Assemblies and Other Opening Protectives

NFPA 252 Standard on Fire Test of Door Assemblies (same as UL 10B)

WINDOW AND DOOR MANUFACTURERS ASSOCIATION (WDMA):

ANSI/WDMA I.S. 1-A Architectural Wood Flush Doors

I.S. 6 Industry Standard for Wood Stile and Rail Doors

I.S. 6-A Industry Standard for Architectural Stile and Rail Doors

UNDERWRITERS LABORATORIES (UL):

UL 10B Standard for Safety for Fire Tests of Door Assemblies (same as NFPA 252)

UL 10C Standard for Safety for Positive-Pressure Fire Tests of Door Assemblies

UL 1784 Standard for Safety for Air Leakage Tests for Door Assemblies

Steel Doors and Frames

AMERICAN NATIONAL STANDARDS INSTITUTE (ANSI):

ANSI/ISDI 102 Installation Standard for Insulated Steel Door Systems

ANSI/ISDI 104 Water Penetration Performance Standard for Insulated Steel Door Systems

ANSI A156.115 Hardware Preparation in Steel Doors and Frames

ANSI A156.115W Hardware Preparation in Wood Doors with Wood or Steel Frames

ASTM INTERNATIONAL:

ASTM E119 Fire Tests of Building Construction and Materials

DOOR AND HARDWARE INSTITUTE (DHI):

Recommended Locations for Builders' Hardware for Custom Steel Doors and Frames
Recommended Locations for Architectural Hardware for Standard Steel Doors and Frames

NATIONAL FIRE PROTECTION ASSOCIATION (NFPA):

Same as for wood doors

STEEL DOOR INSTITUTE (SDI):

SDI-108 Recommended Selection and Usage Guide for Standard Steel Doors and Frames

SDI-110 Standard Steel Doors and Frames for Modular Masonry Construction

SDI-111 Recommended Selection and Usage Guide for Standard Steel Doors, Frames, and Accessories

SDI-112 Zinc-Coated (Galvanized/Galvannealed) Standard Steel Doors and Frames

SDI-117 Manufacturing Tolerances for Standard Steel Doors and Frames

SDI-118 Basic Fire Door Requirements

SDI-122 Installation and Troubleshooting Guide for Standard Steel Doors and Frames

SDI-124 Maintenance of Standard Steel Doors and Frames

SDI-128 Guidelines for Acoustical Performance of Standard Steel Doors and Frames

SDI-129 Hinge and Strike Spacing

ANSI A250.3 Test Procedure and Acceptance Criteria for Factory Applied Finish Painted Steel Surfaces for Steel Doors and Frames

ANSI A250.4 Test Procedure and Acceptance Criteria for Physical Endurance for Steel Doors, Frames, Frame Anchors, and Hardware Reinforcings

ANSI A250.7 Nomenclature for Standard Steel Doors and Steel Frames

ANSI A250.8 Standard Steel Doors & Frames

ANSI A250.10 Test Procedure and Acceptance Criteria for Prime Painted Steel Surfaces for Steel Doors and Frames

UNDERWRITERS LABORATORIES (UL):

UL 63 Standard for Safety for Fire Doors and Frames

UL 10B Standard for Safety for Fire Tests of Door Assemblies

UL 10C Standard for Safety for Positive-Pressure Fire Tests of Door Assemblies

Glass Doors

CONSUMER PRODUCT SAFETY COMMISSION (CPSC):

CPSC 16 CFR 1201 Safety Standards for Architectural Glazing Materials

AMERICAN NATIONAL STANDARDS INSTITUTE (ANSI):

ANSI Z97.1 Safety Glazing Material Used in Buildings, Safety Performance Specifications, and Methods of Test

ASTM INTERNATIONAL:

ASTM C1048 Specification for Heat Treated Flat Glass

HARDWARE

Hinges and Pivots

AMERICAN NATIONAL STANDARDS INSTITUTE (ANSI):

ANSI A156.1 Butts and Hinges

ANSI A156.7 Template Hinge Dimensions

ANSI A156.17 Self Closing Hinges and Pivots

ANSI A156.26 Continuous Hinges

Operating Devices and Locking

AMERICAN NATIONAL STANDARDS INSTITUTE (ANSI):

ANSI A156.2 Bored and Preassembled Locks and Latches

ANSI A156.3 Exit Devices

ANSI A156.5 Auxiliary Locks and Associated Products

ANSI A156.10 Power Operated Pedestrian Doors

ANSI A156.12 Interconnected Locks and Latches

ANSI A156.13 Mortise Locks and Latches

ANSI A156.19 Power Assist and Low-Energy Power-Operated Doors

ANSI A156.23 Electromagnetic Locks

ANSI A156.24 Delayed Egress Locking Systems

ANSI A156.25 Electrified Locking Devices

ASTM INTERNATIONAL:

ASTM F476 Standard Test Methods for Security of Swinging Door Assemblies

UNDERWRITERS LABORATORIES (UL):

UL 305 Standard for Safety for Panic Hardware

Closing Devices
AMERICAN NATIONAL STANDARDS INSTITUTE (ANSI):

ANSI/BHMA A156.4 Door Controls—Closers

Door Locks
AMERICAN NATIONAL STANDARDS INSTITUTE (ANSI):

ANSI A156.2 Bored and Preassembled Locks and Latches ANSI A156.3 Exit Devices

ANSI A156.12 Interconnected Locks and Latches

ANSI A156.13 Mortise Locks and Latches

Miscellaneous Hardware
AMERICAN NATIONAL STANDARDS INSTITUTE (ANSI):

ANSI A156.6 Architectural Door Trim

ANSI A156.8 Door Controls—Overhead Holders and Holders

ANSI A156.14 Sliding and Folding Door Hardware

ANSI A156.16 Auxiliary Hardware

ANSI A156.21 Thresholds

ANSI A156.22 Door Gasketing and Edge Seal Systems

GLAZING

ASTM INTERNATIONAL:

ASTM C1036 Specification for Flat Glass

ASTM C1048 Specification for Heat-Treated Flat Glass

CONSUMER PRODUCT SAFETY COMMISSION (CPSC):

16 CFR 1201 Safety Standard for Architectural Glazing Material

NATIONAL FIRE PROTECTION ASSOCIATION (NFPA):

NFPA 257 Standard for Fire Test for Window and Glass Block Assemblies

FINISH CARPENTRY AND WOODWORK

Carpentry and Woodwork

ARCHITECTURAL WOODWORK INSTITUTE (AWI):

Architectural Woodwork Standards

HARDWOOD PLYWOOD AND VENEER ASSOCIATION:

ANSI/HPVA HP-1-2004 American National Standard for Hardwood and Decorative Plywood

NORTHEASTERN LUMBER MANUFACTURERS ASSOCIATION:

NeLMA Standard Grading Rules for Northeastern Lumber

AMERICAN PLYWOOD ASSOCIATION:

PS 1-95 U.S. Product Standard PS 1-95 for Construction and Industrial Plywood

WESTERN WOOD PRODUCTS ASSOCIATION:

Western Lumber Grading Rules

WOOD MOULDING AND MILLWORK PRODUCERS ASSOCIATION:

WM Series Softwood Moulding Patterns Catalog
HWM Series Hardwood Moulding Patterns Catalog

Laminates

AMERICAN NATIONAL STANDARDS INSTITUTE (ANSI):

ANSI A161.2 Decorative Laminate Countertops, Performance Standards for Fabricated High Pressure
ANSI A208.1 Particleboard
ANSI A208.2 Medium Density Fiberboard for Interior Applications

ARCHITECTURAL WOODWORK INSTITUTE (AWI):

AWI Architectural Woodwork Standards, Section 11

AMERICAN LAMINATORS ASSOCIATION (ALA):

ALA 1992 The Performance Standard for Thermoset Decorative Panels

ASTM INTERNATIONAL:

ASTM D1037 Standard Test Methods for Evaluating the Properties of Wood-Base Fiber and Particle Panel Materials

NATIONAL ELECTRICAL MANUFACTURERS ASSOCIATION (NEMA):

ANSI/NEMA LD 3 High-Pressure Decorative Laminates

FLOORING

Wood Flooring

AMERICAN NATIONAL STANDARDS INSTITUTE (ANSI):

ANSI/HPVA EF 2002 American National Standard for Engineered Wood Flooring

ASTM INTERNATIONAL:

ASTM D2394 Standard Methods for Simulated Service Testing of Wood and Wood-Base Finish Flooring

MAPLE FLOORING MANUFACTURERS ASSOCIATION (MFMA):

Grading Rules for Hard Maple

NOFMA, The Wood Flooring Manufacturers Association: Official Flooring Grading Rules

Tile

AMERICAN NATIONAL STANDARDS INSTITUTE (ANSI):

A108/A118/A136.1 Specifications for the Installation of Ceramic Tile

American National Standard Specifications **A108**. .1A, .1B, .1C, .4, .5, .6, .8, .9, .10, .11, .12, and .13 define the installation of ceramic tile. **A118.1**, .3, .4, .5, .6, .7, .8, .9, .10, and **A136.1** define the test methods and physical properties for ceramic tile installation materials.

A 108.1A Ceramic Tile Installed in the Wet-Set Method with Portland Cement Mortar.

A 108.1B Ceramic Tile Installed on a Cured Portland Cement Mortar Setting Bed with Dry-Set or Latex-portland Cement Mortar.

A 108.5 Installation of Ceramic Tile with Dry-set Portland Cement Mortar or Latex-portland Cement Mortar

A 108.10 Installation of Grout in Tilework

A 118.1 Specifications for Dry-set Portland Cement Mortar

A 118.4 Specifications for Latex-portland Cement Mortar

A 118.6 Specifications for Standard Ceramic Tile Grouts for Tile Installation

A 118.10 Load Bearing, Bonded, Waterproof Membranes for Thin-set Ceramic Tile and Dimension Stone Installation.

A 118.12 Specifications for Crack Isolation Membranes for Thin-Set Ceramic Tile and Dimension Stone Installations

A 137.1 Ceramic Tile

TILE COUNCIL OF NORTH AMERICA, INC. (TCNA):

Ceramic Tile: The Installation Handbook

APPLIED FLOOR FINISHES

Carpet

ASTM INTERNATIONAL:

ASTM D2859 Standard Test Method for Ignition Characteristics of Finished Textile Floor Covering Materials

ASTM D4158 Standard Guide for Abrasion Resistance of Textile Fabrics (Uniform Abrasion)

ASTM E84 Standard Test Method for Surface Burning Characteristics of Building Materials

ASTM E162 Standard Test Method for Surface Flammability of Materials Using a Radiant Heat Energy Source

ASTM E648 Standard Test Method for Critical Radiant Flux of Floor-Covering Systems Using a Radiant Heat Energy Source (NFPA 253)

ASTM E662 Standard Test Method for Specific Optical Density of Smoke Generated by Solid Materials (NFPA 258)

CARPET AND RUG INSTITUTE:

CRI-104 Standard for Installation of Commercial Carpet

CRI-105 Standard for Installation of Residential Carpet

NATIONAL FIRE PROTECTION ASSOCIATION (NFPA):

NFPA 253 Standard Method of Test for Critical Radiant Flux of Floor Covering Systems Using a Radiant Heat Energy Source

NFPA 258 Recommended Practice for Determining Smoke Generation of Solid Materials

Resilient Floor Covering

ASTM INTERNATIONAL:

ASTM F693 Standard Practice for Sealing Seams of Resilient Sheet Flooring Products by Use of Liquid Seam Sealers

ASTM F710 Standard Practice for Preparing Concrete Floors to Receive Resilient Flooring

ASTM F1066 Standard Specification for Vinyl Composition Floor Tile

ASTM F1303 Standard Specification for Sheet Vinyl Floor Covering With Backing

ASTM F1344 Standard Specification for Rubber Floor Tile

ASTM F1516 Standard Practice for Sealing Seams of Resilient Flooring Products by the Heat Weld Method

ASTM F1700 Standard Specification for Solid Vinyl Floor Tile

ASTM F1859 Standard Specification for Rubber Sheet Floor Covering Without Backing

ASTM F1860 Standard Specification for Rubber Sheet Floor Covering With Backing

ASTM F1861 Standard Specification for Resilient Wall Base

Coefficient of Friction Measurements

ASTM C1028 Standard Test Method for Determining the Static Coefficient of Friction of Ceramic Tile and Other Like Surfaces by the Horizontal Dynamometer Pull-Meter Method

ASTM D2047 Standard Test Method for Static Coefficient of Friction of Polish-Coated Floor Surfaces as Measured by the James Machine

ASTM F462 Consumer Safety Specification for Slip-Resistance Bathing Facilities

ASTM F609 Standard Test Method for Using a Horizontal Pull Slipmeter

WALL FINISHES

Paints and Coatings
ASTM INTERNATIONAL:

ASTM D1005 Standard Test Method for Measurement of Dry Film Thickness of Organic Coatings Using Micrometers

ASTM D1212 Standard Test Method for Measurement of Wet Film Thickness of Organic Coatings

ASTM D5146 Standard Guide for Testing Solvent-Borne Architectural Coatings

ASTM D5324 Standard Guide for Testing Water-Borne Architectural Coatings

Vinyl Wallcovering
ASTM INTERNATIONAL:

ASTM F793 Standard Classification of Wallcovering by Use Characteristics

ASTM F1141 Standard Specification for Wallcovering

THE CHEMICAL FABRICS AND FILMS ASSOCIATION (CFFA):

CFFA-W-101-D Quality Standard for Vinyl-Coated Fabric Wallcovering

Stone
ASTM INTERNATIONAL:

ASTM C119 Standard Terminology Relating to Dimension Stone

ASTM C503 Standard Specification for Marble Dimension Stone

ASTM C568 Standard Specification for Limestone Dimension Stone

ASTM C615 Standard Specification for Granite Dimension Stone

ASTM C616 Standard Specification for Quartz-Based Dimension Stone

ASTM C629 Standard Specification for Slate Dimension Stone

SECURITY GLAZING AND DOORS

ASTM INTERNATIONAL:

ASTM F476 Standard Test Methods for Security of Swinging Door Assemblies

ASTM F571 Standard Practice for Installation of Exit Devices in Security Areas

ASTM F588 Standard Test Methods for Measuring the Forced Entry Resistance of Window Assemblies, Excluding Glazing Impact

ASTM F1233 Standard Test Method for Security Glazing Materials and Systems

H.P. WHITE LABORATORY, INC.:

HPW-TP-0500.03 Test Procedure, Transparent Materials for Use in Forced-Entry or Containment Barriers

NATIONAL INSTITUTE FOR JUSTICE (NIJ):

NIJ Std. 0108.01 Ballistic Resistant Protective Materials

UNDERWRITERS LABORATORIES (UL):

UL 752 Standard for Safety for Bullet-Resisting Equipment

UL 972 Burglary-Resisting Glazing Material

UL 1034 Burglary-Resistant Electric Locking Machines

U.S. DEPARTMENT OF STATE

Std. SD-STD-01.01 Certification Standard for Forced Entry and Ballistic Resistance of Structural Systems

ACOUSTICS

CEILING & INTERIOR SYSTEMS CONSTRUCTION ASSOCIATION (CISCA):

AMA I-II Ceiling Sound Transmission Test by the Two-Room Method

ASTM INTERNATIONAL:

ASTM C423 Standard Test Method for Sound Absorption and Sound Absorption Coefficients by the Reverberation Room Method

ASTM E90 Test Method for Laboratory Measurement of Airborne Sound Transmission Loss of Building Partitions and Elements

ASTM E336 Test Method for Measurement of Airborne Sound Attenuation Between Rooms in Buildings

ASTM E413 Classification for Rating Sound Insulation

ASTM E492 Test Method for Laboratory Measurement of Impact Sound Transmission Through Floor-Ceiling Assemblies Using the Tapping Machine

ASTM E989 Standard Classification for Determination of Impact Insulation Class

ASTM E1007 Standard Test Method for Field Measurement of Tapping Machine Impact Sound Transmission Through Floor-Ceiling Assemblies and Associated Support Structures

ASTM E1110 Standard Classification for Determination of Articulation Class

ASTM E1111 Test Method for Measuring the Interzone Attenuation of Open Office Components

ASTM E1130 Test Method for Objective Measurement of Speech Privacy in Open Plan Spaces Using Articulation Index

ASTM E1264 Classification for Acoustical Ceiling Products

ASTM E1374 Standard Guide to Open Office Acoustics and Applicable ASTM Standards

ASTM E1414 Standard Test Method for Airborne Sound Attenuation Between Rooms Sharing a Common Ceiling Plenum

AMERICAN NATIONAL STANDARDS INSTITUTE (ANSI):

ANSI S3.5 Methods for the Calculation of the Speech Intelligibility Index

SUSTAINABLE DESIGN

ASTM D5116 Standard Guide for Small-Scale Environmental Chamber Determinations of Organic Emissions From Indoor Materials/Products

ASTM D6670 Standard Practice for Full-Scale Chamber Determination of Volatile Organic Emissions from Indoor Materials/Products

ASTM E2129 Standard Practice for Data Collection for Sustainability Assessment of Building Products

FIRE RESISTANCE

ASTM E84 Test Methods for Surface Burning Characteristics of Building Materials

ASTM E136 Test Method for Behavior of Materials in a Vertical Tube Furnace at 750°C

UL 723 Tests for Surface Burning Characteristics of Building Materials

INDEX